RINGSEND

JOE CURTIS

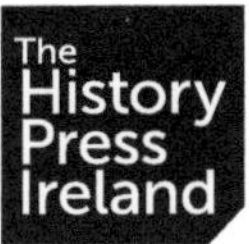

The History Press Ireland

First published 2017

The History Press
97 St George's Place,
Cheltenham, GL50 3QB
www,thehistorypress.co.uk

The History Press Ireland is a member of Publishing Ireland,
the Irish book publishers' association.

British Library Cataloguing in Publication Data.
A catalogue record for this book is available from the British Library.

ISBN 978 0 7509 8411 9

Typesetting and origination by The History Press
Printed and bound by TJ Books, Padstow, Cornwall

CONTENTS

ACKNOWLEDGEMENTS

Many thanks to the following individuals and organisations for assisting me with information or sourcing photos or allowing me to take photos of their premises: Fr Ivan Tonge, Revd John Marchant, Sharon Perry (Abundant Grace Christian Assembly), Gemma Byrne (News Four), Tommy Brown (Ringsend College), Paddy Maguire, Christy Mullen, Gladys Rathorne, Robin Booth, Steven Cull, Patrick Flynn (Shelbourne Greyhound Track), Fergus Morris (Commercial Rowing Club), Dara Breaden (Neptune Rowing Club), Philip Murphy and Gay Byrne (St Patrick's Rowing Club), Mick Curry (Stella Maris Rowing Club), Thomas Hulgrain (CYMS), Paul Ferguson, Gillian Bird (DSPCA), David Lee, Brian Siggins, Frank Pelly, Vivienne Bertram, Dublin Dock Workers Preservation Society, Brian McMahon (ESB Archives), Gary Smyth and Maureen McDonald (Mining Company of Ireland), Sean McDermott (Dublin City Council), Niall Dardis, Sheila Coleman (South Dublin Libraries), Eithne Massey (Dublin City Library and Archives), Jim Cooke, Joe Coughlan, John Wedick (Poolbeg Yacht & Boat Club), Geraldine Smith (Dodder Sea Scouts).

Thanks also to the excellent staff of the National Archives, National Library of Ireland, Irish Architectural Archive, Office of Public Works, Military Archives, Trinity College Dublin, Valuation Office, RCB Library, Central Catholic Library, Diocesan Archives, and St Andrews Resource Centre.

Various photographs are acknowledged individually, and otherwise were taken by the author.

INTRODUCTION

The adjoining villages of Ringsend and Irishtown are reputed to date from the middle of the fifteenth century, but no one knows which village came first. There is also confusion about the meaning of their names. Ringsend is a half Irish and half English word, since the village was located at the north 'end' of a vertical spur of land or headland, called a *'rinn'* in Irish. Irishtown was only a hundred yards south of it and both cut off from Dublin on three sides by the sea and the River Dodder. It seems that Ringsend started off as a maritime business community and Irishtown was built shortly afterwards as a dormitory town, with churches and schools.

The English Parliament made Oliver Cromwell the Lord Lieutenant of Ireland and in 1649 sent him to complete the conquest of Ireland. After the defeat of the Royalist army at the Battle of Rathmines in early August, Cromwell could land unhindered in Ringsend on 15 August 1649, with his army of thousands of soldiers and horses on thirty-five ships. Cromwell's army travelled the 25 miles to Drogheda, and in early September slaughtered the inhabitants, before heading south to Wexford.

Except for the Grand Canal Docks, which opened in 1796, Dublin's docklands developed on the north side of the River Liffey after the building of the new Customs House in 1791.

Originally Ringsend was just a vertical peninsula with Thorncastle Street running down the spine. The South Bull Wall and Poolbeg Lighthouse were built in the eighteenth century. Around 1855, the very wide Cambridge Road was built, linking Thorncastle Street to the South Bull Wall (by this stage called Pigeon House Road). Towards the end of the nineteenth century, the beach along the east side of Cambridge Road was reclaimed, enabling Ringsend Park to be formed. From the middle of the twentieth century, the seashore along the south side of Pigeon House Road and east of the Electricity Supply Board's Pigeon House Generating Station was also reclaimed, allowing expansion of the ESB's activities and the building of the South Bank Quay. Only in recent decades was additional beach reclaimed to create Sean Moore Park and the Irishtown Nature Reserve.

Following the formation of the Pembroke Township in 1863, which included the more prosperous areas of Ballsbridge, Ringsend was no longer controlled by Dublin Corporation, and the township became nearly self-sufficient, with its own electricity and sewerage works, technical school, etc. A new town hall was built in Ballsbridge in 1880, with a fire station extension in 1902. The township was taken over in 1930 by Dublin Corporation.

Ringsend was a thriving port town throughout most of the nineteenth century, and the first seven decades of the twentieth century, until the main Dublin Port activity shifted completely to the North Wall locality, and the 'Celtic Tiger' era (1990-2005) swept away the many industrial premises in Ringsend, including numerous factory chimneys, in favour of shiny office blocks for the multinational companies, and 'luxury' apartment schemes.

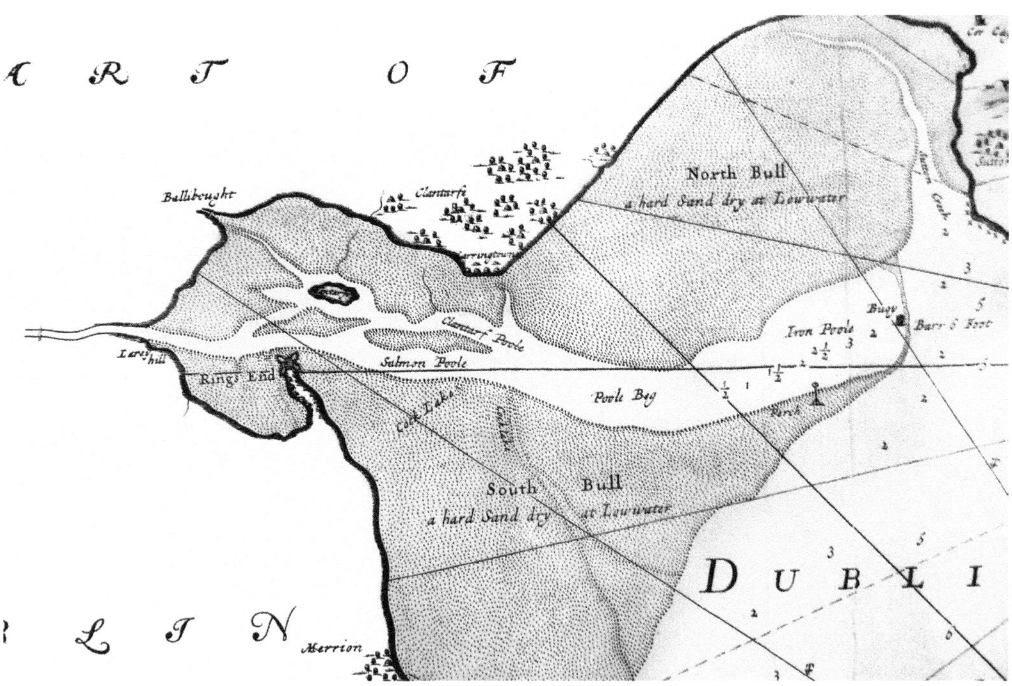

Map showing Ringsend in isolation, surveyed by Captain Greville Collins in 1686. (Courtesy of Irish Lights)

1

MARITIME

BALLAST BOARD

The Ballast Office Committee was established by Dublin Corporation in 1708 to manage the port area and was replaced by the Ballast Board in 1786 (officially called the Corporation for Preserving and Improving the Port of Dublin). After ships have unloaded their cargo, the empty vessel is unstable and ballast (usually sand or gravel) has to be taken on board and dumped at a later stage. The primary function of the Ballast Office was to provide this ballast and ensure that ships' captains did not dig up ballast from the foreshore, etc. From the 1940s, seawater in tanks was used for ballast.

The Ballast Board was superseded by the Dublin Port & Docks Board in 1868, and they built a new headquarters that same year at the corner of Westmoreland Street and Aston Quay. In 1979, they moved to newly built offices in Alexandra Road on the North Wall, and became known as Dublin Port Company in 1997.

Up until 1916, there was a 4ft-diameter copper 'time ball' on the roof of their Westmoreland Street building, mounted on a 15ft-high timber mast and controlled via a telegraph wire from Dunsink Observatory. At 1 p.m. every day, the ball descended the mast, signalling the time to ships offshore. Prior to 1916, Dublin Time was 25 minutes behind Greenwich Mean Time.

The eastern border of Dublin city was originally around the present Townsend Street locality and the wide estuary, which also received the waters from the River Dodder on the south side and the River Tolka on the north side, was shallow and dangerous for shipping, resulting in many shipwrecks over the centuries. There were large sandbanks (called bulls) on the north and south sides of the estuary, connected by a sand bar at the east end. Therefore, the only access for ships was over the sand bar at high tide.

From the early eighteenth century, the land around the mouth of the River Liffey was reclaimed, thus creating the North and South Lotts. Sir John Rogerson (former Lord Mayor of Dublin) acquired some of the south lands, and built his quay in two phases from about 1713 to 1730. From 1869 to 1888, the walls of Sir John Rogersons Quay and Great Britain Quay were rebuilt with deeper foundations, allowing bigger ships to berth.

From 1715 onwards, a breakwater was built to stop sand from the South Bull (part of Sandymount beach) encroaching and silting up the mouth of the River Liffey. The breakwater consisted of closely spaced vertical timber piles (logs) driven into the beach, with the intervening spaces filled with baskets of stones (gabions), stretching out as far as the present Poolbeg Lighthouse. The Charles Brooking map of 1728 shows a short run of piles running out from Irishtown, and a long line of piles much further out into the bay in the vicinity of Poolbeg.

The timber breakwater proved ineffective, so between 1748 and 1759 a stone wall was built alongside, stretching from Ringsend Point as far as the present Pigeon House Harbour. Granite from Dalkey Quarry was transported across Dublin bay in barges for the wall. The second phase of the wall started in 1761, at the site of the proposed Poolbeg Lighthouse (the lighthouse foundations were laid that same year), and proceeded backwards, reaching the site of the present Poolbeg Harbour in 1790, thus completing the 3½-mile-long South Bull Wall. The wall in fact consists of two widely spaced walls, with the void between them filled with rubble stone, and the entire structure was capped off with granite paving. Within the past few decades, large stone boulders (rock armour) have been positioned on both sides of the wall to prevent storm damage.

However, it was not until 1824, when the North Bull Wall was completed, that silting of the river mouth was halted by the scouring effect of tidal water being channelled between the North Bull Wall and the South Bull Wall, and the depth of water at low tide in the spring tides over the sand bar at the port entrance increased from 6ft to 16ft.

In 1760, a caretaker's house (also called the Block House) was built at the end of the first section of the South Bull Wall – the caretaker was John Pidgeon so the house was known as Pidgeon's House. Within a few decades, maps spelt the name as Pigeon. In his spare time, he provided refreshments for the passengers on the packet boats (mail boats) from England. In 1793 a proper harbour was built at the Pigeon House and then a fine three-storey granite-faced hotel in 1795, the latter possibly designed by Robert Pool for the Ballast Board. The packet ships transferred to Howth Harbour (built 1813) in 1818, and then to Kingstown (now Dún Laoghaire) in 1834. The Block House was demolished in 1835.

PIGEON HOUSE FORT

Partly because of the 1798 Rising in Ireland, and partly because of the threat from Napoleon in Europe, the British War Department took over Pigeon House Harbour and Hotel around the turn of the century. However, the mail boats continued to use the harbour until they transferred to Howth in 1818. The hotel became the officers' quarters, and the Revenue House near the east end became married quarters. Soldiers' quarters were built around 1805. In December 1813 the War Department officially purchased the Pigeon House site from the Ballast Board. Both the East Gate cum guardhouse and the West Gate cum guardhouse were built around 1833, while the canteen and prison were built in 1842 and 1845 respectively. The Half Moon Battery out towards the Poolbeg Lighthouse provided a lookout post with five cannons.

An 1880/82 survey of the fort shows a heavily fortified west entrance, comprising an approach area with low palisade fences on both sides, a drawbridge, an inner yard, and the guardhouse. The east entrance was simpler, although still had a drawbridge and guardhouse. Three swivelling cannons were mounted on the east rampart. The Accommodation Schedule comprised 1 commanding officer, 11 officers, 2 staff sergeants, 10 married soldiers, 140 non-commissioned officers and men, 3 hospital patients, and 6 horses for officers. The Chapel School could hold 32 pupils, but was fitted out for 17. The magazine held 1,232 barrels of gunpowder.

The Rathmines and Pembroke Main Sewer passed under the fort, exiting beside the east drawbridge, and on to the sluice-valve station further along the South Bull Wall. Dublin Corporation mains water from the Vartry supply was laid on, filling 55,000-gallon tanks.

Another survey drawing from this period shows the following (proceeding west to east): an outer and an inner drawbridge, two windlass rooms (for winding the drawbridges), guard room/soldiers' quarters, canteen, ball court, prison (near south-west corner), soldiers' quarters, stables and hayloft, four-sided armoury with internal courtyard, shot yard, officers' quarters and garden, engine house (for fire engine), clerks' quarters, stores, magazine, hospital and nearby chapel/school at north-east, east guardhouse, drawbridge. A number of 'hand spike sheds' were scattered throughout – these housed a type of crowbar for winding up the windlass (drawbridge), or for heaving anchor on ships.

Submarine mines (underwater booby-trapped large metal balls filled with explosives) became part of navy warfare in the 1880s/'90s, and a Submarine Mining Station was established by the Royal Engineers around this time, a short distance to the west of the fort, probably with a narrow-gauge tramway to carry the mines down to the harbour.

A newspaper report for 1849 recorded the transfer of four named prisoners from the Richmond Bridewell on the South Circular Road (now Griffith College) to the *Trident* war-steamer in Pigeon House Harbour, and then to the *Swift* convict ship anchored a mile off Kingstown Harbour (now called Dún Laoghaire), for transport to the convict colony of Van Diemen's Land (called Tasmania after 1856, and now part of Australia).

The fort, including harbour, was sold to Dublin Corporation in 1897, as a site for their proposed sewage treatment plant.

In the 1950s, there were four families resident in the former fort, in addition to the Harbour Master and the lifeboat. Gradually the historic buildings were demolished, although the former hotel was restored in 1989 for Dublin City Council offices. Some boundary walls and derelict buildings are still visible, alongside the car park of the Sewage Treatment Plant, and opposite this on the public road.

The Half Moon Swimming Club, founded in 1898, took over the Half Moon Battery in 1910, and is still going strong.

BEGGARS BUSH BARRACKS

Pigeon House Fort was intended to protect the port of Dublin from foreign enemy attack, but Dublin also needed to be protected from attacks by the native Irish. Therefore, various army barracks were built throughout the city, especially in the nineteenth century. One, Beggars Bush Barracks, was built (mostly with squared black calp limestone) in 1827 not far from Ringsend. Later that century, various alterations and additions were completed, including the Chapel School in 1857, an extra four bays to the south-west hospital, the three-storey clock tower in the south centre, the single-storey cookhouse near the rear, and infill brick-built blocks to the officers' quarters on both sides of the front parade ground.

In 1911 the Irish Amateur Boxing Association of Ireland was founded here, with D.P. Mordaunt as its first president.

Following the 1916 Rising, the War of Independence, and the December 1921 Treaty, the barracks was the first in Ireland to be handed over by the British to the Irish Free State, on 31 January 1922. Thereafter, the barracks was only partially used by the army, since the Government Stationery Office was based here from the 1930s. In 1991, the Government built a large office block in the centre of the campus to house the Labour Court (for employment disputes) and the Geological Survey. In 1997, the former three blocks of married quarters alongside Shelbourne Road were converted by Dublin Corporation into senior citizens' flats. In recent years, some other barracks buildings were converted into private apartments, while extensions and additional blocks were built for a similar purpose. The former Chapel School is now the National Print Museum, and the officers' quarters block in the front square is now the Labour History Museum (with arched colonnade filled in).

POOLBEG LIGHTHOUSE

From at least 1735 there was a lightship moored just north of the present lighthouse, and until 1756, ships had to pay a toll when entering Dublin, in order to defray the cost of the lightship. The granite Poolbeg Lighthouse was built in 1761-67, to a design by John Smyth, at the same time as the second section of the South Bull Wall was under construction. The original lighthouse was only 35ft high, with a balcony and staircase on the outside, but these were removed in 1819, and the height increased from three storeys to five, giving a total height of 63ft (base to vane). The height was actually 68ft above high water. Initially the lighthouse was lit by candles, and then oil from 1786. A century later, gas was manufactured and stored in gasometers on site. Fog bells were introduced in 1827, changed to a siren in 1884 and a foghorn in 1965. The fog siren was sounded by compressed air, supplied by an Otto gas engine. Edmondson & Co. of Dublin installed the gas works, engine and siren in 1884.

Robert Callwell, in his manuscript dated 1863, reported that the light was visible at a distance of 12 miles in clear weather. The original lighthouse was whitewashed, then painted black at the beginning of the twentieth century, and finally red in 1935. Since 1969, the lighthouse has been unmanned and fully automated, and the keeper's house later demolished.

From 1837 to 1958, the Ordnance Survey used Poolbeg Lighthouse as the base datum for all levels throughout Ireland, after which Malin Head in County Donegal became the reference level. All buildings and places in Ireland were described as being so many feet above (or below) the benchmark on Poolbeg Lighthouse.

COAST GUARD STATION, 70–80 PIGEON HOUSE ROAD

In 1837, there was a small station near the east end of Sir John Rogersons Quay. Around 1850 a big station was built at Ringsend Point, on the site of a small watch house dating from at least 1816. The new station included ten cottages.

In 1874/75 John Jackson built a new Coastguard Station near the present Poolbeg Yacht & Boat Club for the Board of Works. It comprised a watchtower at the east end, with seven guards' houses alongside, with first-floor party-wall doors linking each house. There were outside toilets and coalhouses, plus a central washroom. The boathouse was near the watchtower. Now all the houses are privately owned, with modern bathroom and kitchen extensions. The foreshore nearby was reclaimed in 1976 for a container terminal, South Bank Quay.

RIVER DODDER

The fast-flowing River Dodder is a major Dublin amenity (although not used for boating), but has tended to cut Ringsend off from the city centre. The first Ringsend Bridge is reputed to date from 1650, replaced several times in the eighteenth century after being swept away by floods. The present single-arch granite bridge was completed around 1812.

The triple-arch Londonbridge dates from 1857 and replaced an earlier timber bridge.

GRAND CANAL HARBOUR

The Grand Canal originally terminated at St James Harbour, west of Dolphins Barn, but a 3.8-mile Circular Line extended the canal to Ringsend Basin, the latter officially opened with great celebrations in 1796. Passenger barges travelled between Dublin and Shannon Harbour, with customers often staying in Portobello Hotel in Rathmines. Goods were also transported by barge, until the advent of the cheaper and faster railways from 1834 onwards.

Three different-sized locks admit ships and barges: the Westmoreland, Buckingham, and Camden. The two-storey Dockmaster's House on the east side of the locks was rebuilt in the 1940s. The lock-keeper's cottage on the west side is now derelict.

There were originally three dry/graving docks for repairing and building ships, but the south one was infilled in the middle of the nineteenth century and is now a slipway (where the amphibian 'Splash' tour enters the water). One of the other docks is now home to *Naomh Eanna* (1958 Aran Islands ferry for CIE, retired in 1987). A unique feature of the dry docks was the method of emptying the water – a sluice valve at the rear was simply opened, and the water flowed into the lower River Dodder alongside.

Grand Canal Harbour is L-shaped, with Pearse Street dissecting the two sections at McMahon Bridge. This bridge was originally a very narrow timber drawbridge built in 1791, known as the Brunswick Bascule, and replaced by the 23ft-wide iron swivel Victoria Bridge in 1857. A new 45ft-wide swivel iron bridge was built (by Ross & Walpole of the North Wall) in 1901 to allow electric trams from Sandymount to proceed into the city centre – prior to this, passengers had to alight from the tram and cross the bridge on foot! Another new lifting bridge was built in 1963 by 'Machine-Fabrik' of Bavaria (Germany), and renamed McMahon Bridge. The present fixed concrete bridge dates from 2007. The smaller section of the harbour has been a colourful marina since 1993, housing permanent houseboats and narrow barges.

DIVING BELL, SIR JOHN ROGERSONS QUAY

This unique piece of equipment was built in 1866 by Thomas Grendon of Drogheda, to a design by Bindon Blood Stoney, the engineer for the Ballast Office, to facilitate faster and cheaper building of quay walls. The 90-ton iron structure consists of a floorless chamber with a tall funnel on top. A barge moved the apparatus into position, and it was lowered to the bed of the River Liffey, with the top of the funnel projecting above the river surface. Six brave divers entered the top of the funnel via an air-lock (compressed air was pumped in), descended a ladder into the chamber, and excavated the muck from the river bed to afford a level foundation for the huge precast concrete sections of quay wall. The bell was used from 1869 to 1885 on the extension of the North Wall Quay.

The bell was discontinued in 1958 but restored as a museum piece in 2000, including a brand new funnel, and viewing portholes cut into the chamber wall. In 2016, the bell was repositioned on stilts on Sir John Rogersons Quay, with a small interpretative centre underneath.

HAILING STATION

The most important building on Sir John Rogersons Quay was the tiny Hailing Station at the corner of Great Brittain Quay. This was the office of the Berthing Master, who controlled the various shipping berths here. It was demolished a few years ago.

BOAT BUILDING

Ringsend has a long and proud tradition of boatbuilding and light shipbuilding, the former generally concentrated on the stretch of River Dodder backing onto Thorncastle Street, and the latter in the dry docks section of the Grand Canal Basin.

The Pembroke Estate map of 1762 by Jonathan Barker depicts boatbuilding activity alongside the River Dodder, backing on to Thorncastle Street.

In 1801 John Clements of Ringsend built the first lifeboat for the Ballast Board, and it was stationed in Pigeon House Harbour. In 1809, Mr Hill and Mr Clements both ran boatbuilding businesses alongside the River Dodder. In 1811, Nicholas Whitthorne of Ringsend built a lighter for the Port Authority for use in Howth, being 40ft long, with a 15ft crossbeam, and 4ft 6in deep. In 1834, John Marshall was in Thorncastle Street. The Dublin Dockyard Company was in Thorncastle Street from 1851 to 1881, but mainly worked on the North Wall, before being taken over by Vickers Ireland. M. Scallan is listed on the street in 1870.

Mat Taylor, originally from Newcastle-upon-Tyne, was a well-respected trainer for the various rowing clubs in Ringsend in the 1870s and '80s. He was also a boatbuilder of renown, supplying the rowing clubs, and he is credited with introducing the sliding seat to Ireland in 1872. Otherwise, it seems that many of the club rowing boats in that era were imported from England.

There were three boatyards on Thorncastle Street in 1906 – Foleys, Murphys (founded 1870), and Harry G. Smith. In 1933, the 15-ton yacht *Theta* was launched from Smiths. Foleys was near Ringsend church, then Murphys, and then Smiths. Foley closed to make way for Whelan House flats in the late 1930s, then Murphys in the 1950s, and finally Harry Smith in 1956 during the actual construction of O'Rahilly House (Harry served his time with Holloway on Sir John Rogersons Quay).

RINGSEND DOCKYARD COMPANY

The Ringsend Dockyard Company (1912-1965), founded by William McMullan, operated from the dry docks leased from the Grand Canal Company and specialised in making steel barges for their landlord. They were taken over by Dublin Shipbuilders in 1919 (which had been set up that same year in Alexandra Basin), and William McMullan remained as managing director. Dublin Shipbuilders closed in 1929, but the Ringsend subsidiary continued trading as Ringsend Dockyard Company (Dublin) Ltd under McMullan (and William Alexander from 1939).

In 1932, Ringsend Dockyard Company made three steel pontoons for the Electricity Supply Board for use on the Shannon/Lock Derg scheme to carry dredging machinery – each was in three parts, with an overall length of 58ft, a width of 13ft and a depth of 4ft 6in.

In 1938 it was reported that Ringsend Dockyard (Dublin) Ltd worked both in Ringsend Dockyard and in the public dock and graving slips at Alexandra Basin on the North Wall. For example, they worked on the Codling lightship, *Guillemot*, the Port & Docks Board dredger, *Sandpiper*, the SS *Shamrock* belonging to Dublin Corporation Sewerage Department, and the Government fishery cruiser, *Muirchu*. In all, twenty-two vessels had either docked or slipped at Ringsend or Alexandra Basin in a six-month period, while twenty-nine vessels had been repaired afloat, including tankers, coasting vessels and steamers belonging to the Commissioners of Irish Lights. Nearly £5,000 was paid in wages to the 130 employees during that six-month period. The Port & Docks Board used either Ringsend Dockyard or Harland & Wolff in Belfast. In 1940, Irish Lights boats serviced included, SS *General McHardy* and SS *Wyndham*.

OTHER BOATBUILDERS

The Ringsend Iron Works operated from Fitzwilliam Quay from about 1800 to 1885. Initially run by Courtney Kenny Clarke, it made boats, steam engines and boilers. Fred Barrington was the operator from 1838 to 1885, generally making barges for the Grand Canal Company in the latter's dry docks in the Basin. In 1846, the *Shamrock*, an iron steamship with screw propeller, was built for the British & Irish Steam Packet Company. Unlike Thorncastle Street, Fitzwilliam Quay did not have direct river frontage.

In 1815, Anthony Hill built the dredger *Patrick* for the Ballast Board, with an endless chain of buckets, presumably using the graving docks in the Grand Canal Basin. In 1825, Mr Morton built (near the drawbridge) a 130-ton rigged schooner for a Bordeaux packet. He also received an order to build a steam-packet for Messrs Rogers Brothers & Co. for the Dublin to Wexford trade. The 1836 Ordnance Survey map shows a shipbuilder's yard on the site where Bolands Mill later operated, but no name is provided.

In 1895, it was reported in the newspapers that P.G. Holloway had started building ships at Sir John Rogersons Quay, to compete with the Brixham ships, and was about to launch a 53-ton vessel for Stephen Sims of Ringsend. Many Ringsend trawlers were built in the fishing village of Brixham in the Torbay region of Devon, where some Ringsend fishermen had ancestors and relatives.

DUBLIN CORPORATION LIFFEY FERRY

Ringsend workers have close ties with the main docks on the North Wall and relied on small ferryboats to transport them to and from their jobs each day. Originally, private operators owned the ferries but Dublin Corporation took over the service from 1920 until 1984, when the East Link Toll Bridge opened. There were two ferry routes: one from Macken Street, beside the Ferryman public house, and the other from Great Brittain Quay. The fare in the early days was ½d (to coincide with the traditional toll on the Halfpenny Bridge), then 1d in the 1950s, and 10p in the 1980s.

The East Link Bridge was privately built, with a lifting central section to allow tall boats to move upriver. The bridge was transferred to Dublin City Council in 2016 and renamed the Thomas Clarke Bridge, in honour of one of the men who signed the 1916 Proclamation.

FISHING

Archer's Survey of 1801 recorded seven fishing 'wherries' in Ringsend, catching cod, ling, haddock, ray and herrings. The Dublin region had eighty-seven boats, while Skerries had the most of that share at thirty-six. Each boat had eight men, and received a parliamentary bounty of £205 a ton, divided into ten shares – eight for the men and two for the owner. There were also twenty 'smacks' and five seine nets occupied in salmon fishing in the bay. The River Liffey also yielded salmon from Islandbridge to Poolbeg, with twelve men based at Poolbeg.

In 1904 there were sixty-three fishing trawlers, individually owned by Ringsend men (some men owned several), landing catches at Dún Laoghaire or Skerries. Ringsend never had a harbour and so trawlers anchored off the South Wall, side by side in a line. Fishing gradually declined after 1906 because of competition from English steam trawlers. In 1937, a company owned the six trawlers in Ringsend.

A 1933 photo in *The Irish Times* shows Ringsend fishermen setting out on a fishing trip: four men rowed the small boat, while six others looked after the nets, and there seemed to be very little space for the fish.

In the 1950s, salmon netting was still practiced on the River Liffey, despite seals killing a lot of fish in previous decades.

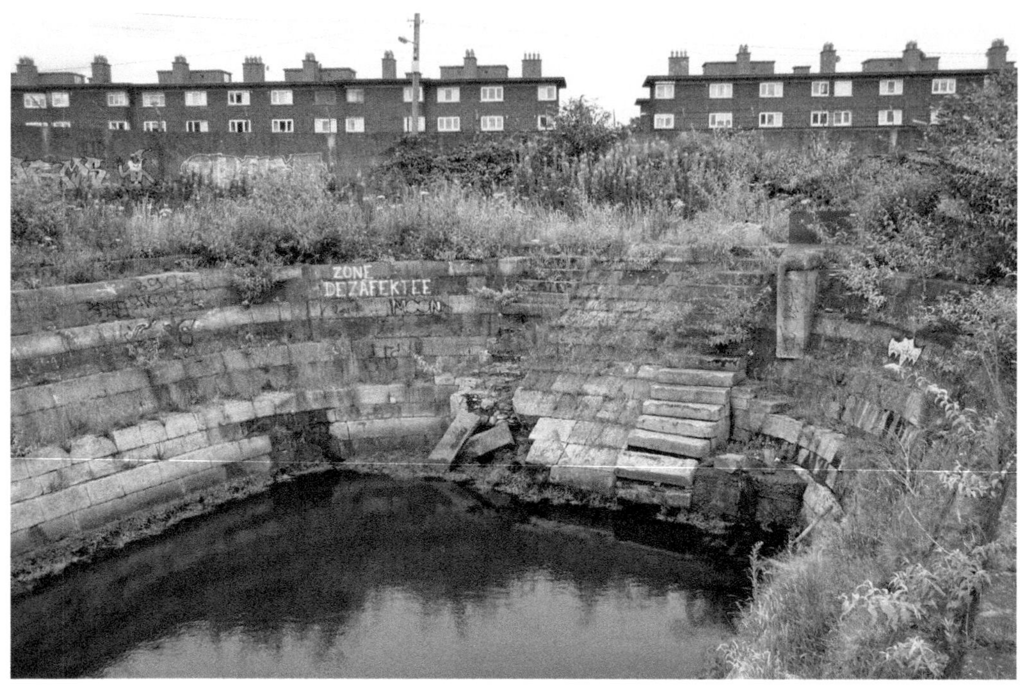

One of the abandoned graving docks in Ringsend Harbour.

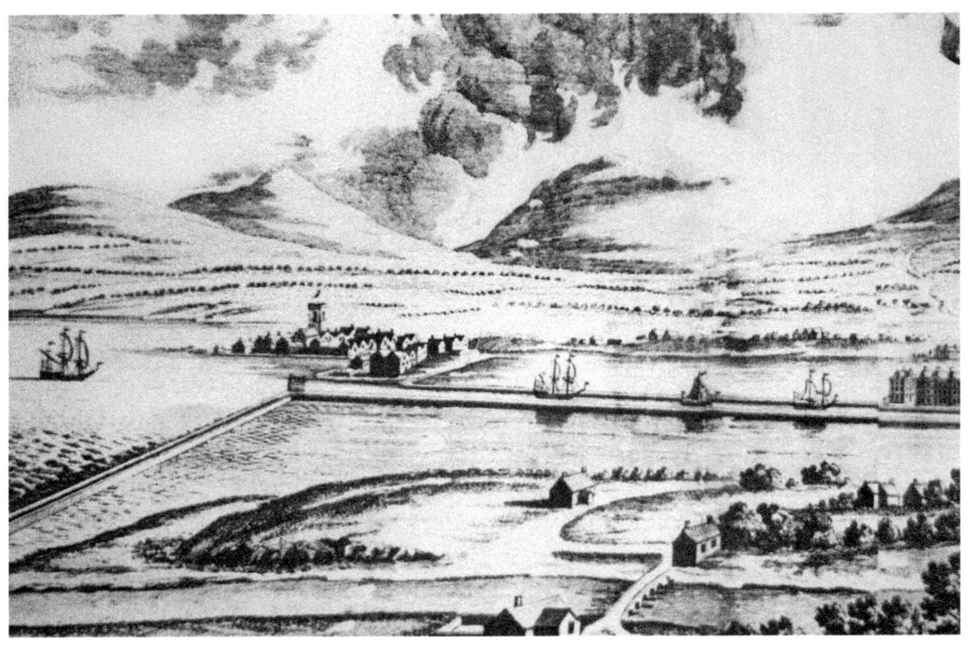

Charles Brooking map, 1728. Ringsend village is on the left. (Courtesy of Trinity College Dublin)

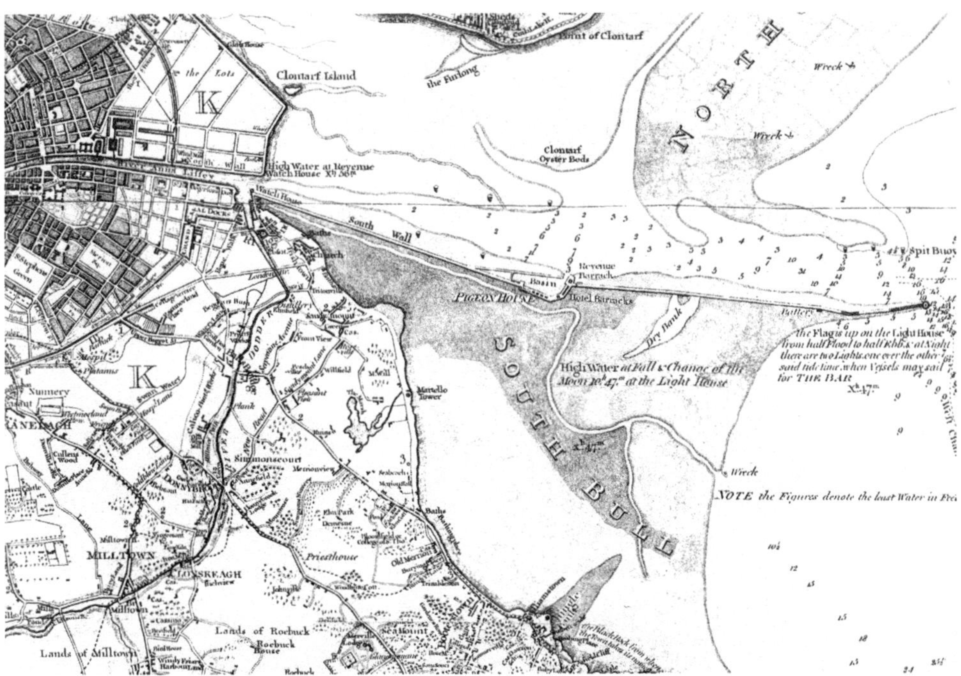

1816 Taylor map, with the South Lotts bringing Ringsend closer to the city centre. (Courtesy of Trinity College Dublin)

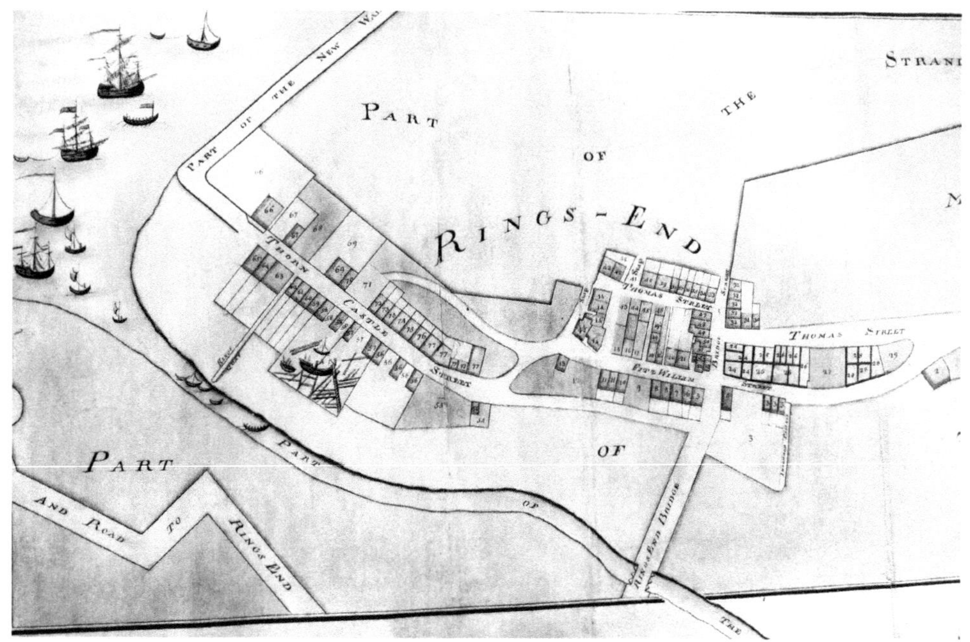

Jonathan Barker map of the Pembroke Estate, 1762. Note the boatyard alongside the River Dodder. (Courtesy of the National Archives of Ireland)

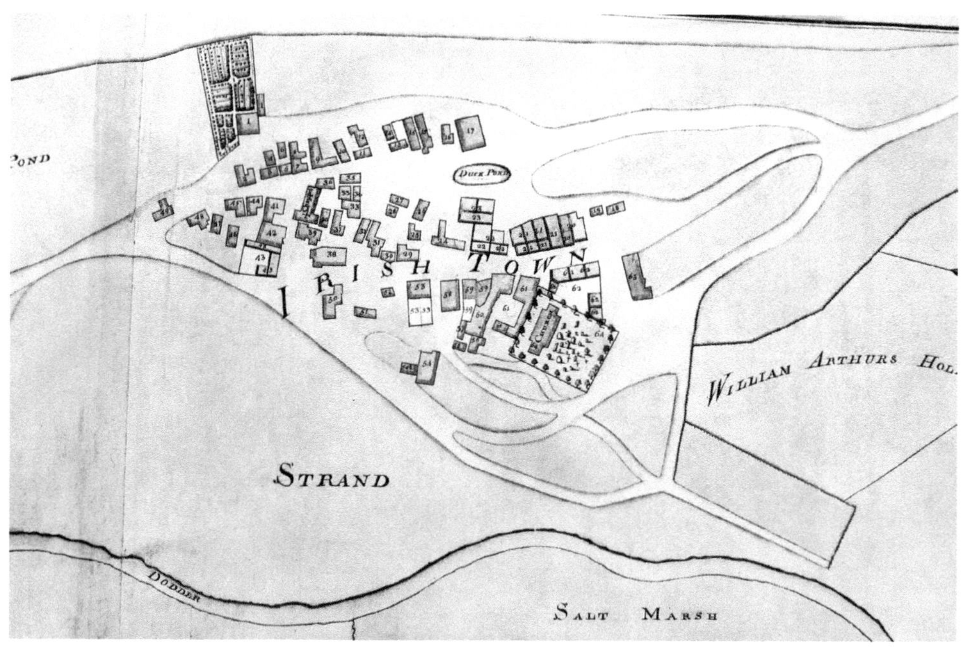

Jonathan Barker map of the Pembroke Estate, 1762. Note the church and the chapel. (Courtesy of the National Archives of Ireland)

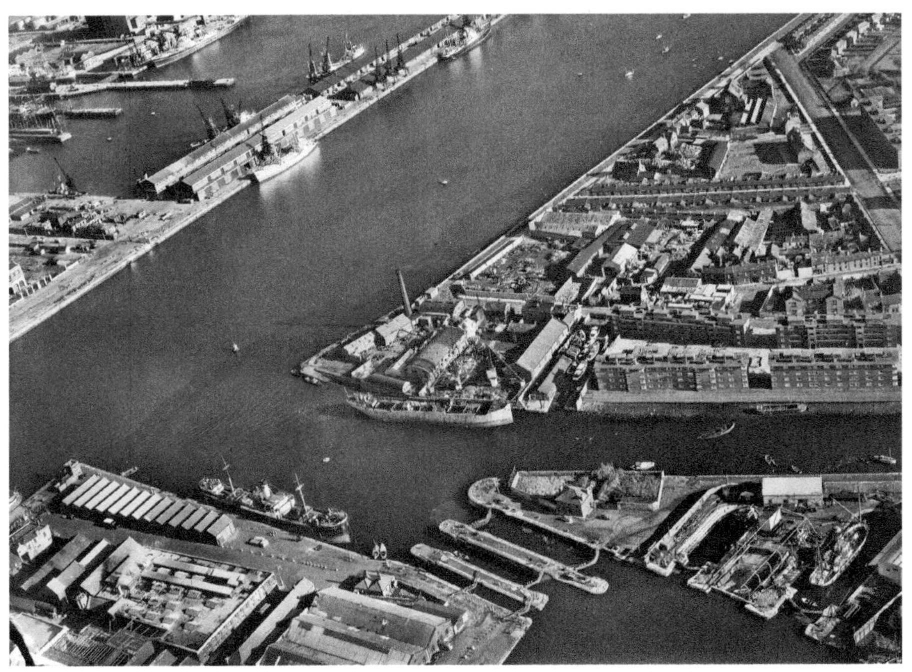

An aerial view of Ringsend in the 1950s. (Courtesy of the National Library of Ireland)

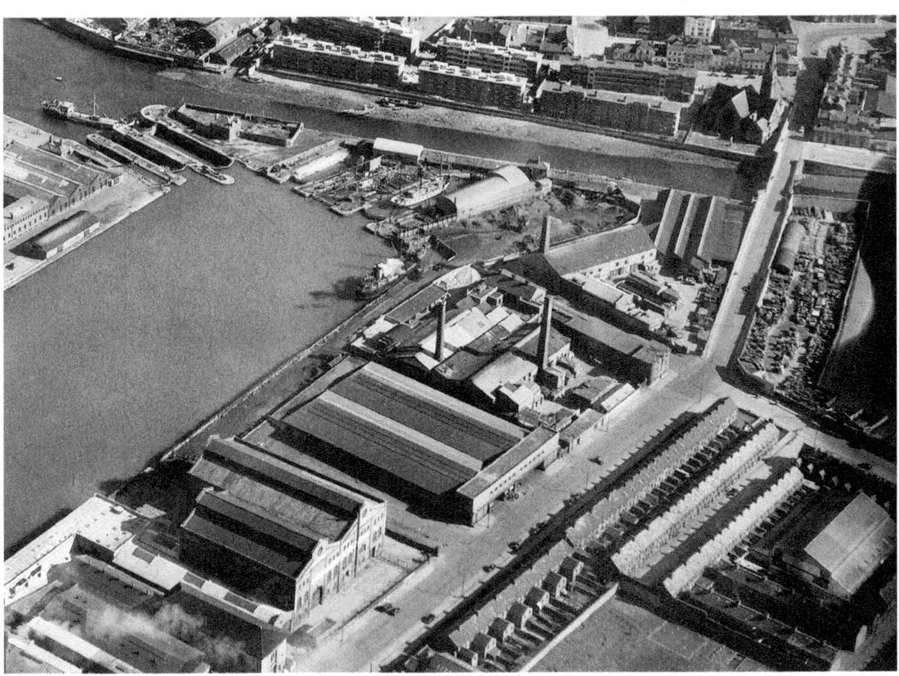

Ringsend Road in the 1950s. On the left can be seen the tram generating station, then the bus depot, and the Irish Glass Bottle Company. (Courtesy of the National Library of Ireland)

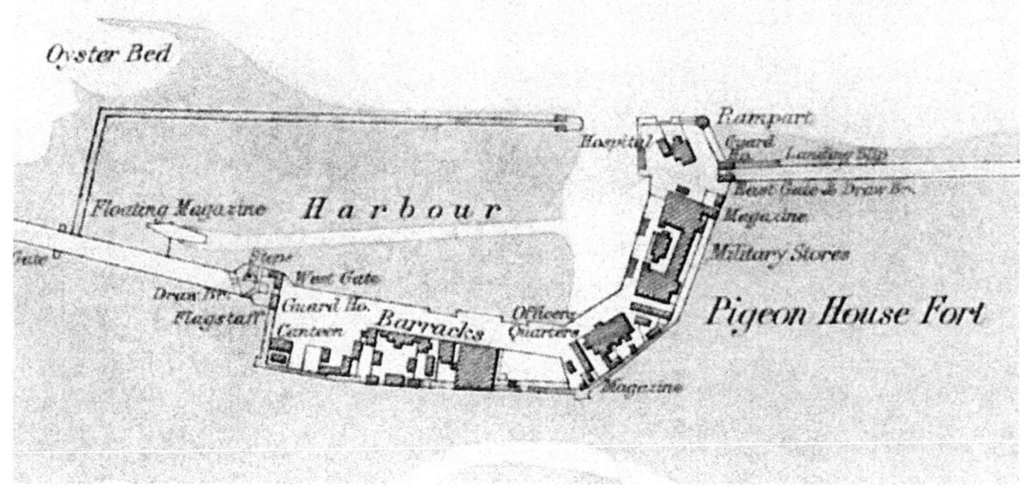

Ordnance Survey map, 1837. Note the 'floating magazine' in the harbour and the 'oyster bed'. (Courtesy of Dublin City Council)

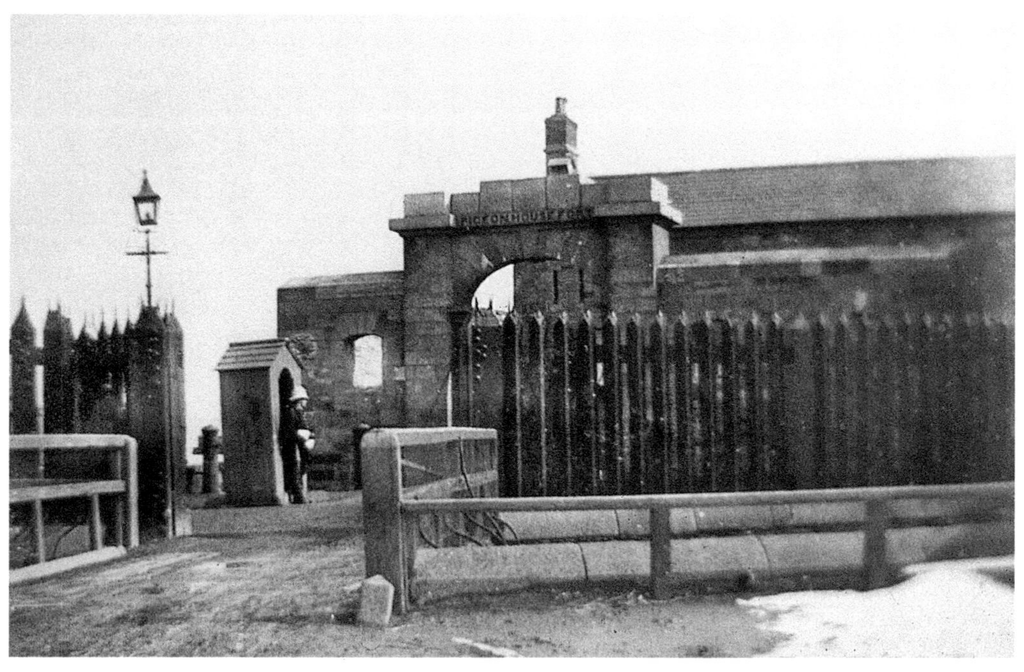

The west entrance to the Pigeon House Fort in the early 1890s. Part of the arched entrance is still standing today. (Courtesy of Dublin City Library & Archives)

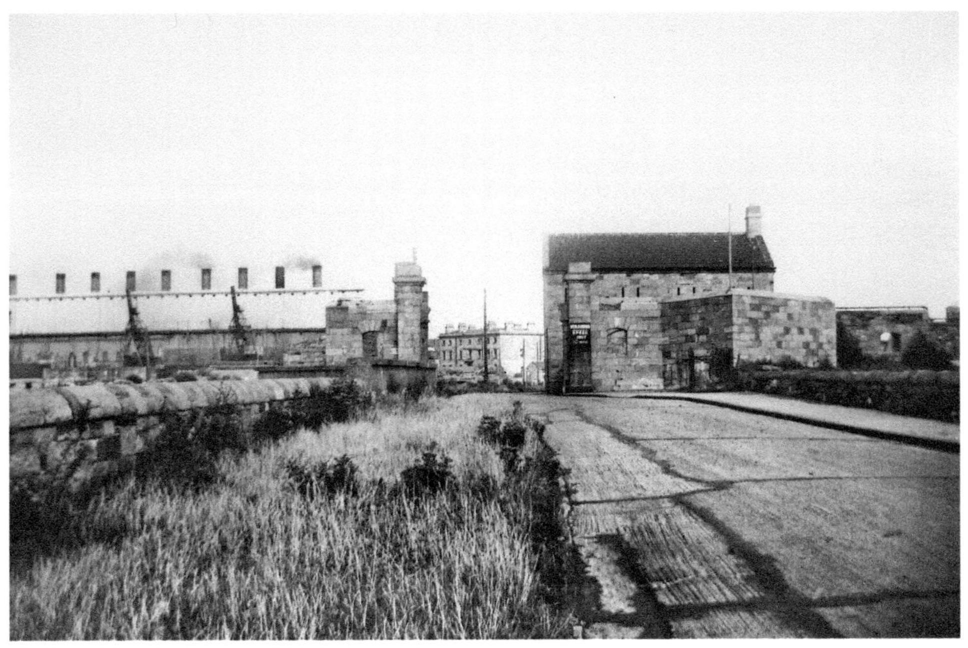

The west entrance to the Pigeon House Fort in the 1950s, with Pigeon House Generating Station in background. The arch over the entrance has been removed by this stage, leaving only the two piers. (Courtesy of Irish Architectural Archives)

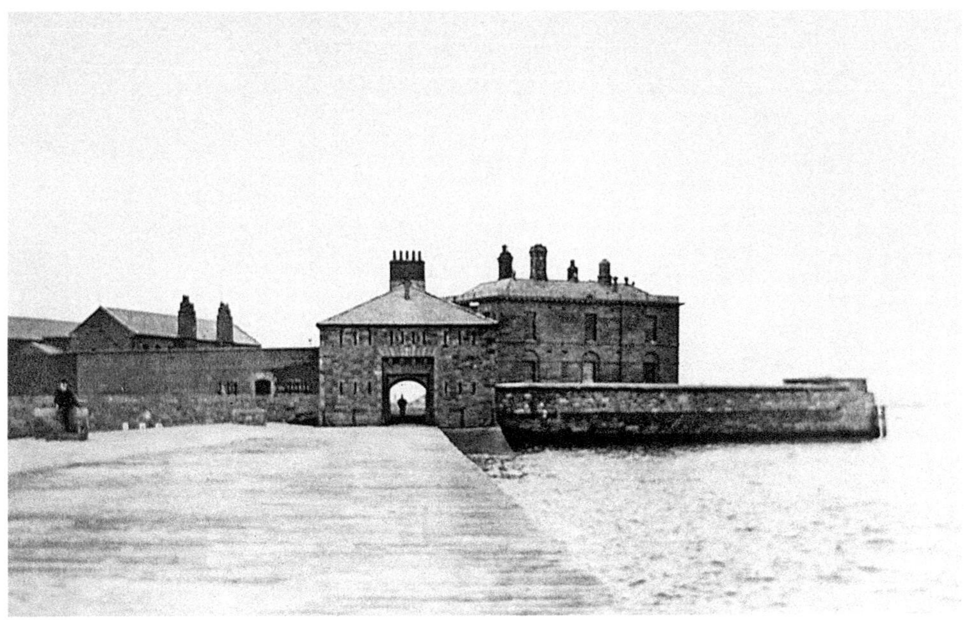

The east entrance to the Pigeon House Fort in the early 1890s, with the former barracks hospital on the right. (Courtesy of Dublin City Library & Archives)

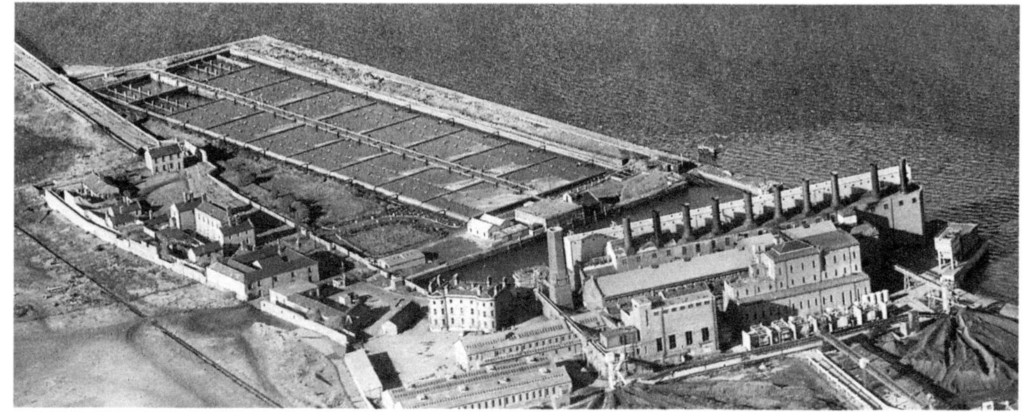

Pigeon House Fort in the 1950s, with the ESB Generating Station on the right. Most of the original harbour is now taken up with the settlement tanks for Dublin Corporation's sewage treatment. (Courtesy of the National Library of Ireland)

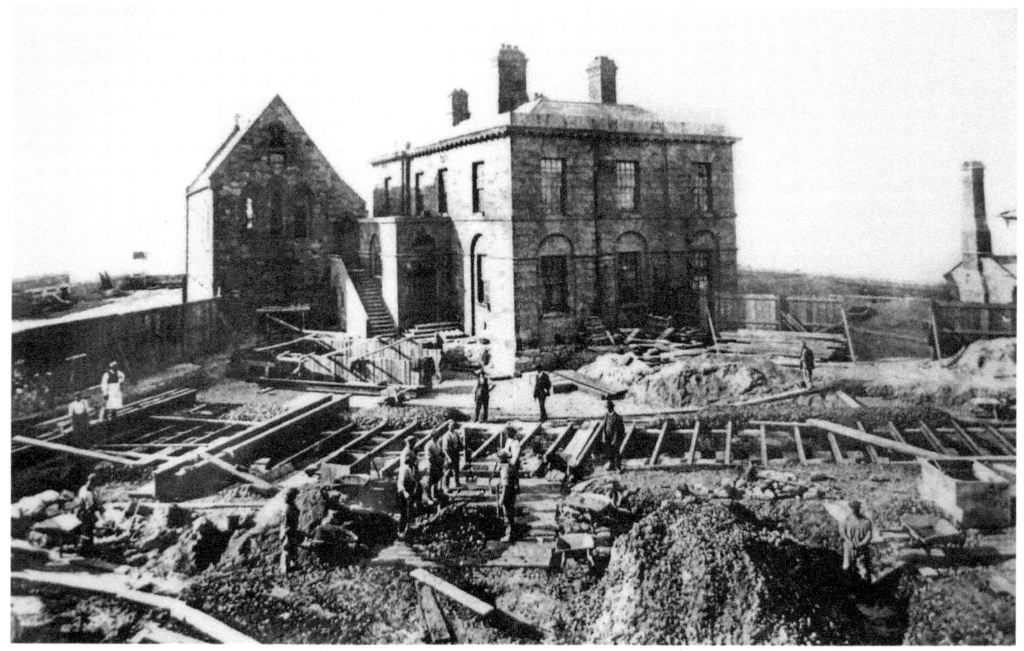

The former barracks hospital and chapel of the Pigeon House Fort, during construction of Dublin Corporation's electricity generating station around 1902/'03. (Courtesy of Brian Siggins)

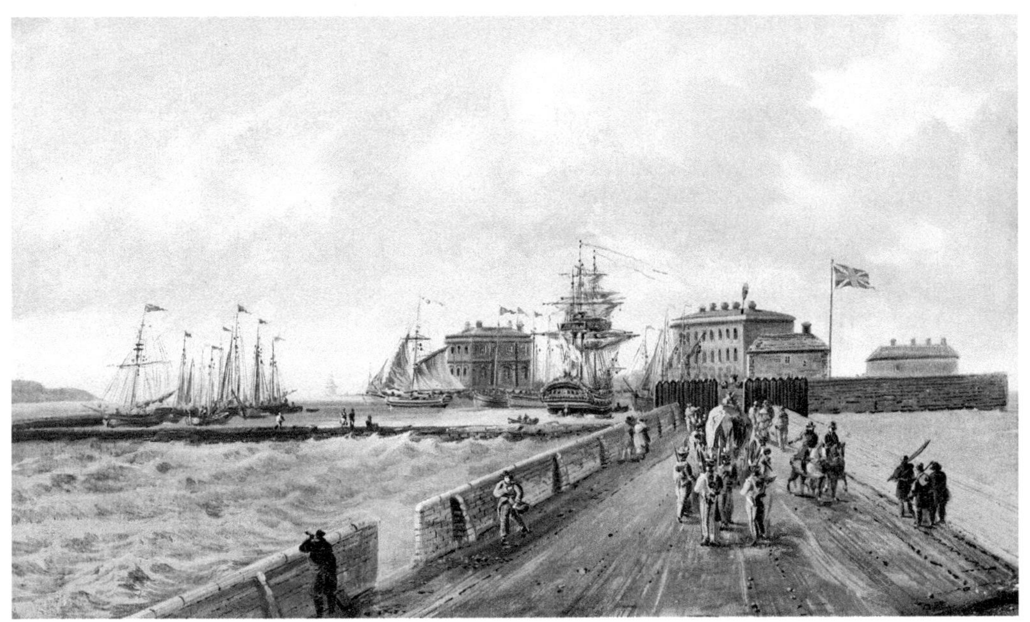

'A View of the Pigeon House, Dublin', by William Sadler the Younger (1782-1839), from the National Gallery of Ireland Collection. (Photo © National Gallery of Ireland)

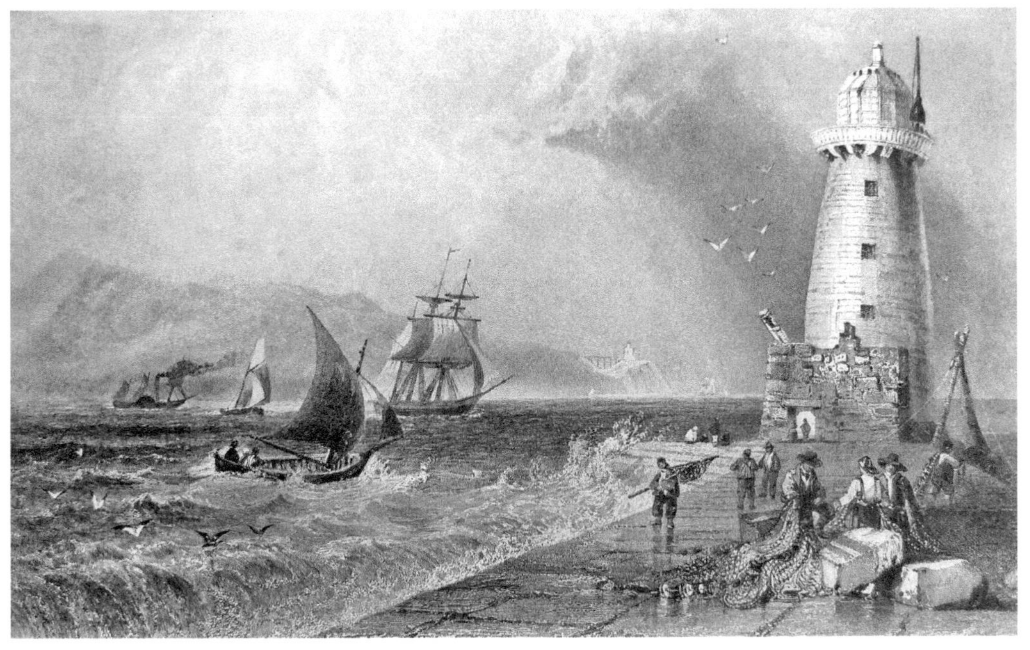

Poolbeg Lighthouse in the nineteenth century. (Courtesy of Irish Lights)

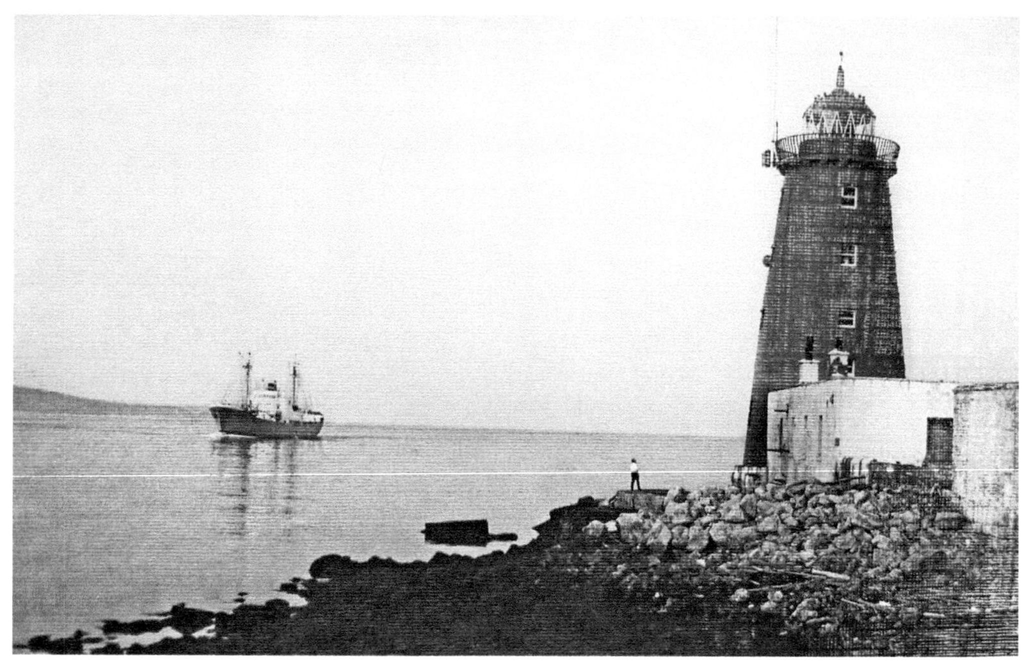

Modern view of the Poolbeg Lighthouse. (Courtesy of Irish Lights)

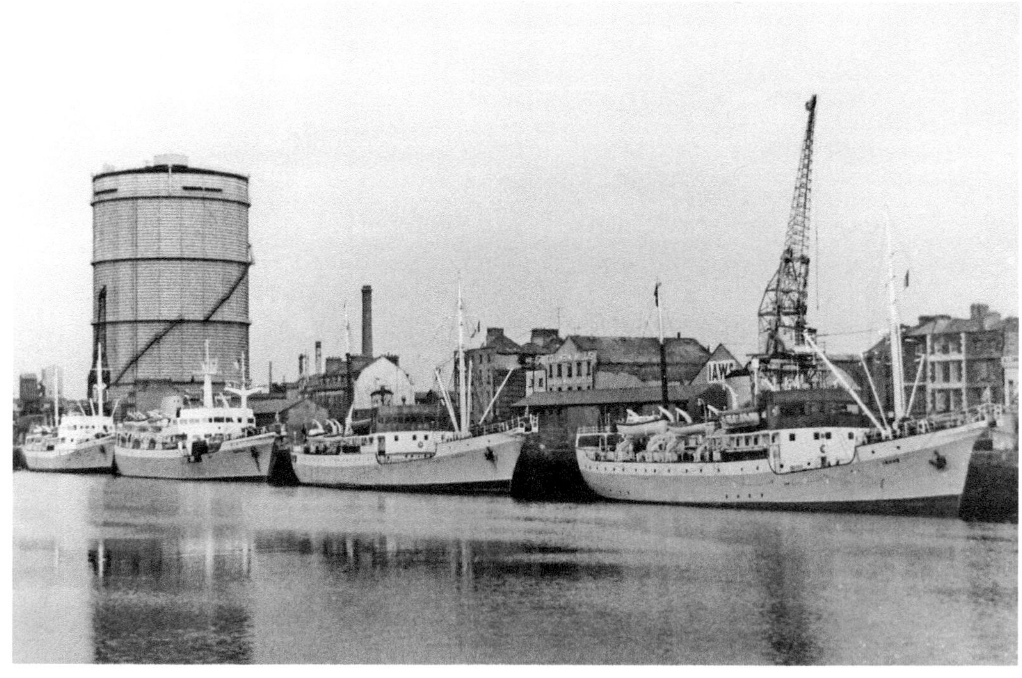

Lighthouse tenders alongside Sir John Rogersons Quay in 1971. From left to right: *Atlanta, Granuaile, Isolde, Ierne*. The gasometer on the left was an enormous landmark. (Courtesy of Irish Lights)

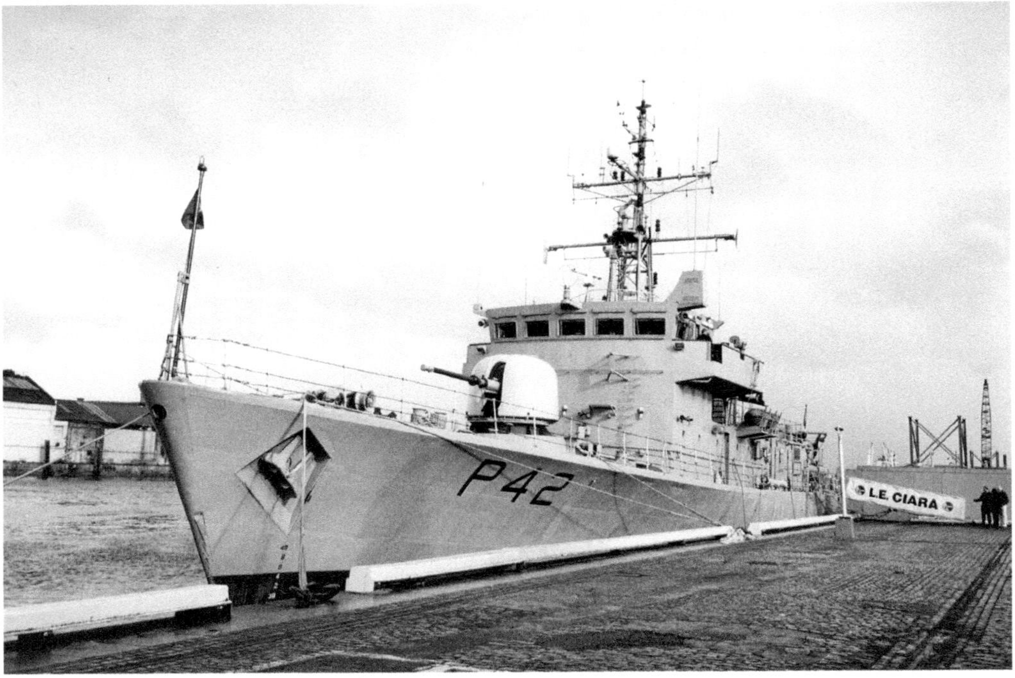

Irish naval ship, the LE *Ciara* on Sir John Rogersons Quay in October 2001.

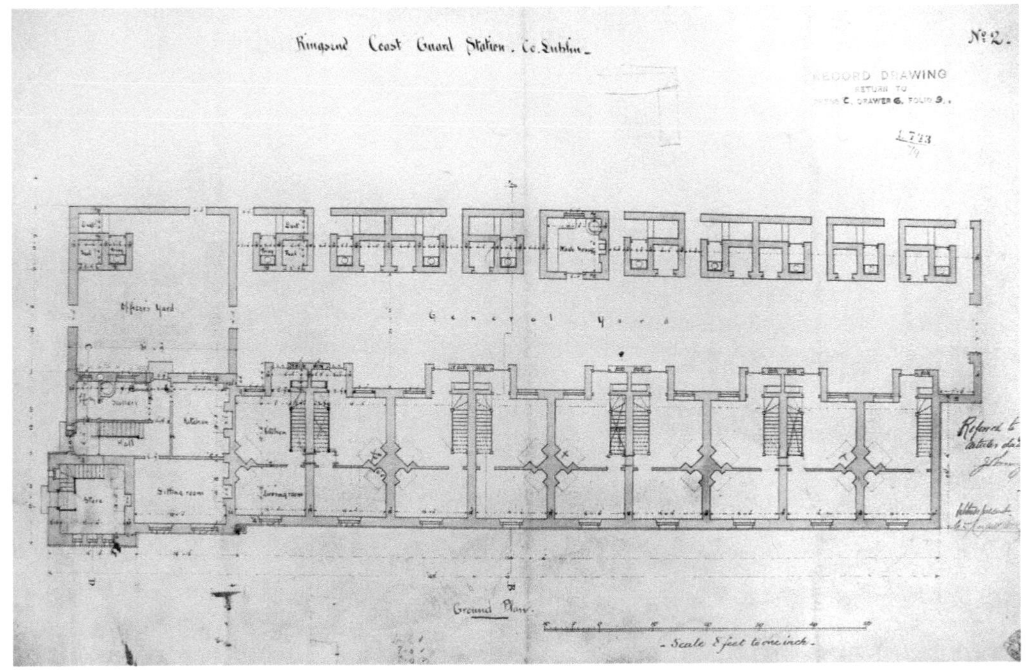

Plan of the ground floor of the former Coastguard Station on Pigeon House Road. Originally the toilets and coalhouses were in the back gardens. (Courtesy of the Office of Public Works)

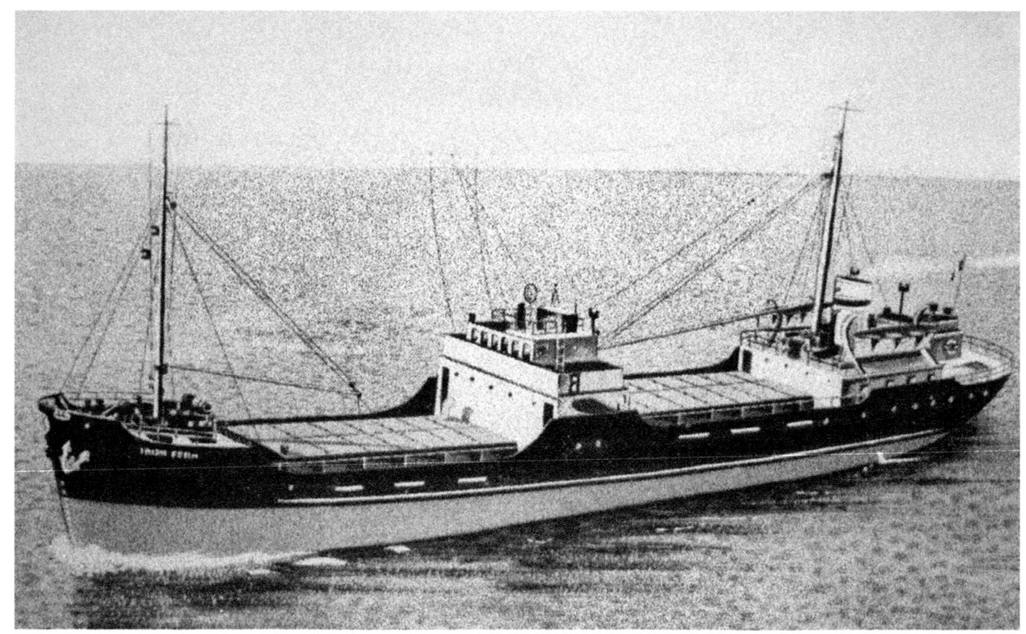

The *Irish Fern* in 1954, built by the Liffey Dockyard on the North Wall. (Courtesy of Irish Shipping)

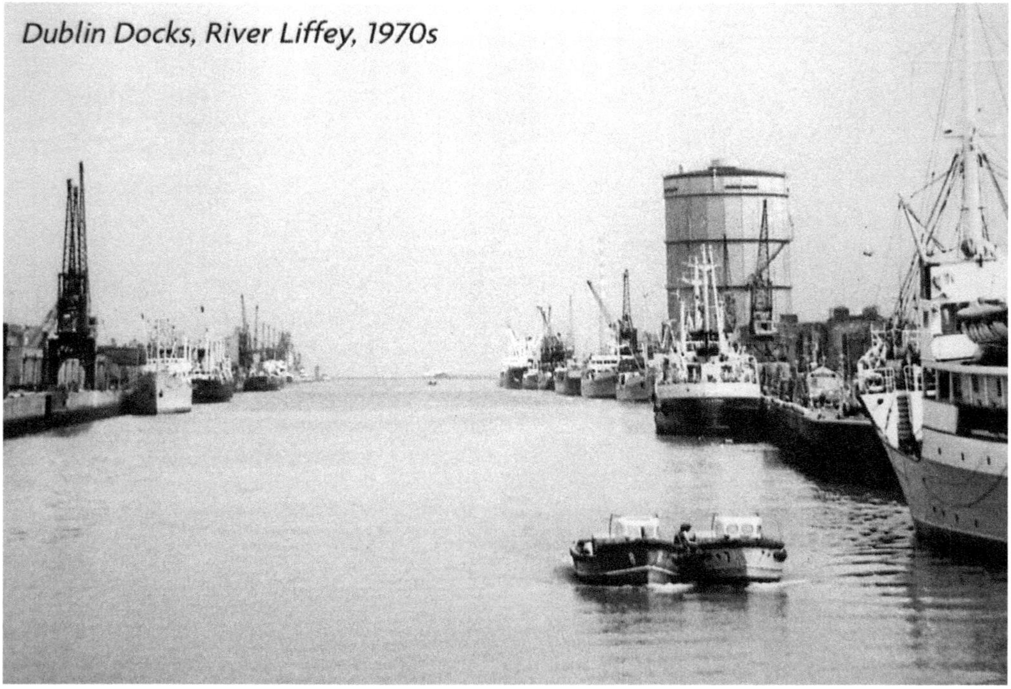

Sir John Rogersons Quay in the 1970s, with the famous gasometer in the background. (Courtesy of Dublin City Library & Archives)

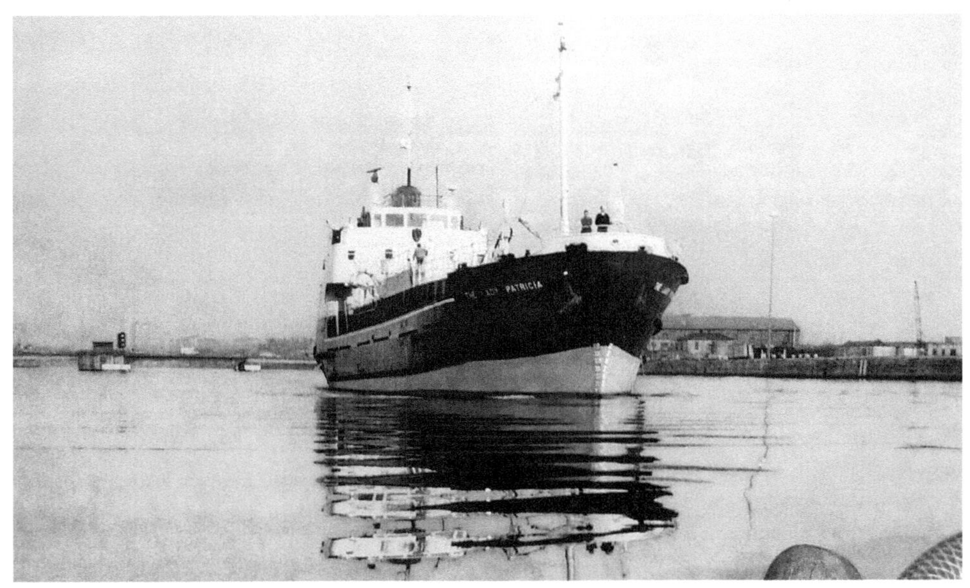

One of the Guinness ships, the *Lady Patricia*. (Courtesy of St Patricks Rowing Club)

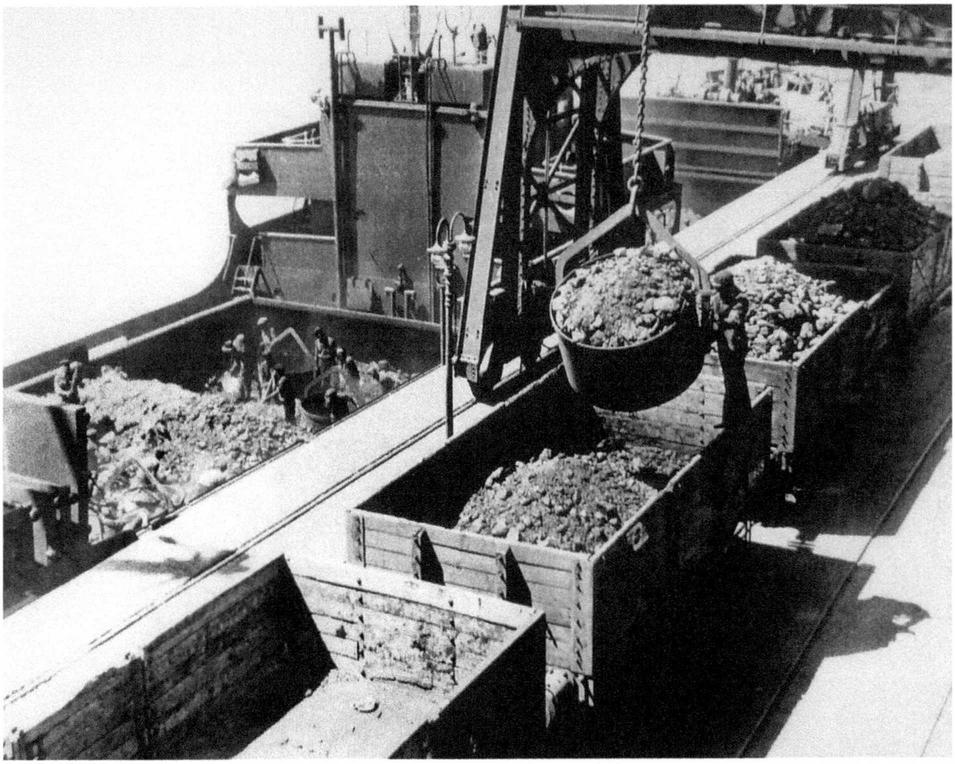

Dockers in the hold of a ship, hand-shovelling coal into giant bins, in the 1940s. (Courtesy of Dublin Port Company)

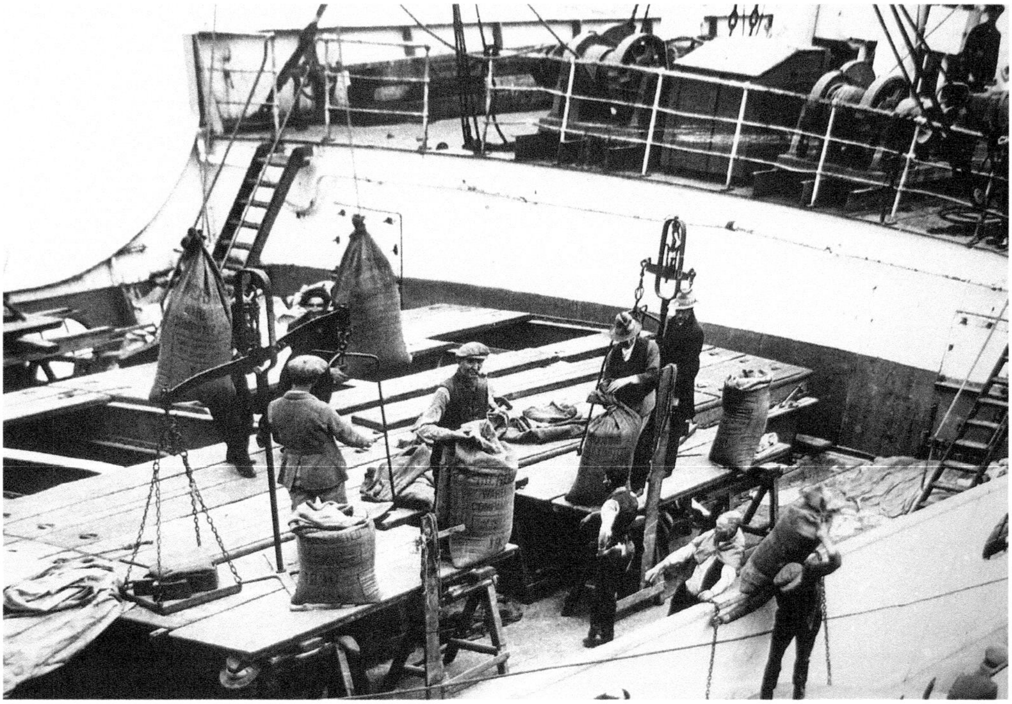

Grain being weighed on a ship in the 1930s. (Courtesy of St Andrews Resource Centre)

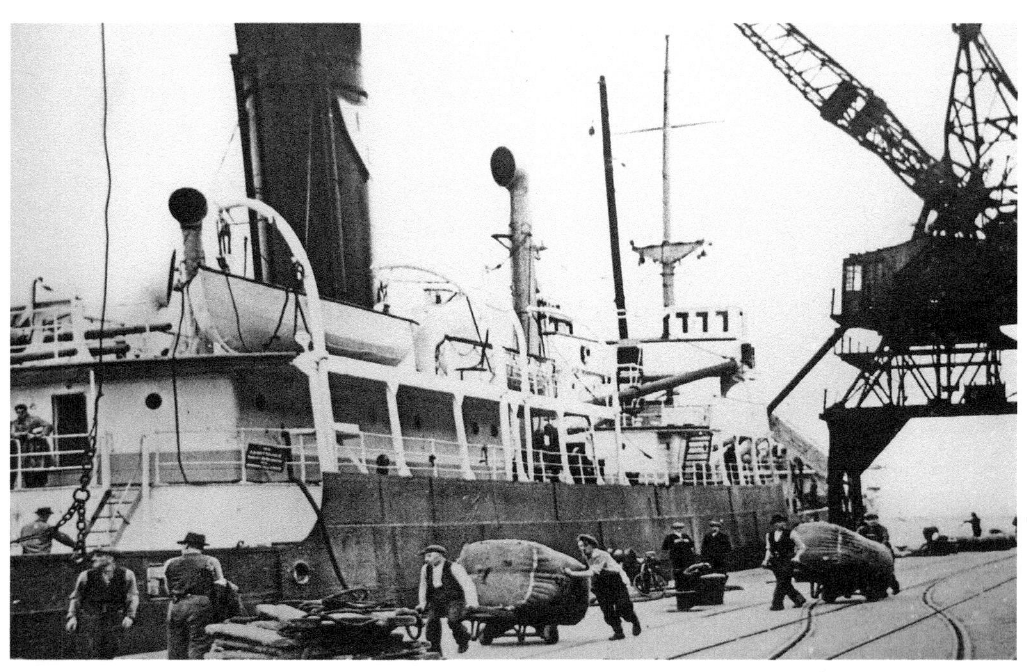

Labour-intensive dock activity in the 1950s. (Courtesy of St Andrews Resource Centre)

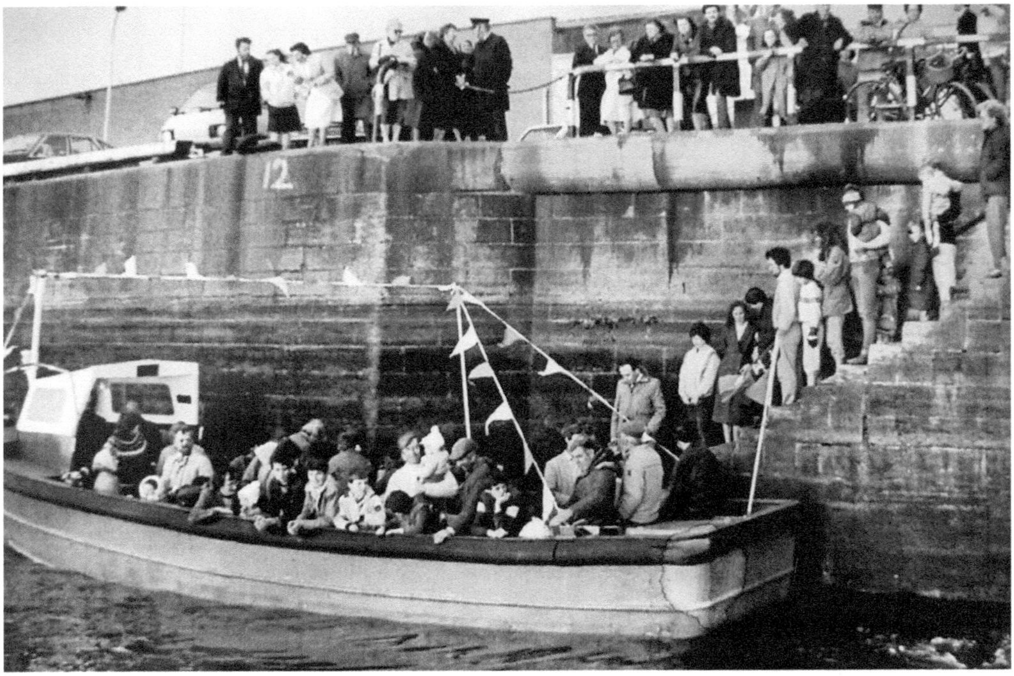

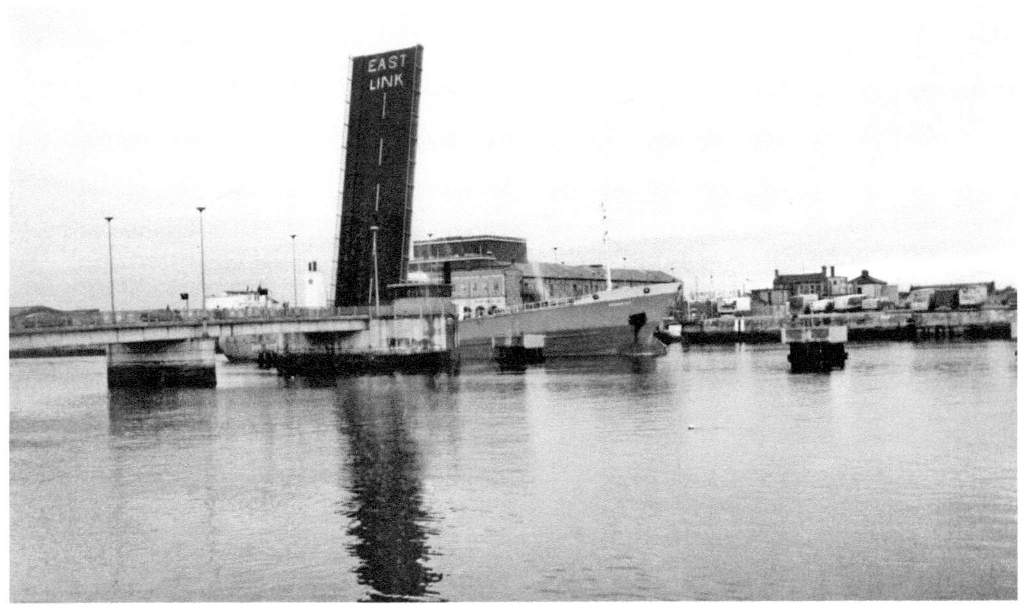

The last Liffey ferry crossing in October 1984. Many Dubliners claim to have been aboard! (Courtesy of Dublin Dock Workers Preservation Society)

The East Link Toll Bridge (now renamed Thomas Clarke Bridge) can be lifted to allow ships to travel up the River Liffey.

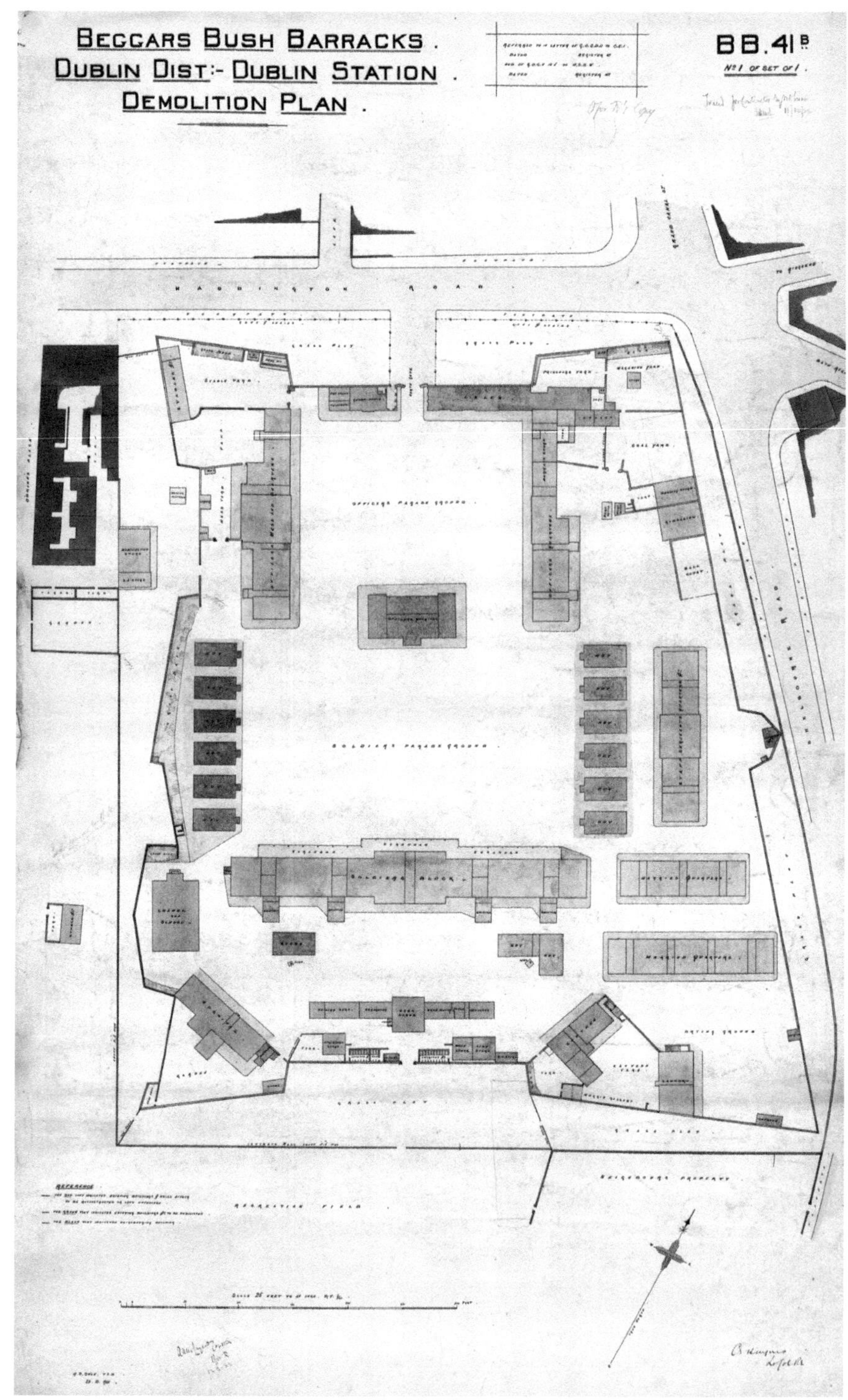

1903 plan of Beggars Bush Barracks. (Courtesy of the Military Archives)

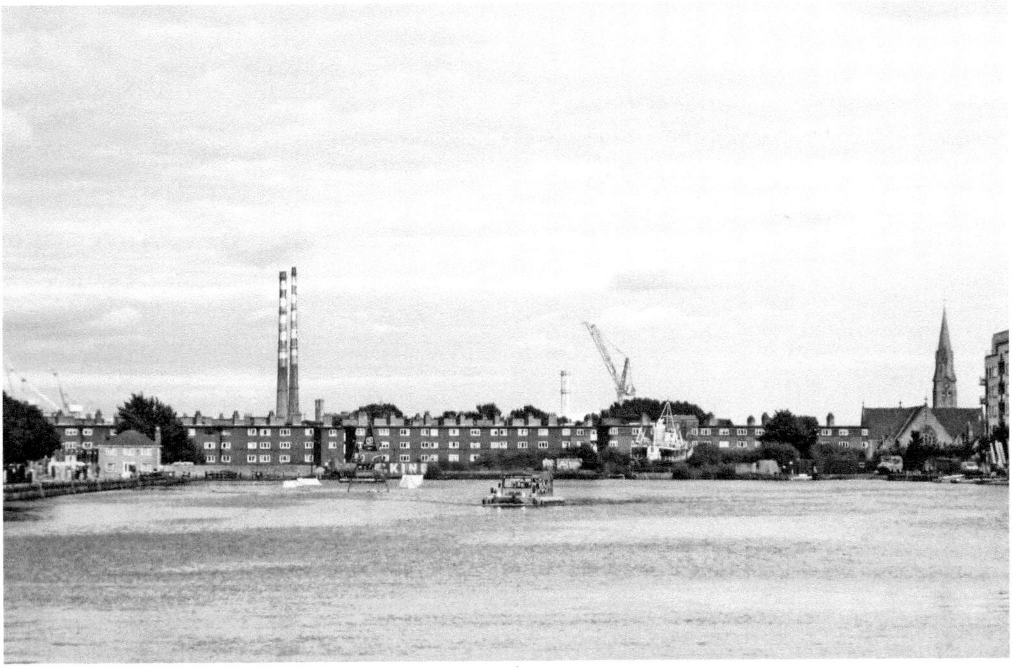

Ringsend in a nutshell, with St Patrick's church on the right and Poolbeg chimneys on the left.

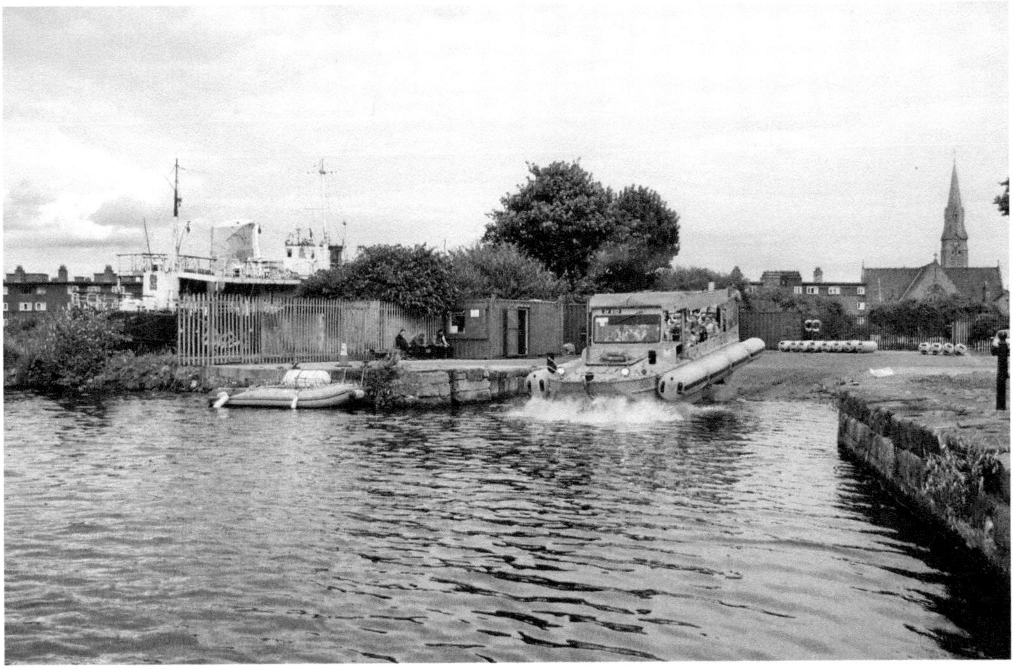

The 'Splash' amphibian vehicle enters Ringsend Basin from the infilled graving dock.

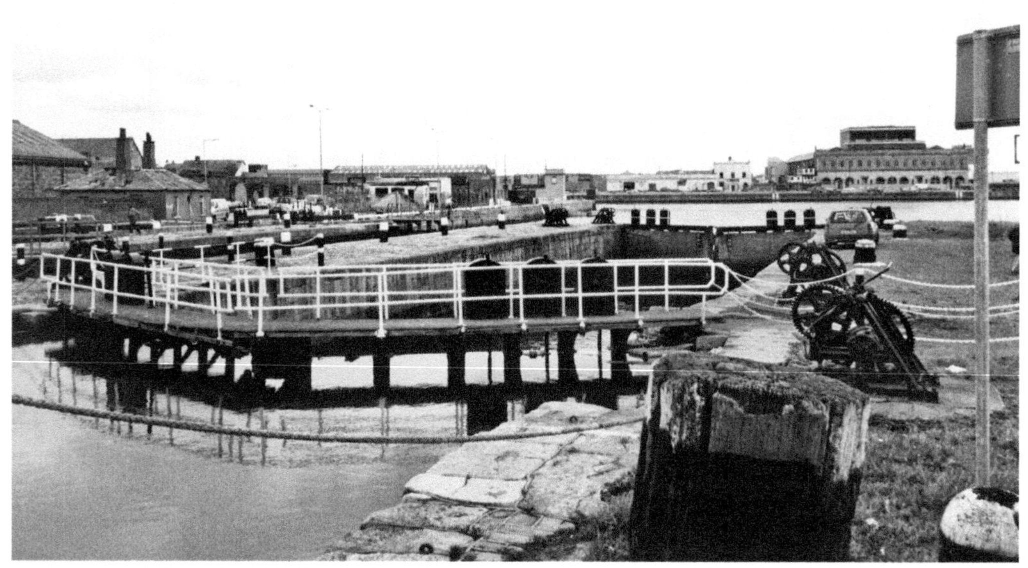

Grand Canal locks, with the lodge on the left, and the Point Depot visible at top right.

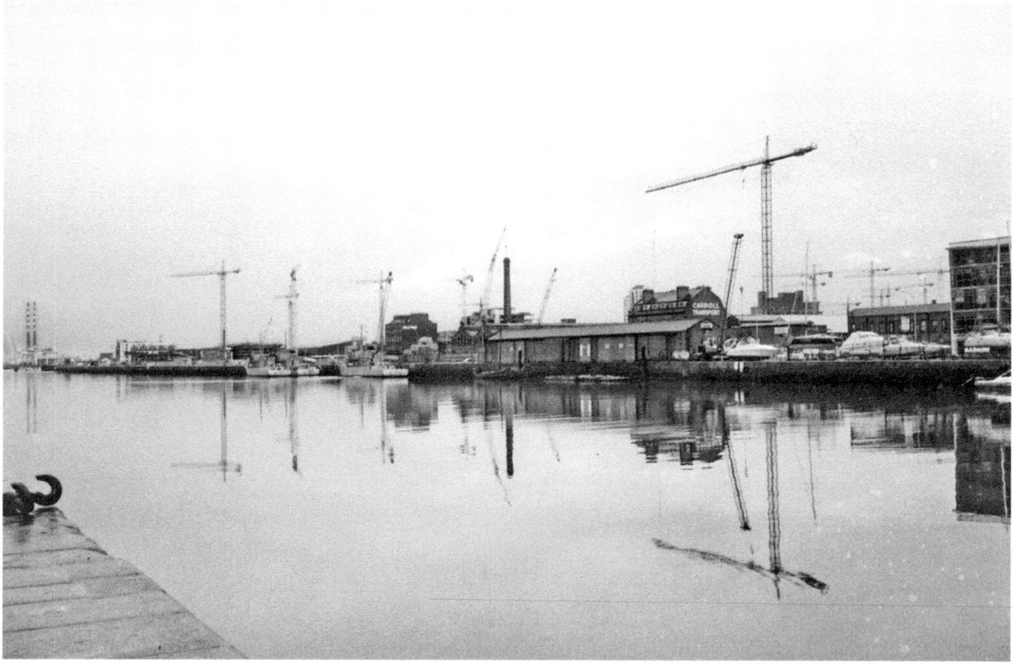

Sir John Rogersons Quay during the 'Celtic Tiger' era, where the tranquil waters belie the storm ahead.

2

PUBLIC ENTERPRISE

PIGEON HOUSE ELECTRICITY GENERATING STATION

Street lighting in Dublin from the 1820s consisted of gas lamps, each of which had to be hand-lit every evening. In 1892, Dublin Corporation opened an electricity generating station in Fleet Street, mainly for street lighting, but which also supplied some business premises.

In 1897, the Pigeon House Fort and Harbour in Ringsend was sold to Dublin Corporation, primarily as a site for a proposed sewage treatment works, but they also built a coal-fired three-phase electricity generating station on part of the site, which opened in July 1903. Thereafter Fleet Street did not generate electricity, although it continued in operation as a distribution station. The Pigeon House station was extended northwards in 1911 and 1913 (necessitating the demolition of the hotel's two-storey annex, and the former hospital and chapel school in the old fort), to cater for the increasing demand for electricity. The Corporation had a lovely showroom at 39 Grafton Street, fitted out as typical rooms in the modern home, designed to entice households to change from gas to electricity.

The Electricity Supply Board (ESB) was established by the state in 1927, and they took control of the Pigeon House Generating Station in 1929. Initially Pigeon House lay idle because the new Ardnacrusha hydro-electric scheme on the River Shannon supplied Dublin, but later, Ringsend became part of the National Grid. The station was decommissioned in 1976, closed in 1982, and now lies derelict. The 250ft-high redbrick chimneystack was a noted landmark, but was reduced in height some time ago.

The 831ft-long and 7ft-diameter Liffey Tunnel was bored under the River Liffey in 1928, to allow electrical cables from Pigeon House Generating Station, and water mains, to traverse the Liffey. The 107ft-deep South Shaft is in Thorncastle Street (beside St Patrick's Rowing Club), while the 111ft-deep North Shaft is in the former Harbour Master's office on the North Wall. The men building the tunnel had to work in compressed air and some of them got the dreaded 'bends'.

POOLBEG GENERATING STATION NO. 1

The ESB signed a contract in 1969 for the new oil-fired Poolbeg Generating Station, including a 680ft-tall concrete chimney and an open jetty for 35,000-ton oil tankers (including Russian oil), all of which was completed in 1971. An extension was completed in 1978, including the second chimney almost as tall as the first. The pair of chimneys were painted red and white, which instantly gave them iconic status. The project entailed a large amount of land reclamation, and the creation of a manmade public beach called the White Bank (also called the Shelley Bank). The station was de-commissioned in 2010, and the two chimneys were recently capped-off, when they were made Protected Structures by Dublin City Council.

POOLBEG GENERATING STATION NO. 2

A combined gas cycle generating station, recognisable by its four steel chimneys, was built to the east of the site in 1994, operating on both Kinsale natural gas and oil, and this was extended in 1998 and 2011. Staff facilities include a recreation block and outdoor tennis courts.

RINGSEND GENERATING STATION

This station was built in two stages, 1956 and 1966, some distance to the west of the Pigeon House Station, on newly reclaimed land south of the Corporation's sewerage works. The project included a new wharf for the oil tankers and colliers, and a high-level conveyor across Pigeon House Road. By this date, coal from the colliers was no longer shovelled manually by dockers into large buckets but moved by mechanical grabs, which could do the job faster. The station was closed in 1988, used as an ESB training centre for many years, and demolished in 2007. The Synergen Dublin Bay Power Plant, recognisable by a single steel chimney, was built on part of the site in 2002, and is a joint venture between the ESB and Statoil Company of Norway, utilising both gas and oil. Until recently, the ESB staff had their own pitch & putt course behind the station.

PEMBROKE ELECTRIC LIGHTING, SOUTH LOTTS ROAD

The Pembroke Township built a coal-fired electricity generating station at Margaret Place, off Bath Avenue, supplying streetlights in the Ballsbridge and Donnybrook areas, which went operational in June 1900. The station included a refuse destructor, built in 1898 by Horsfall Furnace Syndicate Ltd of Leeds, for £2,188, capable of handling 32 tons of refuse a day – the steam produced was re-used in generating electricity. When the ESB became operational in 1929, Pembroke Township linked in to that supply, and the generating station became redundant. The ESB still use the brick-built station as a workshop, and later acquired the adjoining premises of Packing Cases Ltd (makers of timber boxes from 1920s to 1956) as a site to build offices, all now accessed from South Lotts Road.

Sportsco is the name of the ESB staff recreation facility on the South Lotts Road, built in 1979 at the rear of the former Pembroke Generating Station. Facilities include a 82ft swimming pool, sports hall and gym, all of which are also open to the public. The site was originally the University College Dublin (UCD) Recreation Grounds.

SEWERAGE

In the nineteenth century, Dublin's sewers simply discharged into the River Liffey, in the hope (not always realised) that the foul matter would be carried out to sea by the daily tides. However, between 1886 and 1906, Dublin Corporation laid interceptor sewers along the north and south quays, with a connecting tunnel under the Liffey opposite Marlborough Street, and thence to a new main lift pumping station on the west side of the Coastguard Station on Pigeon House Road, and finally to filtering and settlement beds at Pigeon House Harbour. The Corporation had bought the harbour in 1897 from the War Department of the British Government, since it formed part of Pigeon House Fort. The pumping station, comprising four boilers supplying steam to four engines, connected to four pumps, lifted the waterborne sewage up a height of 23ft into an 8ft sewer, and onwards to the outfall works at the Pigeon House Harbour, comprising eighteen concrete tanks (roofless compartments). The sewage solids settled in these chambers, and the water was skimmed off into the River Liffey by means of a slowly rotating arm. In due course, the sludge in the chambers was lifted into a holding tank, discharged into a ship alongside the works, and dumped a few miles out at sea. The first ship, called the TSS *Shamrock*, was 148ft long, and was built in 1906 in the Liffey Dockyard on the North Wall. The ship made 400 trips per year, with loads of 377 tons. When the first ship retired in 1958, the MV *Seamrog II* was built by the Liffey Dockyard, and lasted until 1984. The final (second-hand) ship was the *Sir Joseph Bazalgette* (which was built for Thames Water in England 1963), and this 1,000-ton vessel was used until 1999, when dumping of sewage at sea was banned by the European Union.

The Grand Canal Drainage Tunnel was a major project started in the 1970s. It was a 12ft-diameter tunnel running underground alongside the Grand Canal, comprising one segment for surface water (rainwater) and the rest for foul sewage, designed to intercept various old sewers along its route. At Grand Canal Street (Maquay Bridge), the surface water was diverted into the Grand Canal Basin, while the sewerage carried on down Bath Avenue, picking up the Rathmines and Pembroke sewer at Londonbridge Road, and on to a new main lift pumping station in Ringsend (behind the present Recycling Centre), which opened in 1985. In the forecourt, there are a few engineering items from the old pumping station on display, but pride of place goes to the twin cast-iron entrance gates from the former Nelson's Pillar (Nelson's head is in the reading room of Pearse Street library).

In 2003, a new sewage treatment works was completed across the road from the 1906 settlement tanks, and the former became redundant. The new works handles the sewage from Sutton Pumping Station, by means of an undersea steel pipeline, and also the output of Dún Laoghaire Pumping Station. This state-of-the-art facility converts the raw sewage into Biofert Fertiliser, and also Biogas, the latter supplying 60 per cent of the works' energy needs. The cleansed water is run off into the Liffey.

The original main lift pumping station was electrified in 1924. In February 1969 a leak of naphtha gas from the Dublin Gas Company near the Grand Canal Locks entered the sewers and emerged in the old pumping station, leading to a massive explosion, with serious damage to the building and the collapse of the redundant 120ft chimney. The brick building was repaired (but not the chimney) and continued in use until it closed in 1985, and was demolished in the 1990s. Sadly, Joseph Murphy, one of the men in the station, was killed in the accident. He is remembered by a small headstone in the nearby new pumping station.

In 1881, the townships of Pembroke and Rathmines jointly built a sewage pumping station on Londonbridge Road beside the River Dodder – Dodder Lodge was the caretaker's home. Small syphon buildings (still there) on both sides of the Dodder allowed the sewage to flow in a low-level sewer underneath the river. The sewer continued onwards, and then passed through the Pigeon House Fort, before discharging the raw sewage into Dublin Bay at Whitebanks at ebb tide by means of a sluice valve (the valve building is still there). This pumping station was electrified in 1915 and operated until 1985, when it linked up with Dublin Corporation's new station in Ringsend. The old building was recently converted into private apartments, with the old brick chimney as a showpiece. The City Morgue was nearby, beside the South Syphon House, but the former is now gone.

DUBLIN GAS COMPANY

Town gas is manufactured by a process called carbonisation: bituminous coal is heated to 1,000°C in a retort (an airless oven), the gas is cleaned/purified and stored is a gasometer (a large holder seated on a water tank to prevent escape of the gas). Tar and ammonia are also driven off during the baking process and the original coal is reduced to coke (which can be recycled and used to heat the ovens).

The manufacture of town gas was carried out on a large site between Pearse Street and Sir John Rogersons Quay, since at least the 1830s. Initially the Hibernian

Gas Company was based on Pearse Street, beside Victoria Bridge, with the Alliance Gas Company immediately behind it, fronting on to Sir John Rogersons Quay, until they amalgamated (with others) in 1847 to form the Alliance & Dublin Consumers Gas Company (generally known as the Dublin Gas Company). The company motto was '*Ex Fume Dare Lucem*', Latin for 'From Smoke Comes Light' (burnt coal gives gaslight).

The company expanded to South Lotts Road, building two large gasholders in 1871 (now gone) and another one in 1885 (now a block of apartments).

A report in 1888 recorded that the Alliance and Dublin Consumers Gas Company had four stations, two in Dublin, one in Kingstown (Dún Laoghaire), and one in Bray. The site in Pearse Street occupied 61 acres, running back to Sir John Rogersons Quay. About 125,000 tons of coal and cannel, shipped in from Newcastle in England, were carbonised to produce 1,350 million cubic feet of gas, by means of 1,550 retorts (five retort houses). The purifiers used were oxide of iron or bog ore from Kings County (Offaly), and lime.

The Dublin Gas Company operated its own fleet of colliers to import supplies of coal, each around 400-500 tons gross (Glenbride, Glenageary, Glencree, Glencullen), unloading alongside the works in Grand Canal Basin. When the gas company changed from coal to oil in 1968, the colliers were retired.

The famous waterless gasometer on Sir John Rogersons Quay, just east of the Ferryman pub, was built in 1934, to a height of 250ft, and was demolished in the mid-1990s. From the 1930s, the gas company built their own kitchen cookers and gas meters, a little further east along the quay.

Bord Gais, a semi-state company, was set up in 1976 when natural gas was discovered underneath the Irish Sea off the coast at Kinsale, and they took over the Dublin Gas Company in 1987.

During the Celtic Tiger years, the former gas company sites had to be decontaminated by the Dublin Docklands Development Authority, by removing the soil down to a depth of many feet, and the spoil shipped to the continent. Perfume was sprayed into the atmosphere to offset the smell of gas and tar.

The Dublin Gas Company had lovely showrooms on D'Olier Street, having been remodelled in the 1930s in the Art Deco style. It is now occupied by the School of Nursing of Trinity College.

TRAMS

Horse-drawn trams, running on iron rails, were introduced in Dublin in 1872, with a variety of private companies operating the various routes. The Dublin City Tramways Company ran a route from D'Olier Street to Sandymount, via Great Brunswick Street (called Pearse Street from 1920), Westland Row, Lower Merrion Street, Merrion Square North, Lower Mount Street, Northumberland Road, Beggars Bush, Bath Avenue, Londonbridge Road, Tritonville Road, Sandymount Road, Seafort Avenue, Beach Road, to Sandymount Martello Tower. Ringsend was not on a tram route because of constraints imposed by the Victoria Bridge over the Grand Canal Basin.

In 1881, three smaller companies amalgamated to form the Dublin United Tramways Company (DUTC). In 1896 the Dalkey route was electrified, with the main power station in Shelbourne Road, Ballsbridge. Other routes were electrified in stages immediately after this, although the Sandymount route was only electrified from Nelson's Pillar (O'Connell Street) to Haddington Road, with horse-drawn trams on the remaining section for a short time after.

In 1899/1900 a new central power station to drive the trams was built on Ringsend Road by the DUTC. The large steel-framed building housed a coal-fired boiler house, 140ft by 78ft, and an engine/generator room, 200ft by 60ft, with twin steel chimneys, 250ft high. Thereafter, the original electricity generating plants at Shelbourne Road and Clontarf were redundant and became electricity sub-stations.

The DUTC built a new iron swivel bridge over the Grand Canal Basin in 1901, and thereafter double-decker trams served Ringsend. No. 1 tram terminated at Thomas Street in Ringsend, whilst No. 2 and No. 3 carried on to Sandymount Green and Tower respectively. The single-decker No. 4 continued its route via Bath Avenue, constrained to a lowly stature by the low-level Bath Avenue railway bridge. The old 1872 tram depot at Gilford Road in Sandymount was extended in 1900 to accommodate the new electric trams.

With the advent of cheaper ESB electricity in the 1930s, the tram generating station on Ringsend Road became redundant and a new three-storey ESB transformer station was built in 1934/35 at the south-west corner of the depot, in fine Art Deco style. The 'M' letters at the top are a reference to William Martin Murphy, of tram company fame, who is also associated with the infamous 1913 Dublin Lockout by employers.

In the mid-1920s, private bus companies began to compete with the trams, and by 1932, the No. 4 tram to Sandymount (via Bath Avenue) was made redundant and immediately replaced by a bus – by this stage the DUTC was also in the bus business. By 1940, the Nos 1, 2, and 3 trams were also replaced by buses. The DUTC built a new bus station on Ringsend Road in 1939/40, in the yards beside their former generating station. Córas Iompair Éireann (CIÉ) took over the buses in the 1950s.

The former generating station was stripped of its plant in the 1930s and used as a bus station. The two steel chimneys (concrete lined), which were nicknamed the Tramway Twins, were hand-demolished in 1942. G.A. Brittain Ltd, car assemblers, used the old generating station in the 1950s and '60s, after which the building was demolished. It is now the yard on the west side of Ringsend Bus Station.

The 1930s ESB sub-station was occupied by Bovril (makers of Virol health drink in the early days) from 1953 to 1980, then the Shelbourne Pierrot Snooker Club (Pat Quinn) in the 1980s, and currently Windmill Lane Recording Studios.

TRAINS

The first passenger train in Ireland was opened in 1834 by the Dublin and Kingstown Railway Company, running between Westland Row and Kingstown (Dún Laoghaire), and was built by the famous contractor, William Dargan. Later the line was known as the Dublin and Wicklow Railway, then the Dublin, Wicklow & Wexford, and finally the Dublin & South Eastern Railway. The railway line skirted the south side of Ringsend, and a very small site in Ballsbridge (near the present Railway Cottages) was the original workshop for engine and coach building. In 1837 a bigger site on Grand Canal Street, sandwiched between Barrow Street and the Grand Canal Basin, was chosen for the works. Additional land, previously used by the Boston Lime Works, on the north side of the track, was acquired in 1878. The first engine made by the company was called *Princess*. The factory closed in 1925, when its operations were transferred to Inchicore Works.

The Grand Canal Street site was initially a whiskey distillery, known as the Dock Distillery, operated by Aeneas Coffey from 1830 to 1837. He was a Frenchman of Irish parentage, and he invented the Coffey Still – this was an improvement on the Robert Steins (Scottish) two-column continuous still. Coffey started Aeneas Coffey & Sons in London in 1835, which later became John Dore & Co. Ltd.

In 1935 the Grand Canal Street site was used by the Doneda Clothing Factory and also a chemical works. From 1958 to the 1970s, International Meat Company Ltd had a major business here, slaughtering cows, sheep, pigs, etc. Now Pembroke Square apartments and Grand Canal Dock Dart Station occupy this prominent location.

DUBLIN PORT COMPANY

We sometimes forget that the Port Authority is a major employer on both sides of the river mouth, employing crane drivers, pilots (guiding ships in to Dublin Port), Customs and Excise officers, administrative staff, etc., currently amounting to about 140 people. Prior to the advent of containerised transport, hundreds of dockers (casual labourers) were employed by Stevedores to load and unload ships by hand.

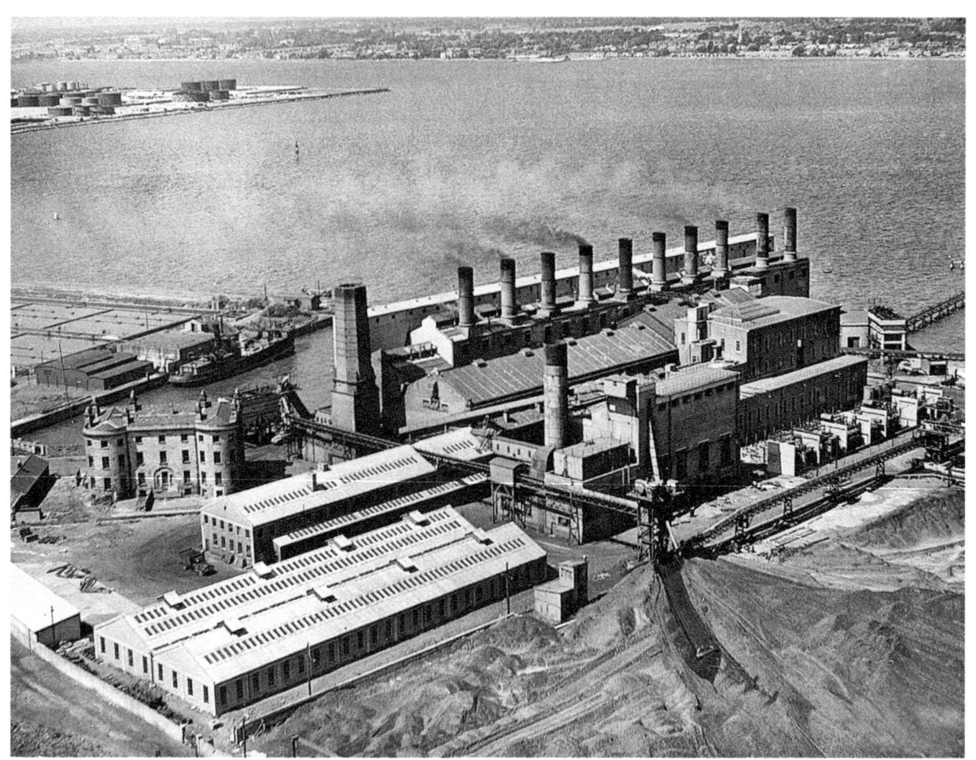

A 1951 view of Pigeon House Generating Station, with a huge heap of coal at lower right. Note the former Pigeon House Hotel on the left, with the harbour behind and a sewage sludge ship. (Courtesy of ESB Archives)

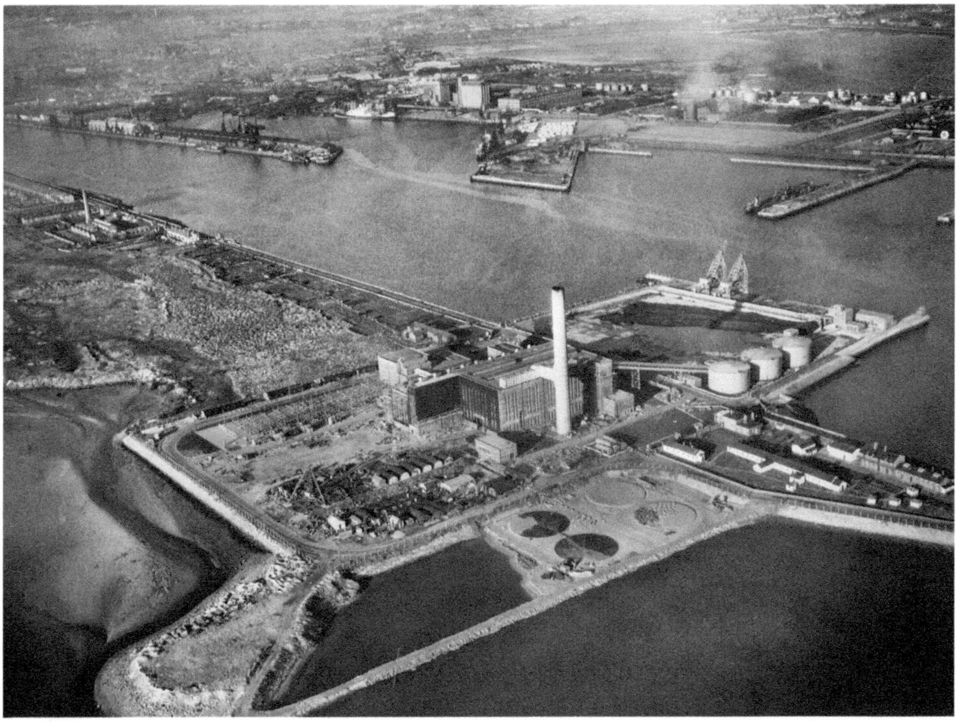

A 1950s view of Ringsend Generating Station, with the former St Catherine's Hospital on the right. (Courtesy of the National Library of Ireland)

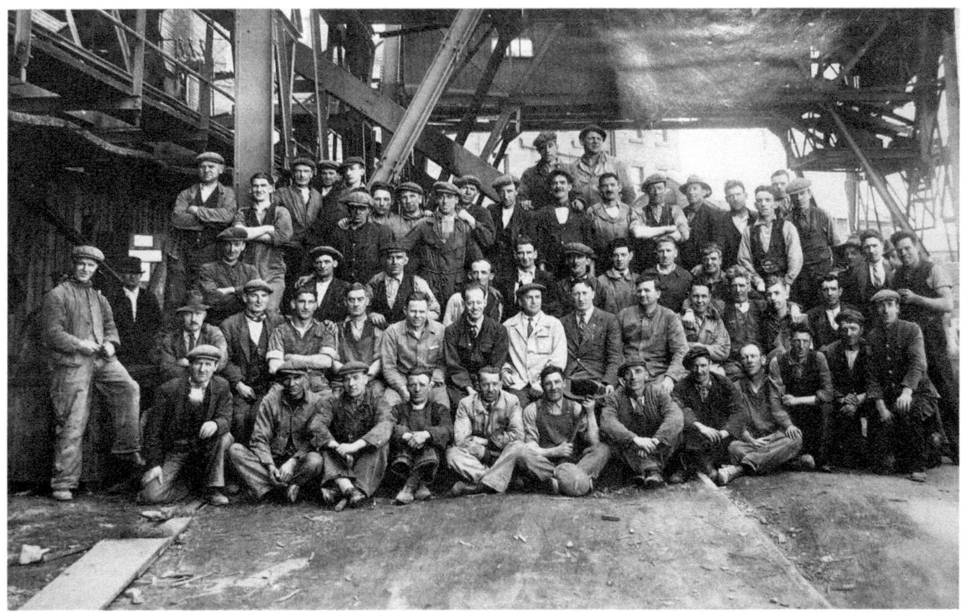

Workers at the Pigeon House Generating Station, 1938. (Courtesy of NewsFour)

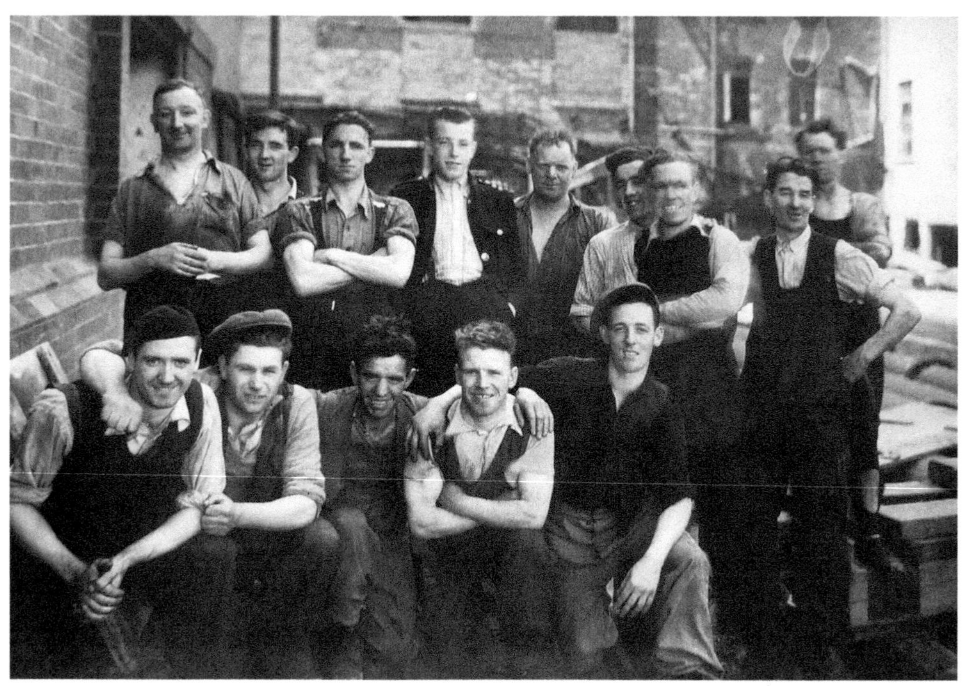

A group in the Pigeon House Generating Station, 1939. (Courtesy of NewsFour)

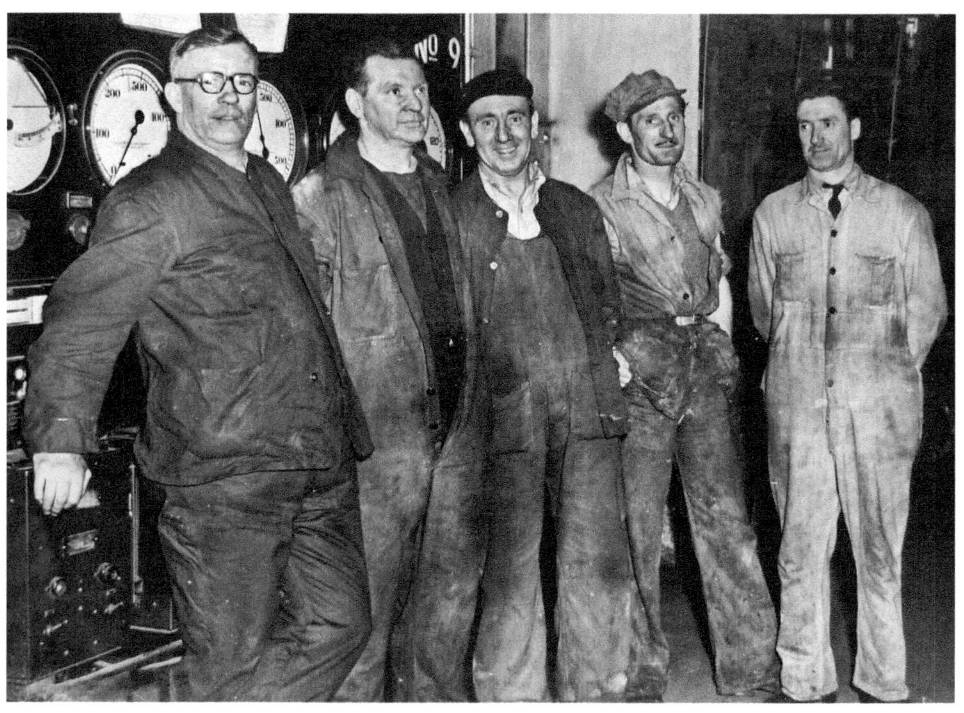

Workers at the Pigeon House Generating Station, 1951. (Courtesy of NewsFour)

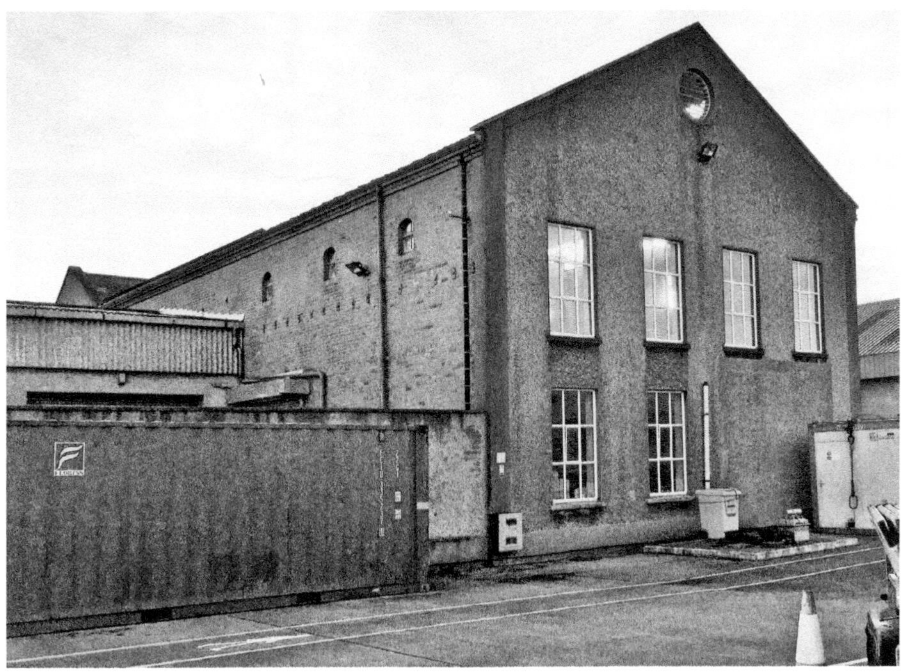

The former Pembroke Electricity Station on South Lotts Road is now a workshop for the ESB. (Courtesy of ESB Archives)

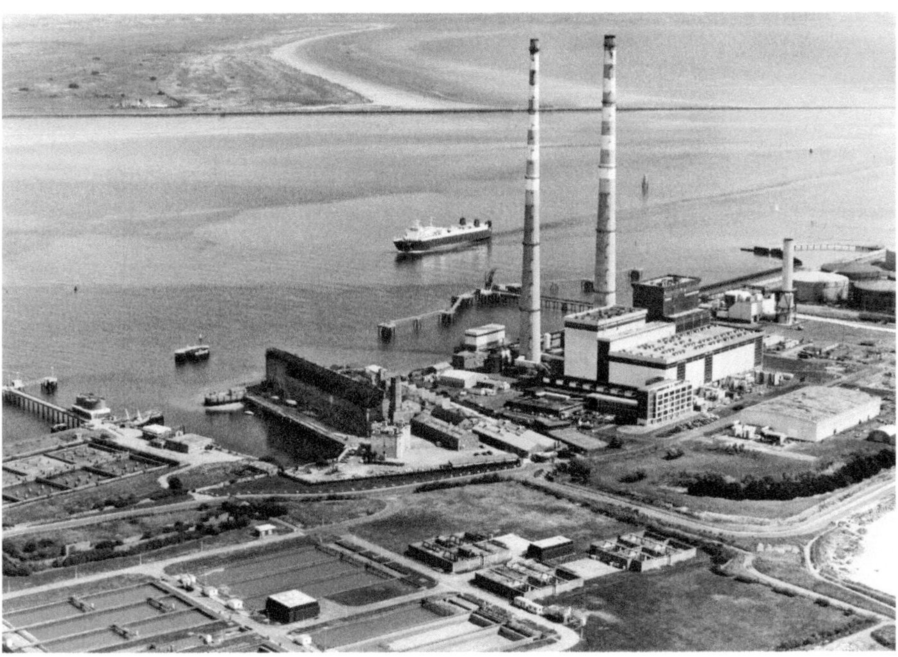

The iconic chimneys of Poolbeg Generating Station, with Dollymount Strand in the background. (Courtesy of ESB Archives)

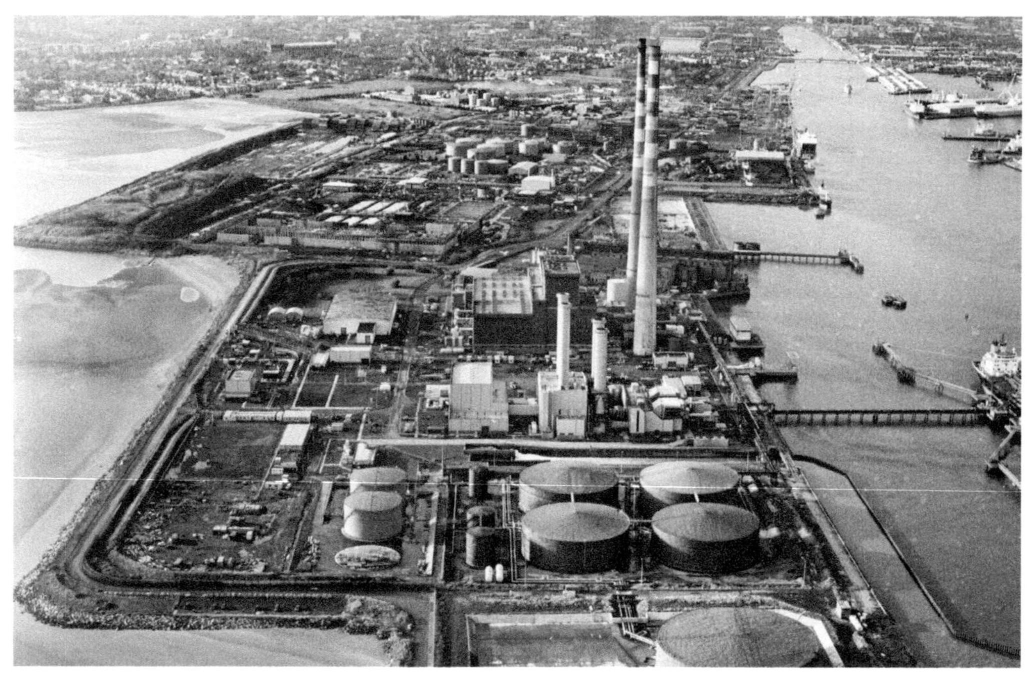

Poolbeg Generating Station, looking towards Ringsend. (Courtesy of ESB Archives)

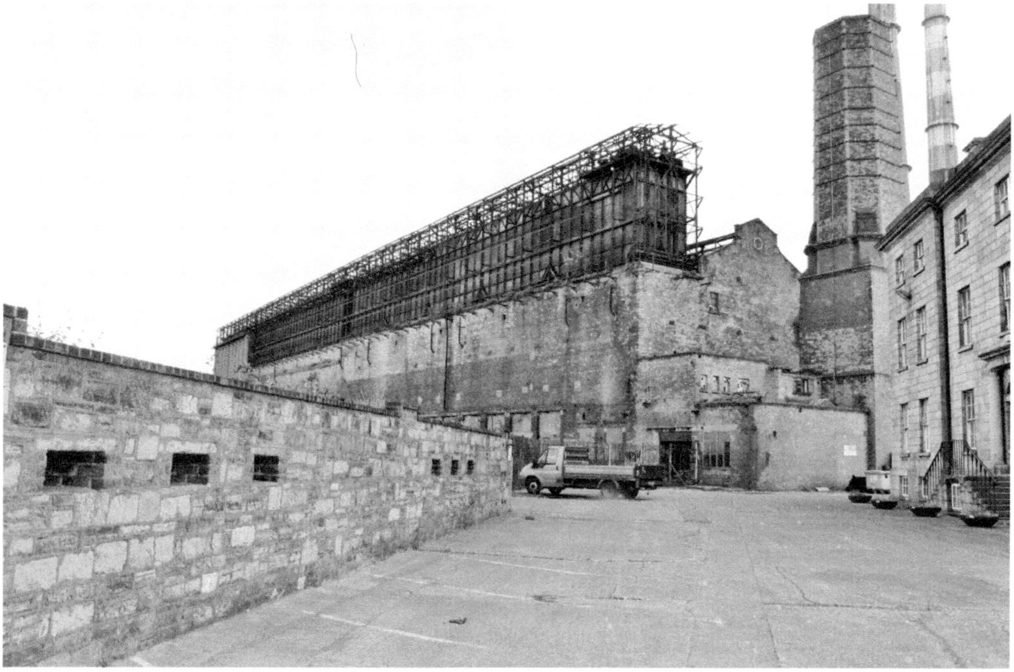

Current view of the original Pigeon House Generating Station, with the front entrance of the former hotel on the right. Part of the harbour is still behind the former fort wall on the left.

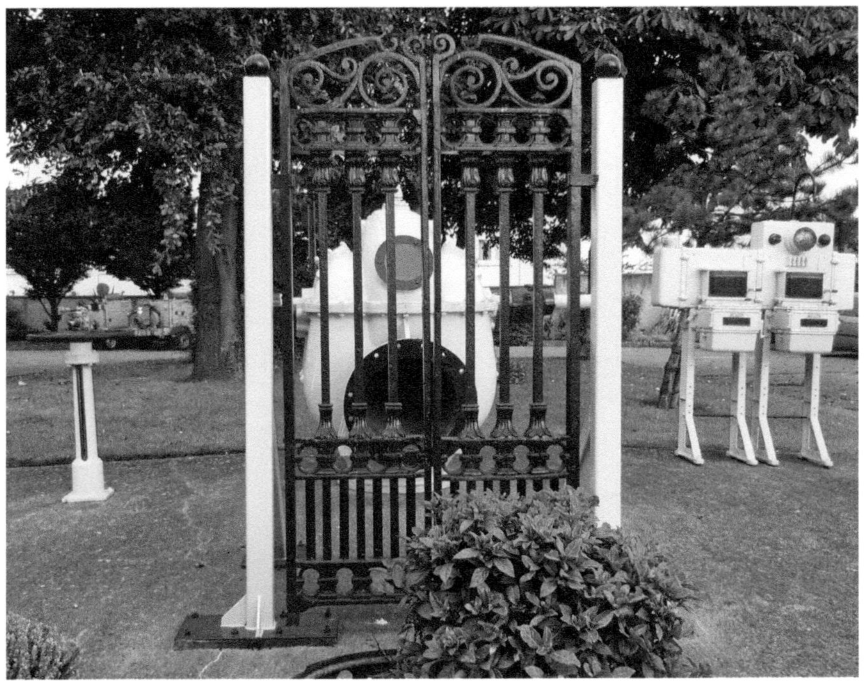

These are the gates of the former Nelson's Pillar from O'Connell Street, in the grounds of the sewage pumping station, at the north end of Sean Moore Road.

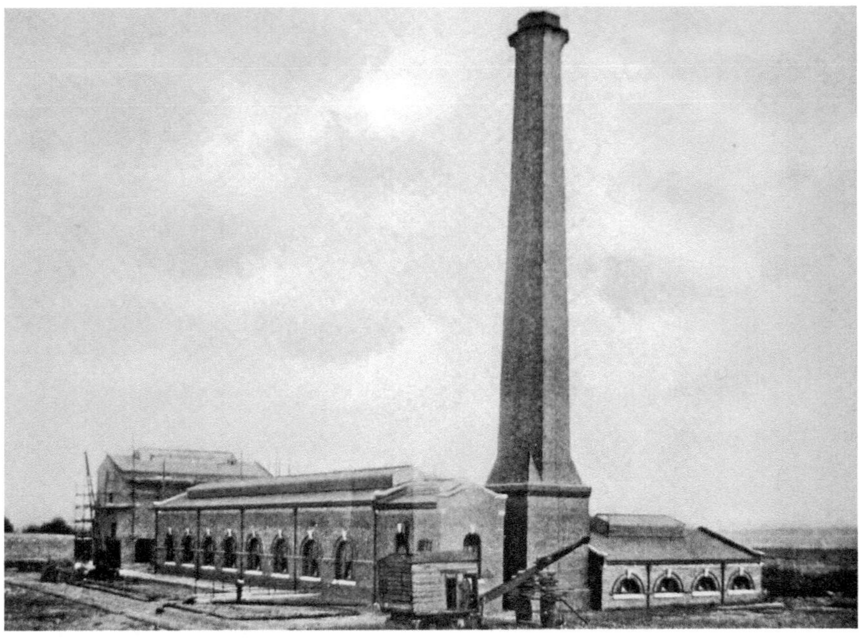

The former Dublin Corporation Main Lift Sewage Pumping Station, beside the Coastguard Station on Pigeon House Road. (Courtesy of Michael Corcoran)

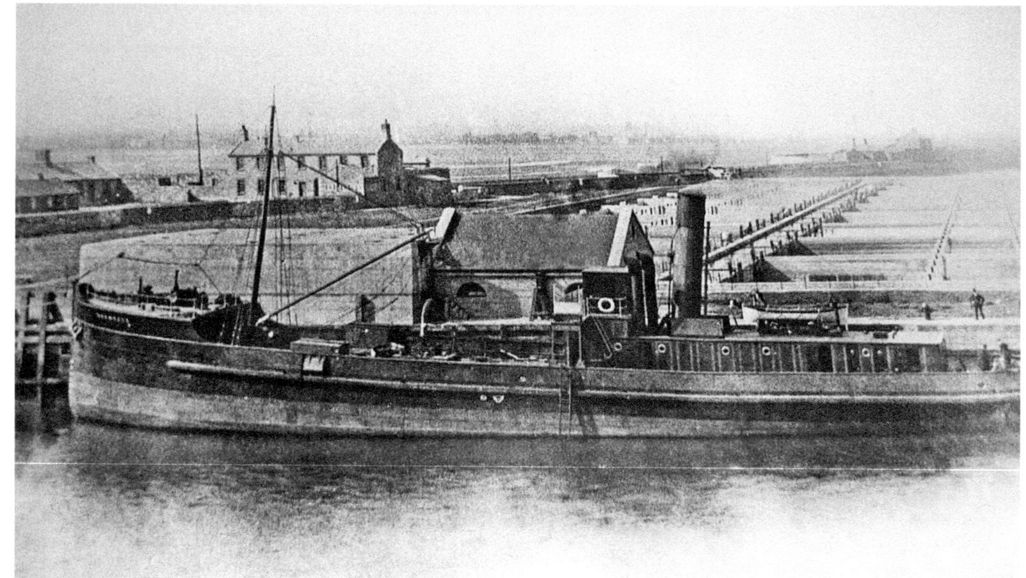

The *Shamrock* sludge ship in Pigeon House Harbour, alongside the sewage settlement beds, early 1950s. Note the former fort buildings in the background on the left. (Courtesy of Dublin City Council)

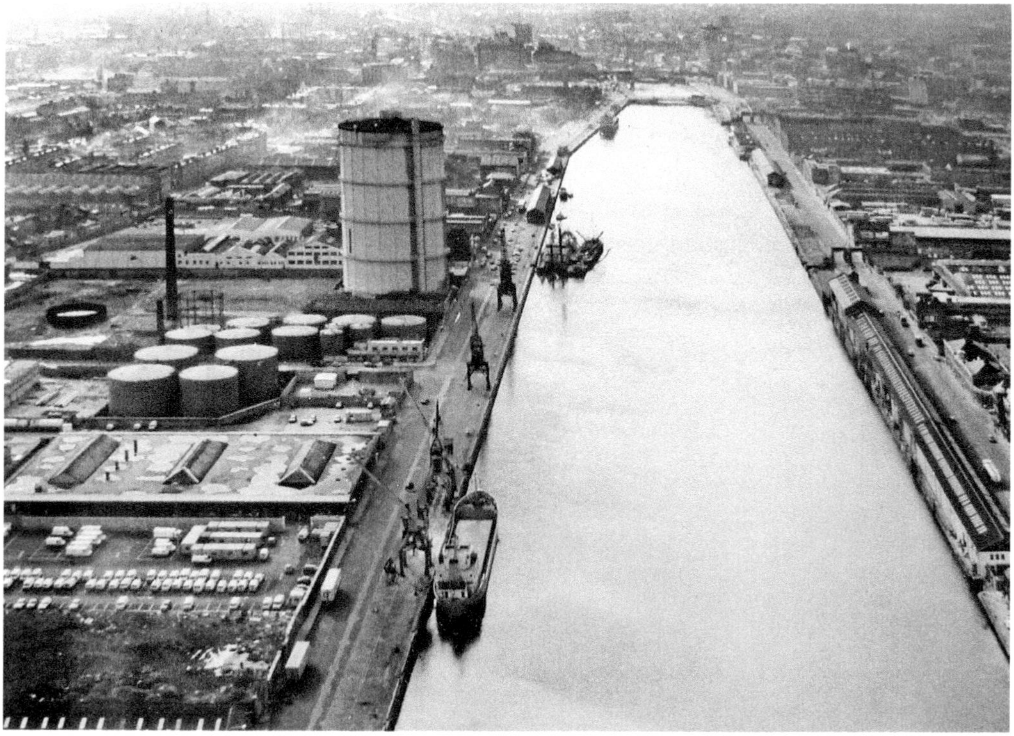

Sir John Rogersons Quay, 1950s. (Courtesy of Dublin City Library & Archives)

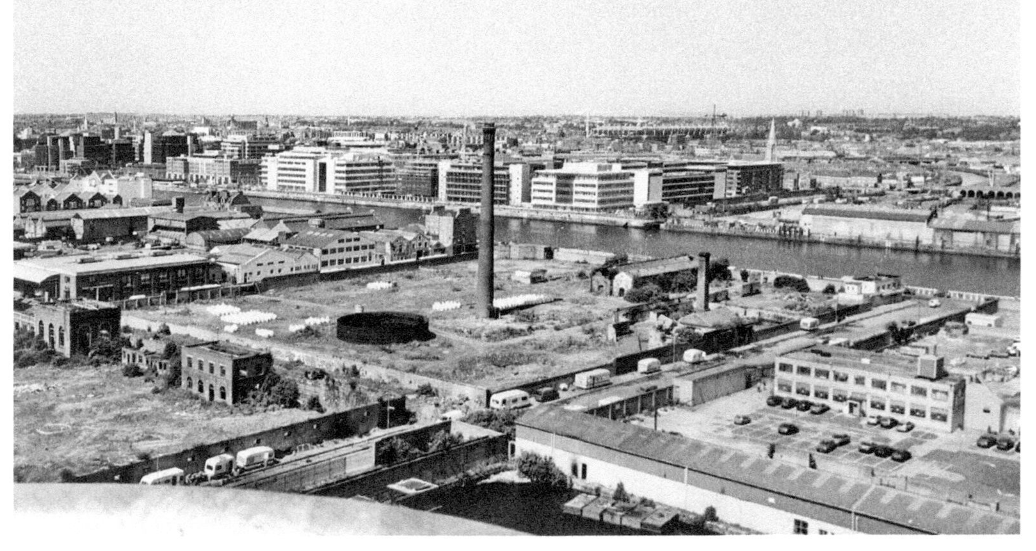

The former Dublin Gas Company site in 2000, looking north-west.

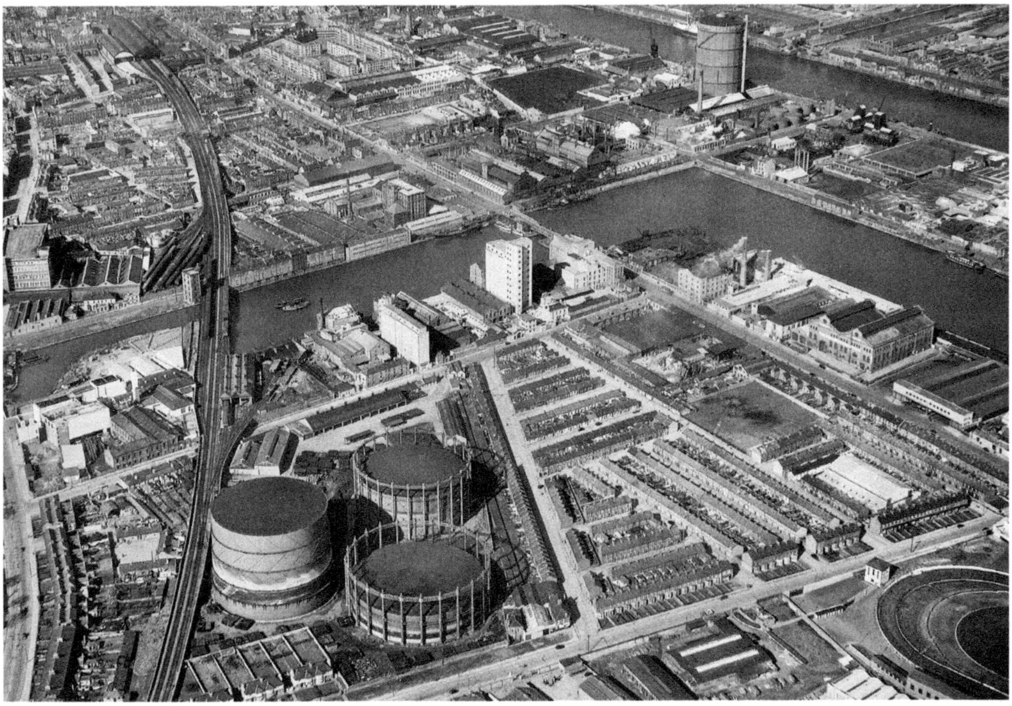

Ringsend Basin in the 1950s, looking north-west. (Courtesy of the National Library of Ireland)

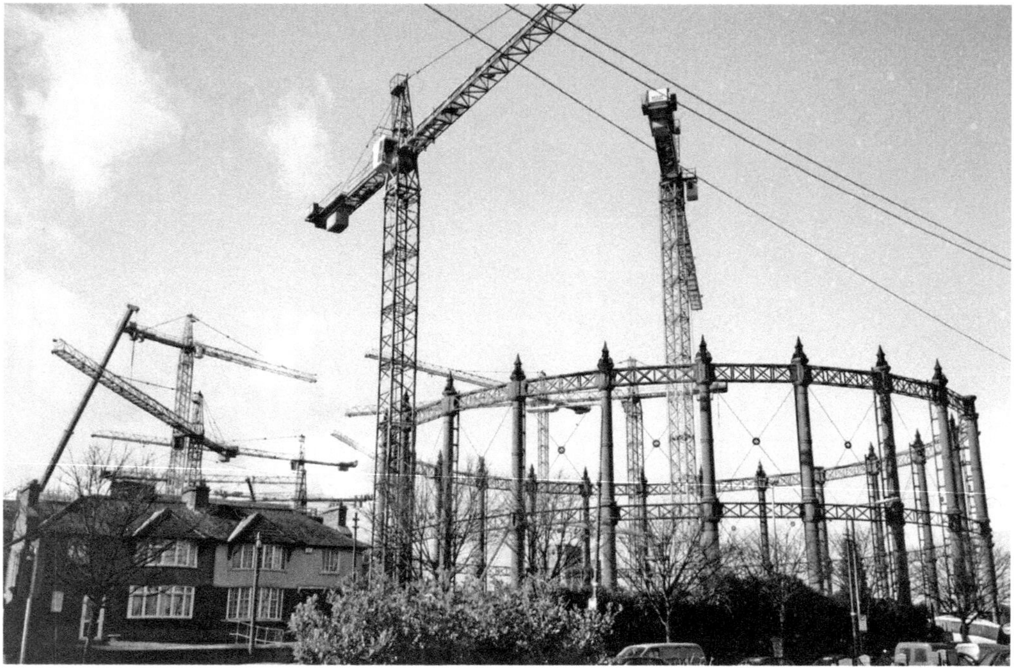

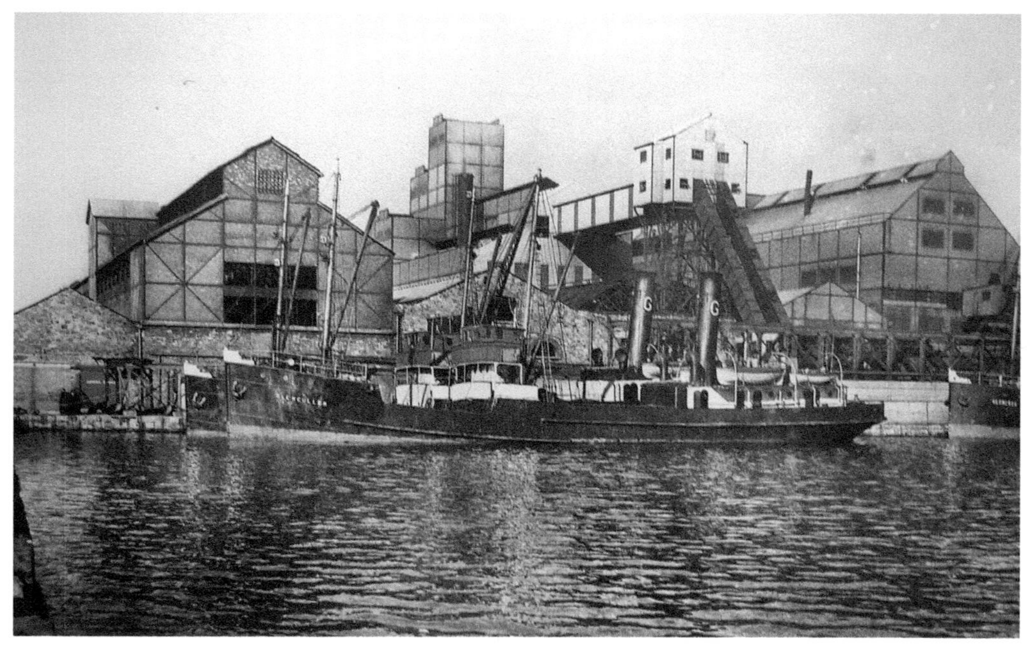

A modern view of the 1885 gasometer frame on South Lotts Road, before it was converted to apartments.

The *Glencullen* collier unloading coal on Hanover Quay, alongside the Dublin Gas Company. (Courtesy of Airbnb)

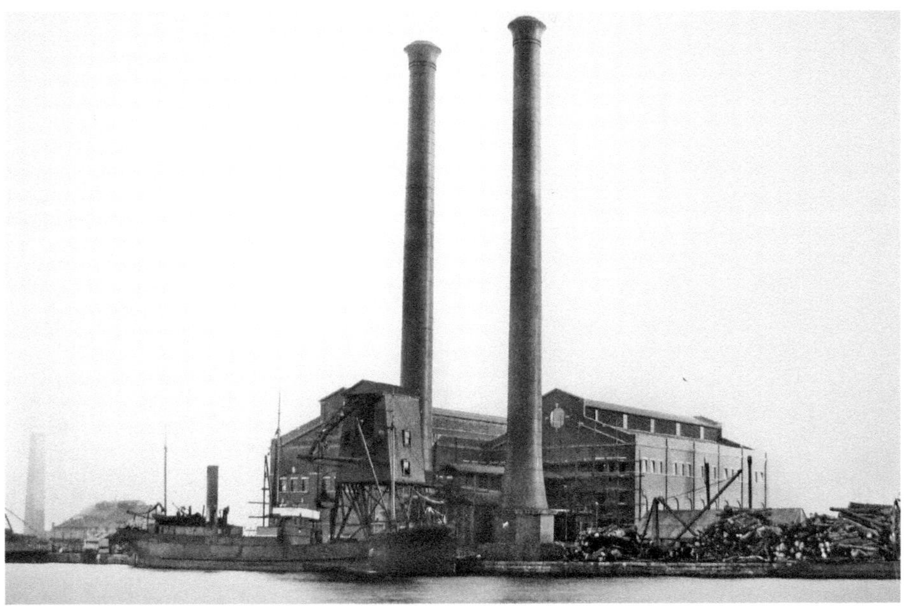

The generating station for the tram company on Charlotte Quay, as seen from the Grand Canal Basin. (Courtesy of Irish Architectural Archive)

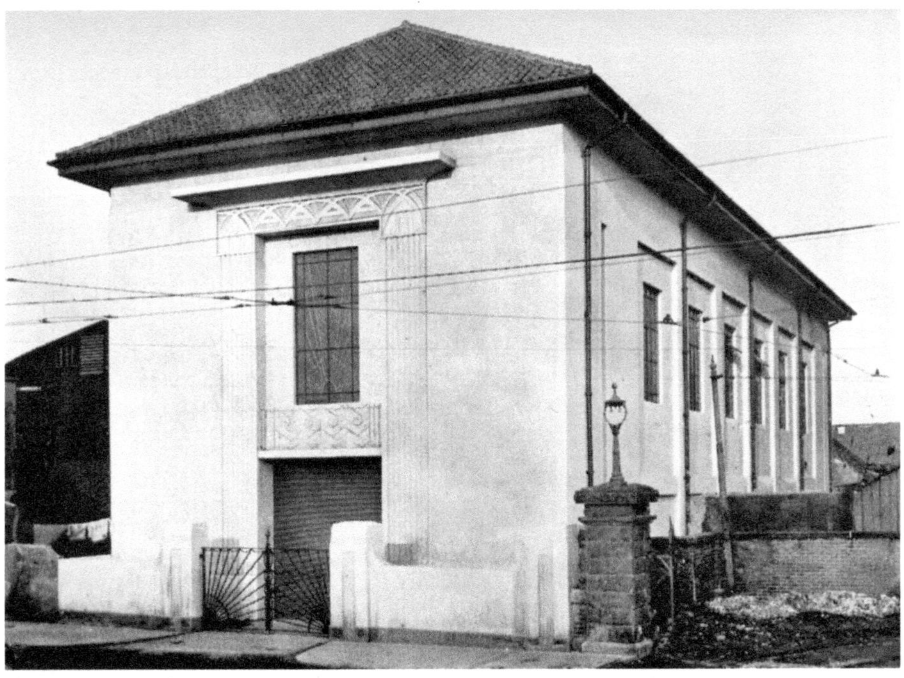

The ESB built a sub-station on Ringsend Road for the tram company, and their adjoining generating station became redundant. Later used by Bovril, it is now used by Windmill Lane Studios. (Courtesy of ESB Archives)

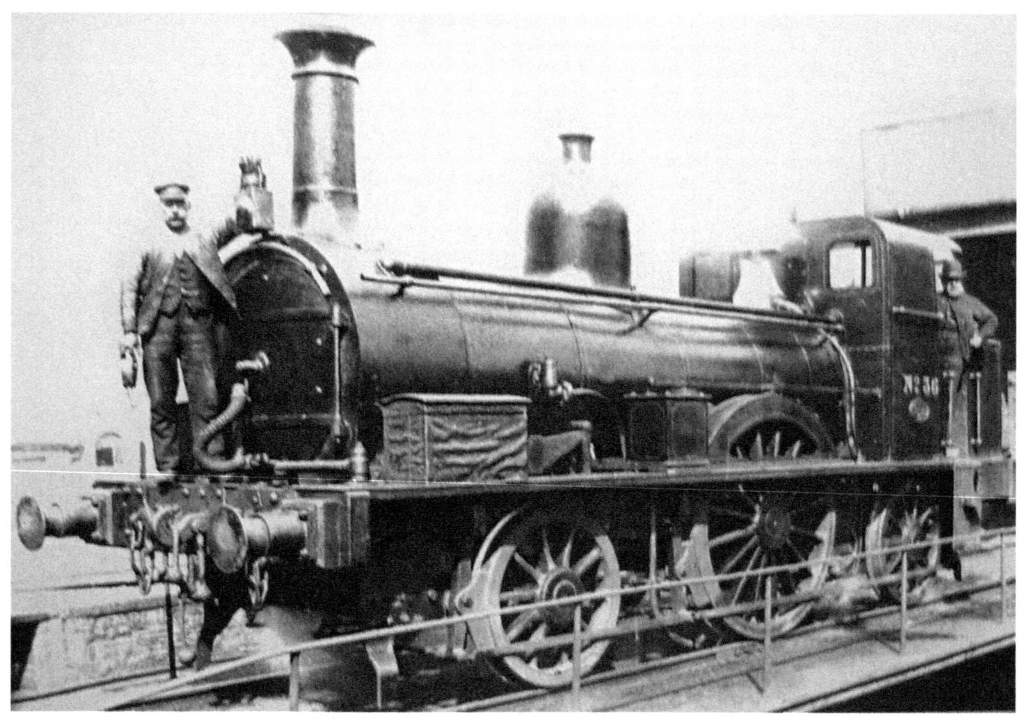

J. Wakefield 2-2-2 WT engine built in 1877 at Grand Canal Street for the Dublin & South Eastern Railway Company. (Courtesy of Irish Railway Records Society)

3

GLASS BOTTLES

Glass bottles were made in four locations around Ringsend, namely, Fitzwilliam Quay, Ringsend Road/Charlotte Quay, Thorncastle Street, and Cambridge Place, the latter two being the smallest.

A newspaper reported that there were three main glass-bottle factories in Dublin in 1874, all producing black glass:

1. Ringsend Glass Bottle Company, Fitzwilliam Quay. Their bottles were denoted by an 'R' on the base. The company also made clear-glass bottles. In 1870/71 new premises were built on the site of old glassworks, with a 100ft chimney. The owners were William Arthur, Robert Smyth, and Robert William Smyth.
2. The Irish Glass Bottle Company on Charlotte Quay, founded by J.A. & Robert King. Their bottles had a 'K' on base. New premises built in 1870 at east end of Charlotte Quay.
3. Dublin Glass Bottle Company on North Lotts. This was the oldest in Dublin, founded in 1821. A 'D' or 'DBC' on base of bottles denoted their wares. They also produced clear-, blue-, green-, and amber-coloured glass bottles.

RINGSEND GLASS BOTTLE COMPANY, FITZWILLIAM QUAY

There was a glassworks on Bridge Street, backing on to Clarkes Metal Foundry on Fitzwilliam Quay, from at least 1830 (a map of that date also shows a Glass House in ruins immediately to the south), operated at different times by William Hodgens, Patrick Joseph Nolan, Martin Crean, and Elijah Pring. In 1845 it was called the National Glass Company of Ireland, makers of crown window glass. In 1854, Samuel Davis and William Arthur took over, changing the name to the Ringsend Bottle Company, makers of bottles for wine, porter, spirits, amber flasks, ginger beer, sodas, and carboys.

In 1882, the Ringsend Bottle Co. Ltd was inviting the public to buy shares, noting that the company had been purchased that year for £11,500, and was producing 38,000 gross (a gross is 144) of bottles annually, using Siemens machines. The directors were Robert Smyth, Frederick Barrington (from the adjoining Ringsend Foundry), David B. Chambers, Richard Greening, and William Arthur (managing director). A manager's house was included in the premises.

IRISH GLASS BOTTLE COMPANY, RINGSEND ROAD

The Irish Glass Bottle Company was founded in 1870 by James A. & Robert King, when a new premises and furnace were built at the east end of Charlotte Quay. All gas-fired in 1891 (from gas manufactured on site from coal), employing 300 workers, with a weekly output of 1,300 gross bottles.

In 1926 the Irish Glass Bottle Company and the Ringsend Bottle Company merged, under the former's name, but a receiver ran the company until 1931. The business was idle for nine months in 1931, with 200 men left unemployed. In January 1933 a Belgian company took over – Societe de Participation Verrieres s.a. – under the chairmanship of Joe McGrath. The directors were R.J. Duggan and F.F. Warren, while Franz Winkleman and H.C. Cropp were general managers, and P. Clarke was the company secretary. The new company immediately introduced bottle-making machines, thus ending the age-old tradition of manual blowing by skilled craftsmen, although they still employed 160 people. By June 1936, the company was making 130,000 bottles a day, using 600 different moulds. Some 250 men (no women) operated in three shifts, keeping the furnaces at a constant 1,550°C. Grey sand (which made up 50 per cent of the glass ingredients) was shipped in from France to be melted down – the other lesser ingredients were soda ash, limestone, and cullet (broken glass).

A 1935 map shows the glass works on both sides of South Dock Road (the present Arup building at 50 Ringsend Road was probably built later by IGB in the 1950s). In the 1830s, the site immediately beside Ringsend Bridge was known as a sal-ammoniac manufactory, and later as Ringsend Chemical Works.

In 1936, a new division, complete with a 120ft chimney and another of 75ft, was built at 16-18 Ringsend Road (previously used by Richardson & Fletcher fertilisers), for the manufacture of sheet and plate glass, used in windows, necessitating an additional ninety men. The new building was 245ft by 71ft, and four storeys over a basement, supported on 167 piles, 25ft long. G & T Crampton was the builder and W.H. Byrne the architect. J & C McGloughlin of Pearse Street was responsible for the steel frame and corrugated-steel roof. This sister-factory ceased making sheet glass in 1960 and was later used for bottle making.

The company directors in 1952 were: Joseph McGrath (chairman), Joseph Griffin (joint MD), Franz Winkelmann, a former German (joint MD), Richard G. Duggan, Frederick F. Warren, Robert A. Petit (French), Maurice de Brouwer (Belgian), Paul E.M.J. Mols (Belgian), and Patrick McGrath.

In 1967, the main factory moved to a 24-acre site on the present Sean Moore Road, and employed up to 800 workers in the 1970s. A training centre opened in 1972. Senator Paddy McGrath was chairman in the 1970s, retiring in 1987. The company continued to use the sites on Ringsend Road (Nos 12-18 and 40-50), and also Fitzwilliam Quay. In 1972, IGB sold the Fitzwilliam Quay premises (86,000 sq. ft) to Modern Display Artists and by 1991 the two sites on Ringsend Road were also empty. Sadly, the Irish Glass Bottle Company ceased trading in 2002.

Recent years saw the demolition of the main factory on Sean Moore Road, and it now awaits redevelopment. The older premises on Ringsend Road was demolished in the early 1990s and apartments built, although part of No. 50 at the corner of South Dock Road survives, being used by Arup Associates.

The workers of the Irish Glass Bottle Company bought 15 acres of land in Goatstown in 1958 as a sports grounds, where they developed a soccer pitch, a pitch & putt course, a clubhouse, indoor and outdoor bowls, etc. After previously selling 5 acres of the site, the remaining 10 acres were sold for 20 million in 2002.

HIBERNIAN BOTTLE WORKS, 83 THORNCASTLE STREET

In 1890, the site at 83 Thorncastle Street was listed as Scallans Yard. The Patent Machine Bottle Blowing Company was in occupation in 1891 but the following year, the Hibernian Glass Bottle Works and John Little were on the site. Edward & John Burke Ltd were the owners shortly afterwards and became a major public company, with another large premises at 16 Bachelors Walk, exporting drinks all over the world, including stout and whiskey, and also became owners of Cantrell & Cochrane. The Ringsend bottle factory closed in 1927, when the work was transferred to Liverpool. The company also built a brewery in New York in 1933, when Prohibition ended. Sir John G. Nutting, a baronet, was the managing director for many years, and spent part of his fortune on upgrading St Helens House in Booterstown (the present Radisson Blu Hotel).

NATIONAL BOTTLE WORKS, CAMBRIDGE PLACE

In 1877, Cornelius Canning & Robert Good, glass-bottle manufacturers, went bankrupt. Their estate included Old Bottle House Yard, Cambridge Place, and also a yard at the rear of Mary Genevieve Page, Thorncastle Street, which was formerly part of the yard of the Salt Works. By 1900, the National Bottle Works was operated by Mrs Atkinson, then Mrs Weldrick in 1915, and it was gone by 1926.

BOTTLEMAKERS HALL, IRISHTOWN ROAD

The Bottlemakers Hall, beside St Patrick's Dispensary (now Primary Care Centre), was built in 1916 and officially known as the Irish Bottle Makers Trade Protection Society. It was used as a social/snooker club, with J. Longmore as secretary for many decades, until the building was sold in 1964. The house and rear hall are still standing, but empty.

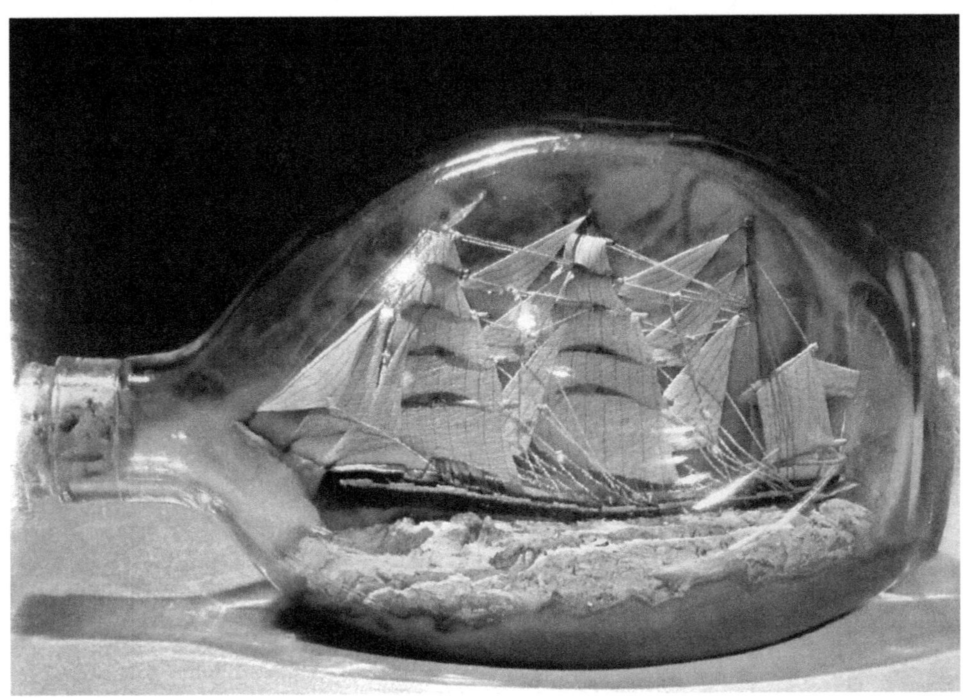

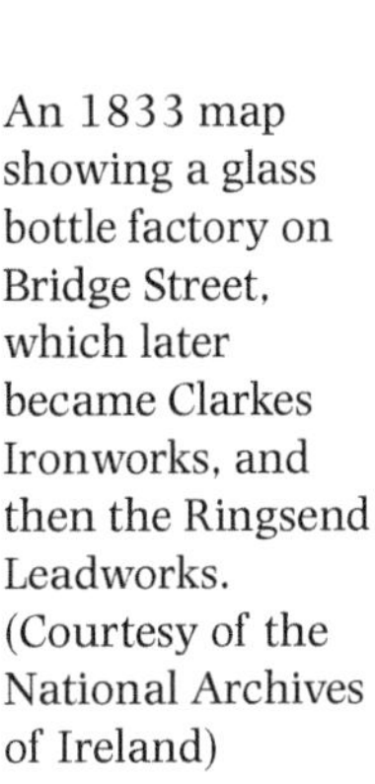

Ringsend is synonymous with glass and sailing. (Courtesy of the Irish Glass Bottle Company)

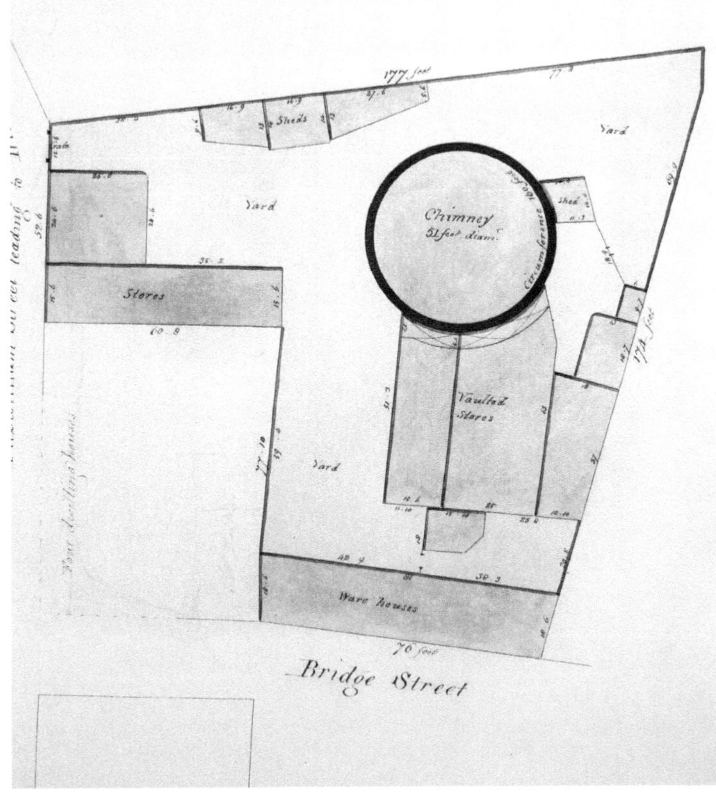

An 1833 map showing a glass bottle factory on Bridge Street, which later became Clarkes Ironworks, and then the Ringsend Leadworks. (Courtesy of the National Archives of Ireland)

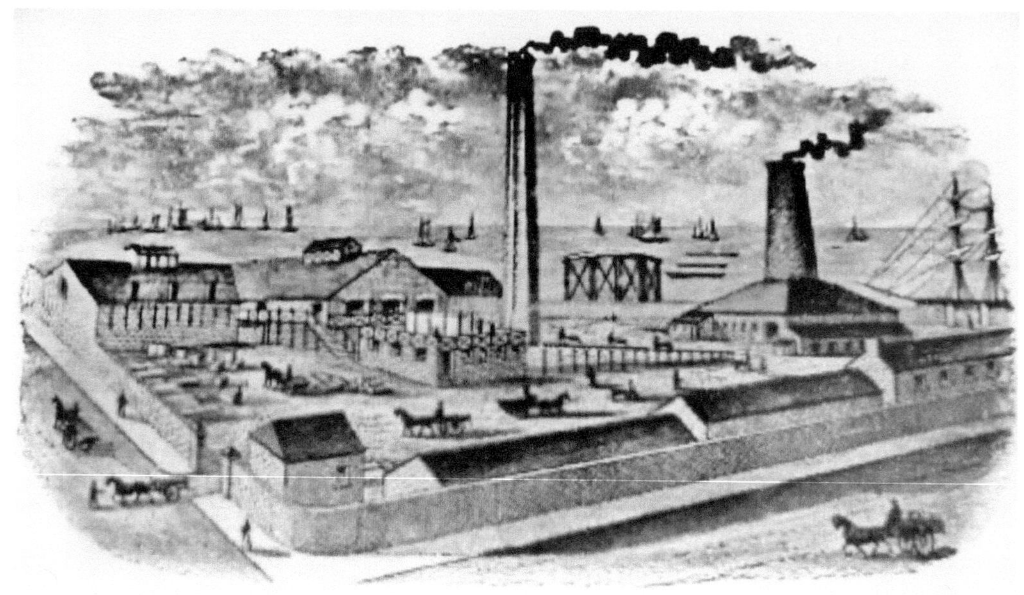

An 1892 advertisement for the Irish Glass Bottle Company/ James A. & R. King, on Ringsend Road. (Courtesy of Irish Architectural Archive)

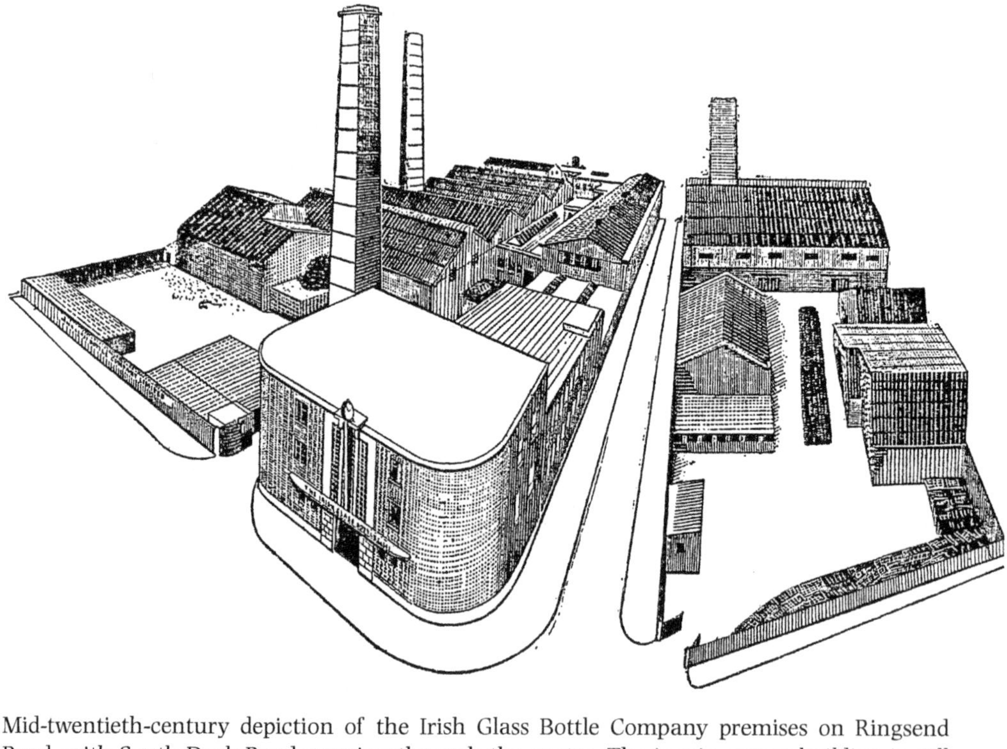

Mid-twentieth-century depiction of the Irish Glass Bottle Company premises on Ringsend Road, with South Dock Road running through the centre. The iconic corner building is still standing. (Courtesy of the Irish Glass Bottle Company)

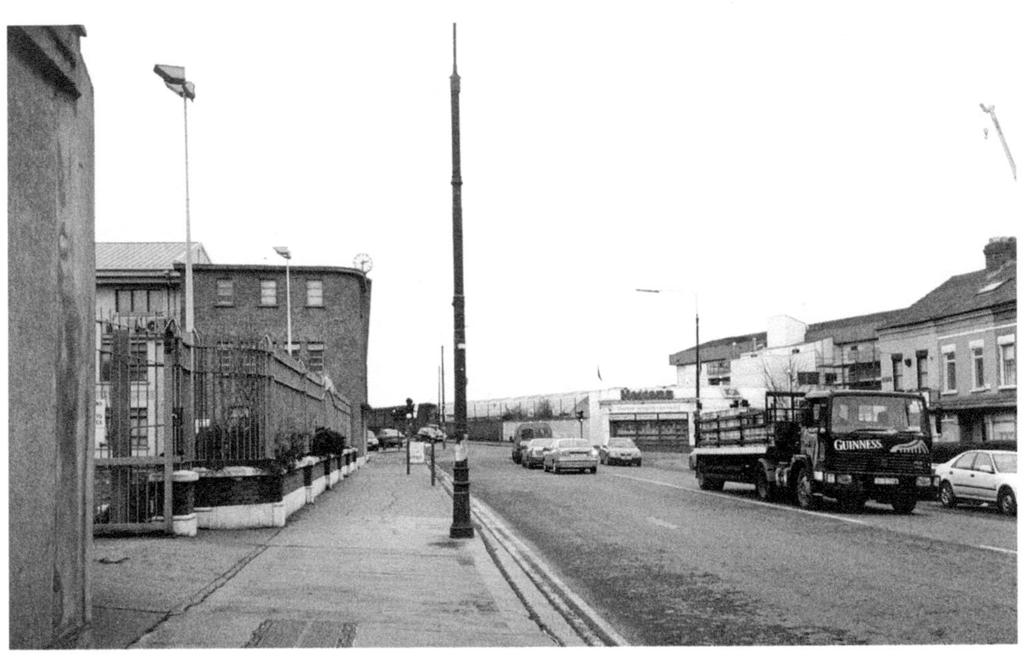

Ringsend Road in 2001, with the Irish Glass Bottle Company on left and Shelbourne Greyhound Stadium on the right (behind Heitons Builders Providers).

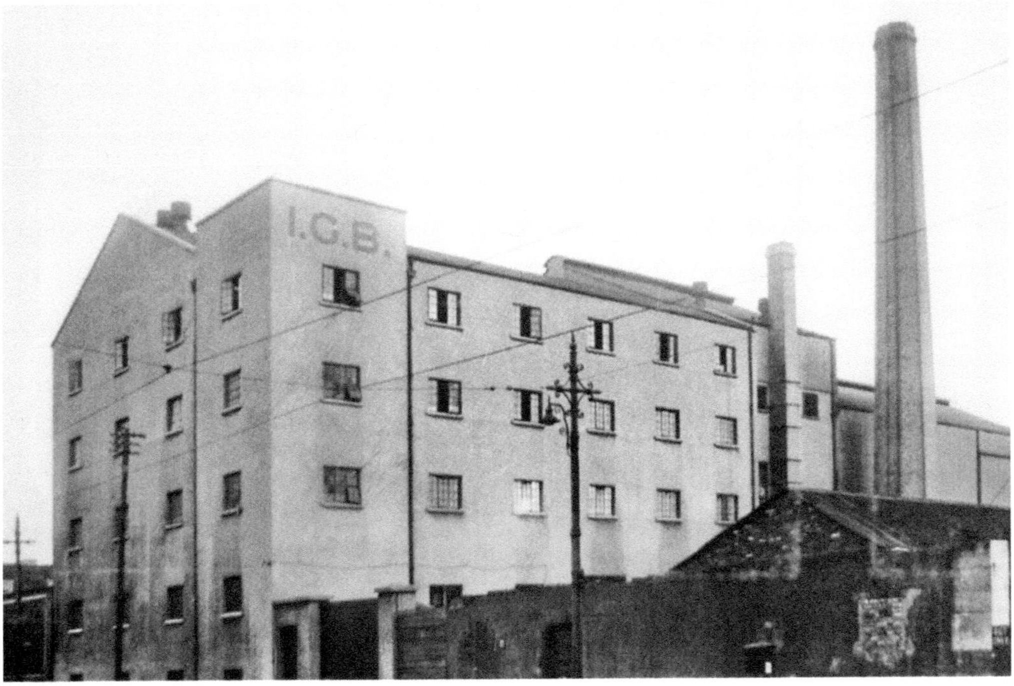

The Irish Glass Bottle Company factory for making sheet glass was on Ringsend Road, opposite the present Maxol garage. (Courtesy of the Irish Glass Bottle Company)

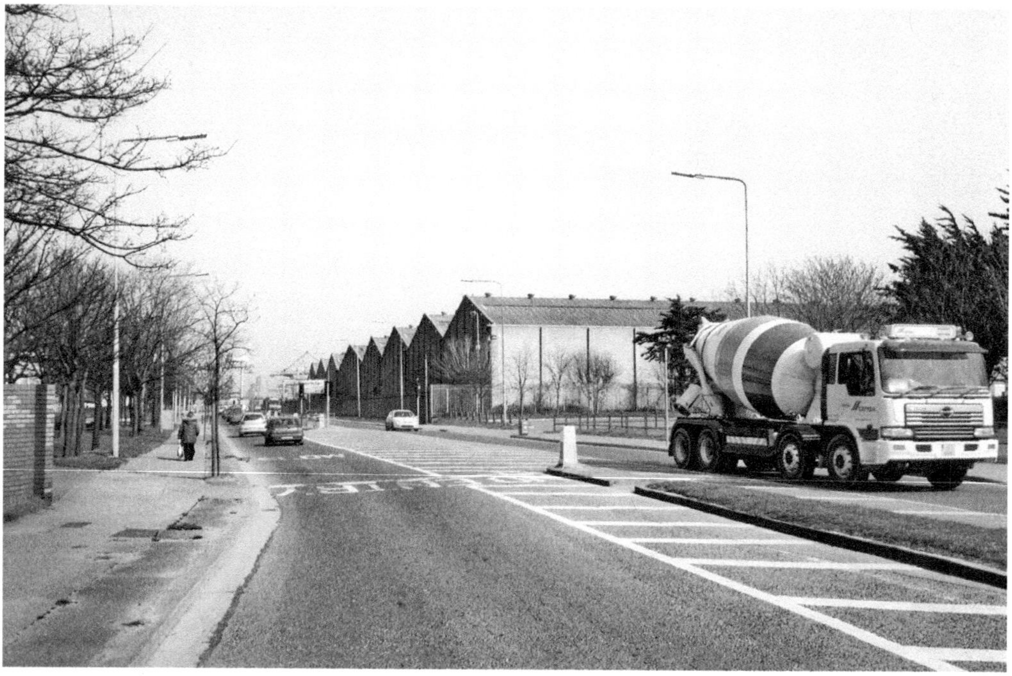

The empty premises of the Irish Glass Bottle Company on Sean Moore Road in 2007.

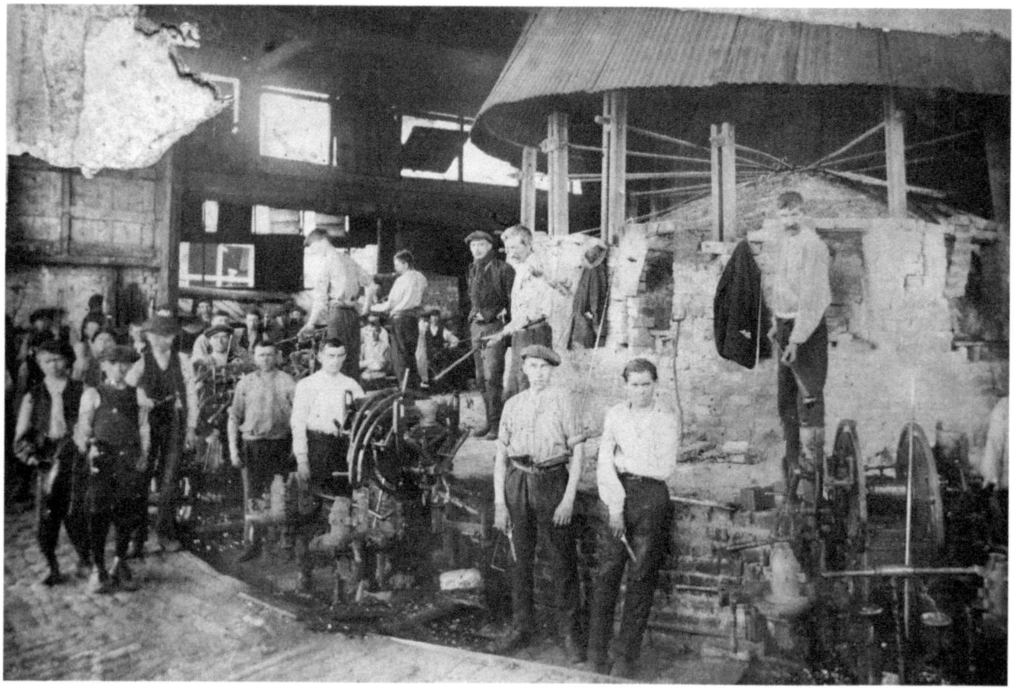

Men and boys at work in the Irish Glass Bottle Company. (Courtesy of NewsFour)

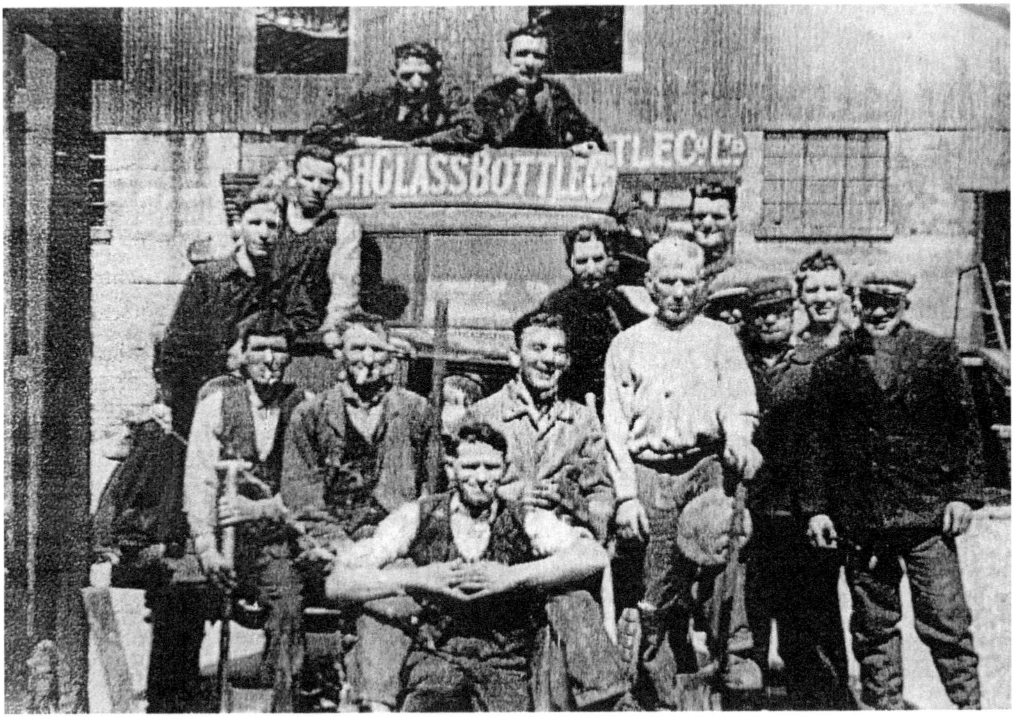

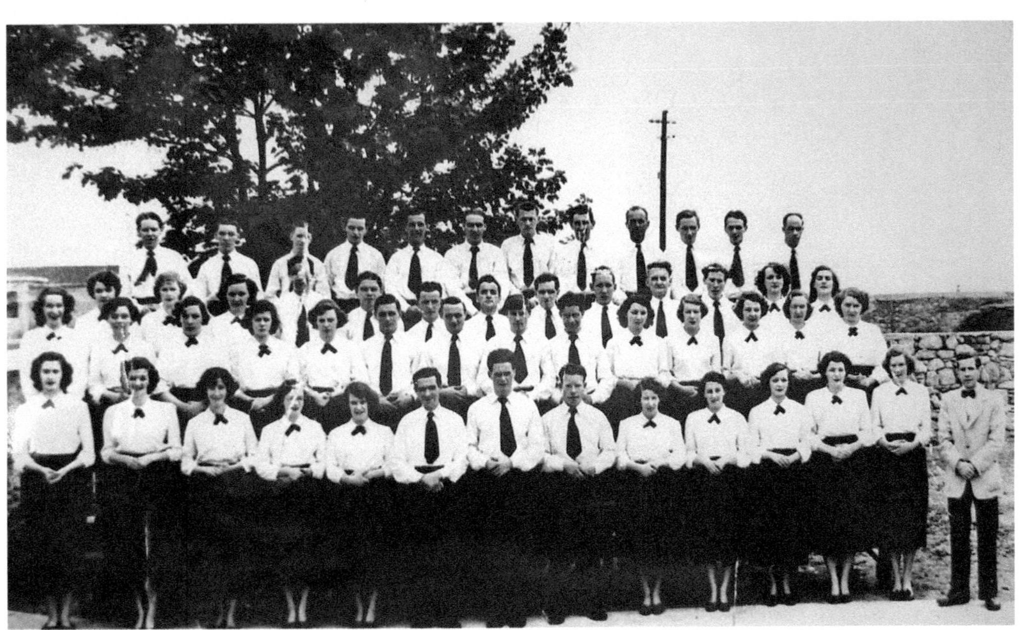

Workers at the Irish Glass Bottle Company. (Courtesy of NewsFour)

A 1950s choir at the Irish Glass Bottle Company, with conductor Alec Gordon on the right.
(Courtesy of NewsFour/Elizabeth Byrne)

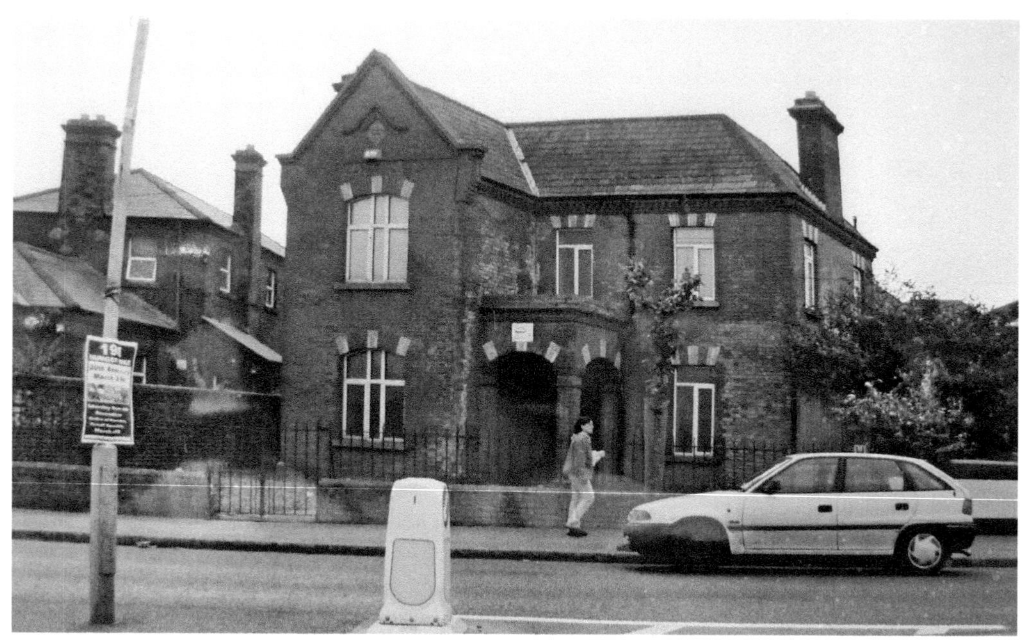

The Bottlemakers Hall on Irishtown Road (the hall itself was behind the house), with St Patrick's Dispensary on the left. (Courtesy of NewsFour)

4

FLOUR MILLING & BREAD

BOLANDS MILL, RINGSEND ROAD/BARROW STREET

Patrick Boland started a small bakery at 138 Capel Street in 1823, living over the shop, and his son, also Patrick, was born there in 1840. Patrick (Junior) took over Pims Flour Mill in Ringsend in 1873 (this steam-powered flour mill was started in 1847 on the site of a shipbuilder's yard, but caught fire in 1862). Within a year or two, he founded branches in Dún Laoghaire and Grand Canal Street/Quay. The company went public in 1888 and the assets were listed as the Metropolitan Bakery at 133-136 Capel Street, City of Dublin Bakery in Grand Canal Street/Quay, Bolands Flour Mills in Ringsend, and the Model Bakery in Dún Laoghaire (there were also retail shops at 14 Cumberland Street and 9 Upper Georges Street).

A report by the Institution of Mechanical Engineers in 1888 (as recorded by *Grace Guide to British Industrial History*) and another in the *Irish Builder* provide interesting facts. The mill was built in 1847 for Pims, utilising twenty-two pairs of grinding stones, and when Bolands acquired it in 1873, they added eighteen more pairs in a new extension. In 1880, the twenty-two original pairs were replaced by a complete roller plant, made by J. Harrison Carter of London, capable of producing 200 sacks of flour per day (twenty-four-hour operation). The other eighteen pairs of stones were still in use, producing 150 sacks of flour per day.

The new seven-storey (including basement) extension held 3,000 tons of wheat, mostly shipped in from places such as Australia and California, with the floors supported on cast-iron columns. It contained a separator and a cockle machine for preliminary cleaning of the grain, and a Simons automatic weighing machine. Large elevators lifted and distributed the grain to various hoppers. In the cleaning department, the wheat passed through a Victor smutter, two Seek polishers and two Throop brush machines. The 1846 Fairbairn beam-engine was supplied with steam from two Lancashire boilers, made by Barrington of Dublin.

In the Roller Mill building (1847), the basement contained shafting and pulleys for operating the machines. The ground floor had three rows of roller mills, the first floor had three scalpers for separating broken particles of wheat from the semolina middlings and flour, the second floor had wheat graders, the third floor had purifiers, and each of the fourth and fifth floors had eight centrifugals. The noise of the machines was deafening. The roller mill had two steam engines (coal-fired), made by Fairbairn, supplied with steam from a boiler 18ft long and 10ft diameter, made by Bewley Webb & Co. of Dublin.

In the mid-1950s, two giant concrete grain silos were built, one of 7,000-ton storage capacity, with drying machinery (badly needed for the native grain crop) capable of handling 20 tons an hour, and the other of 5,000 tons and drying plant of 12 tons an hour. Both silos were demolished in 2016 as part of a residential redevelopment currently underway.

BOLANDS BAKERY (CITY OF DUBLIN BAKERY), GRAND CANAL QUAY/STREET

The City of Dublin Bakery was built in 1874 by Bolands, comprising 15,000 sq. ft of buildings on a site of 3½ acres, including a two-storey building at the Grand Canal Quay entrance, for the manager's residence, offices, and retail shop. There was also a brewery on the premises for making barm (used in breadmaking).

By the 1880s there were 530 staff on the payroll, with twenty-four horse-drawn bread-vans delivering throughout Dublin (the vans were actually manufactured on the premises). The bakehouse was 100ft by 120ft, with a double-arch roof on iron beams and a central line of cast-iron columns. There were two rows of ovens (ten in each row) heated by coal and fired from the side, seven kneading machines, and a line of moulding boards, on which dough was shaped into loaves of bread. In a smaller bakehouse there were four ovens for making fancy bread.

In 1951, a multi-storey bakery was built on the Grand Canal Street side, by G & T Crampton. Bolands built their own garage and motor repair shop in nearby Sandwith Street in 1956. Bolands also made biscuits, from at least 1895, but ceased this side of the business in 1914. Biscuit production re-started in 1957, in the Model Bakery in Dún Laoghaire, and a new factory (133,000 sq. ft) was built in Deansgrange in 1962, employing 270 workers.

Bolands merged with Jacobs Biscuits in the 1970s, to become Irish Biscuits, and much of the work was transferred to the Jacobs factory in Tallaght. United Biscuits took over in 2004, moved production to England, and closed the Tallaght factory.

The original Grand Canal Street bakery was bought by developer Treasury Holdings in 1984, and they added an extra storey to the main building, re-clad the exterior with expensive stone, and the premises is now partly occupied by the National Asset Management Agency (NAMA).

The Boland family became very wealthy, living in a mansion on the north side of Dublin, and they have a big monument in Glasnevin Cemetery in the O'Connell Circle.

EASTER RISING, 1916

The 3rd Battalion of the Irish Volunteers, under Eamon de Valera, had six companies. 'A' Company was active around Beggars Bush Army Barracks, while 'C' Company occupied Bolands Bakery on Lower Grand Canal Street, and was the headquarters of de Valera. 'D' Company occupied Bolands Mills on Ringsend Road/Barrow Street. The Battle of Mount Street Bridge was the main event of the Rising in this part of Dublin, inflicting serious casualties on the British Army as it made its way into the city, after disembarking at Kingstown (Dún Laoghaire).

Immediately after the Rising, the Government awarded compensation to people and businesses damaged during the fighting. Bolands Bakery and Mills submitted a claim for £958, and was awarded £761. The damage to the buildings and equipment was very slight, and about two-thirds of the claim was in respect of bread baked on Easter Monday night which could not be distributed. Sir Patrick Dunns Hospital submitted a claim for £26 in respect of mattresses, pillows, sheets etc. that were saturated with blood from wounded soldiers and civilians.

A marble plaque in the nave of St Patrick's church is in memory of the deceased members of 'D' Company, 3rd Battalion, Dublin Brigade, Old IRA. Sean McMahon Bridge, over the Grand Canal Basin, commemorates the captain of the 'B' Company, 3rd Battalion.

During the First World War, 1914-1918, James Beckett Ltd, well-known building contractors, based in South Dock Works on Ringsend Road, was engaged in munitions work for the War Department. In March 1916 they obtained an electrical supply from the tramway generating station across the road, to power their machinery. One wonders if de Valera was aware of this factory so near his headquarters in Bolands factory!

DOCK MILLING COMPANY, 38-40 BARROW STREET

William Brown & Co. operated the Dock Flour Mills in Barrow Street from at least 1865. It was destroyed by fire in 1885 and rebuilt, comprising four storeys over basement, plus attic space, size 63ft by 35ft internally, with the screening room as an annex. The business was known as the Dock Milling Company during the twentieth century and grew into a very large operation. It was sold to Bolands Mill in the late 1980s and the site was later redeveloped.

RINGSEND BAKERY, RINGSEND ROAD

Following the closure of the le Brocquy lubricating oil company in 1896, occupying a long narrow site just north of the present Shelbourne Dog Track, R.N. Campbell started the Ringsend Bakery around 1904. Kennedy Bakery took over in 1917, soon employing about fifty workers. There was a fire in 1947, but thankfully the thirteen horses were saved. In the 1950s and '60s, McFerran & Guilford, builders' providers, were doing business here, and became known in the 1970s as Heiton McFerrans. The Watermarque office block was built on the site during the recent 'Celtic Tiger' boom.

HANOVER STREET FLOUR MILLS

The 1836 Ordnance Survey map shows a windmill sandwiched between Hanover Street East and Windmill Lane. This was originally an oil mill, but in 1862 it was raised by two storeys and fitted out as a flour mill. In 1869, a new granary with four lofts and a new chimney were built. Originally there were only pairs of grinding stones, then a mixture of stones and rollers, but by 1885 all were rollers, producing eight sacks of flour an hour. The mill, also known as Windmill Lane Mills, was continuously owned by Walter Brown & Co., and closed in the early 1960s, upon the death of Walter Brown. Older readers may remember 'Dainty' self-raising flour and 'Browns Best' for soda bread.

In recent decades, the old mill and other nearby buildings were used by the Windmill Lane recording studios, and fans of rock band U2 decorated the boundary walls with very colourful street art. Today, a new office block is being built around the original stone mill.

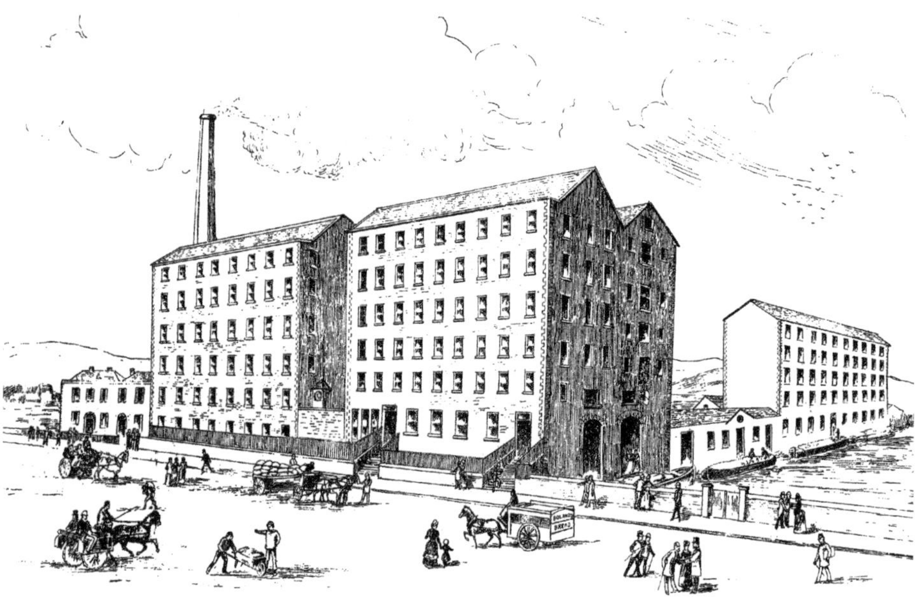

Bolands flour mill on Ringsend Road, 1888. (Courtesy of Irish Architectural Archive)

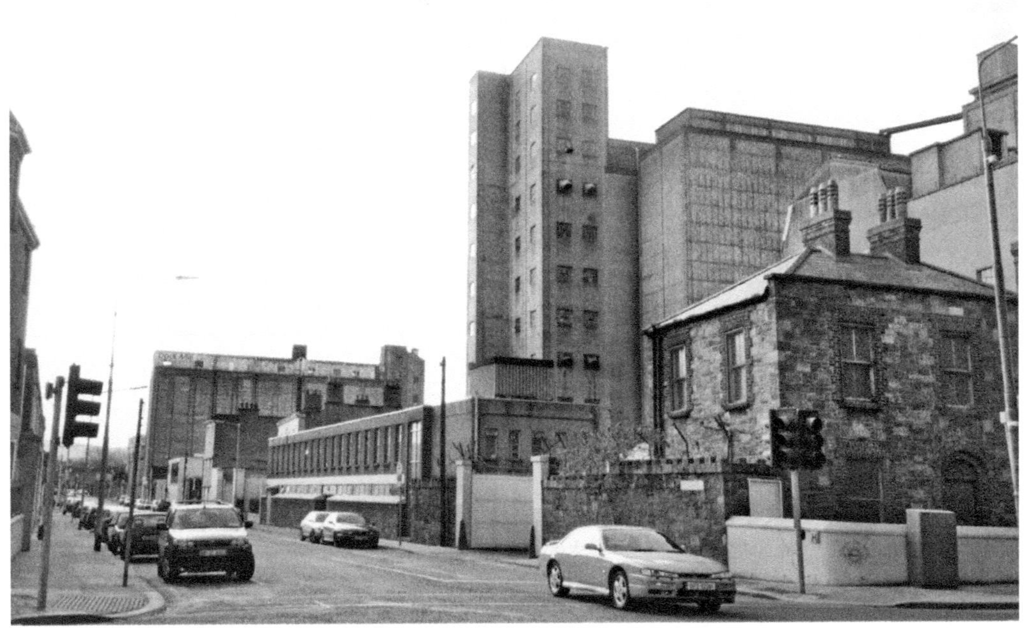

Barrow Street looking south, 2000. The former Bolands Mill on the right, and the Dock Mill grain silo can be seen in the distance.

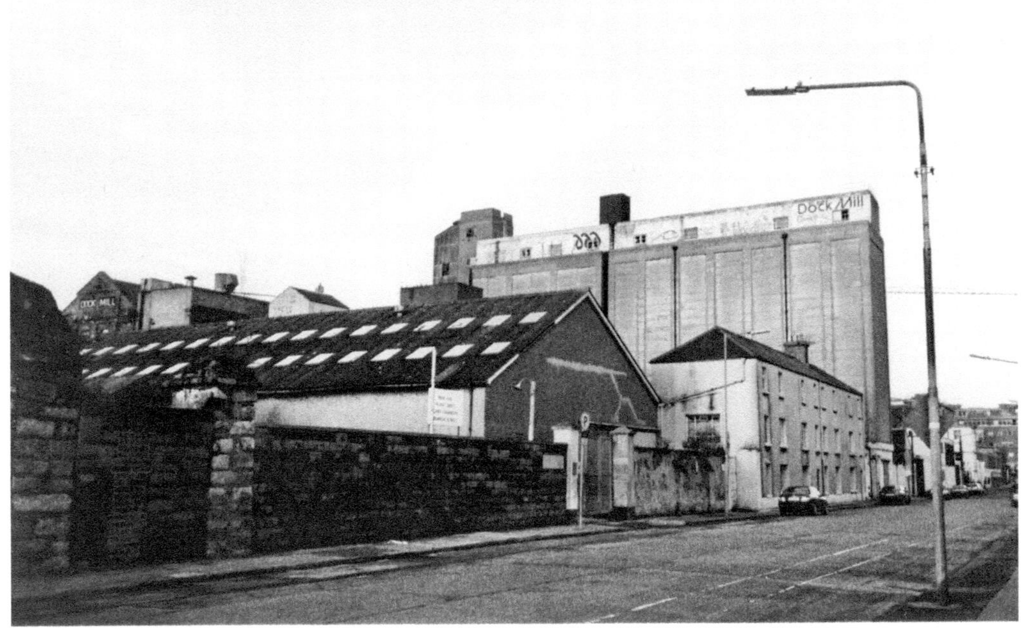

The former Dock Mill grain silo on Barrow Street in 2001, looking north, with the Irish Rail Depot on the left.

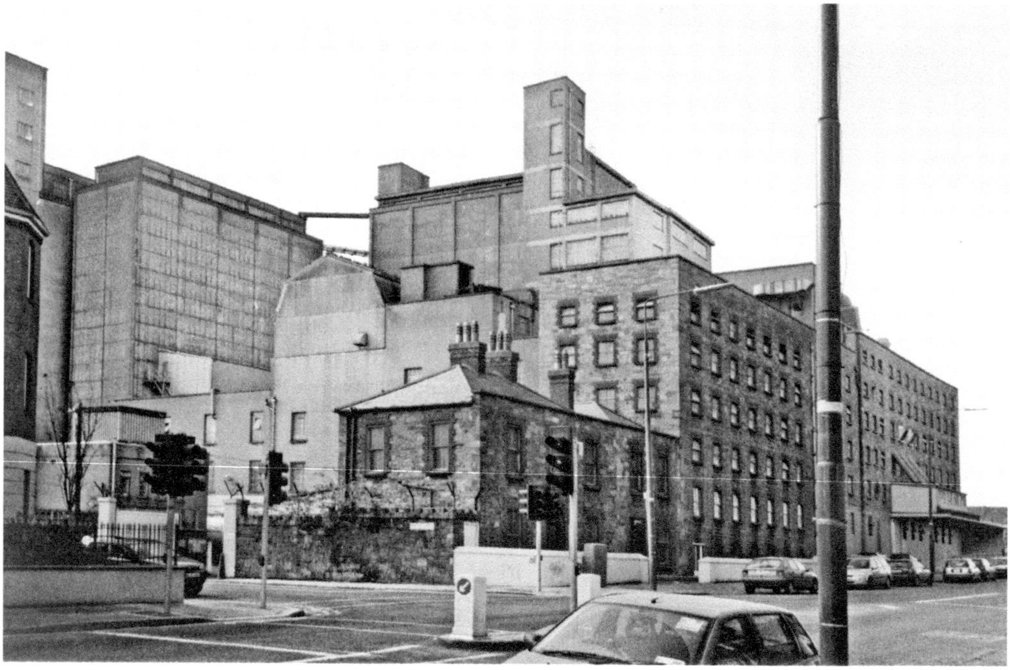

Bolands Mill on Ringsend Road in 2000. The site is currently being redeveloped.

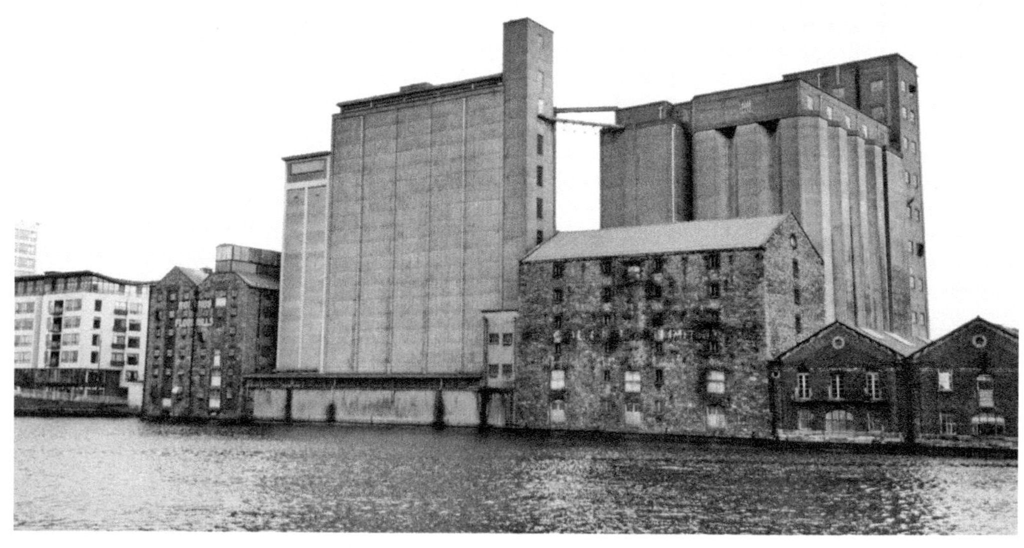

Bolands Mill backing on to Ringsend Basin in 2001. The giant grain silos have now been demolished.

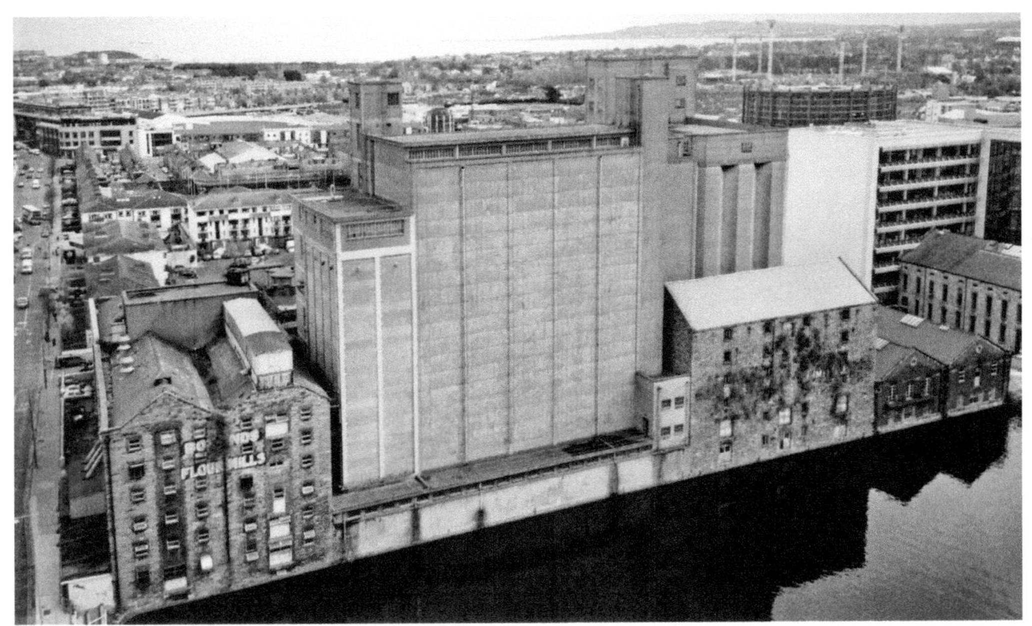

Bolands Mill in 2008. The redeveloped former gasometer on South Lotts Road is just visible in the distance on the right.

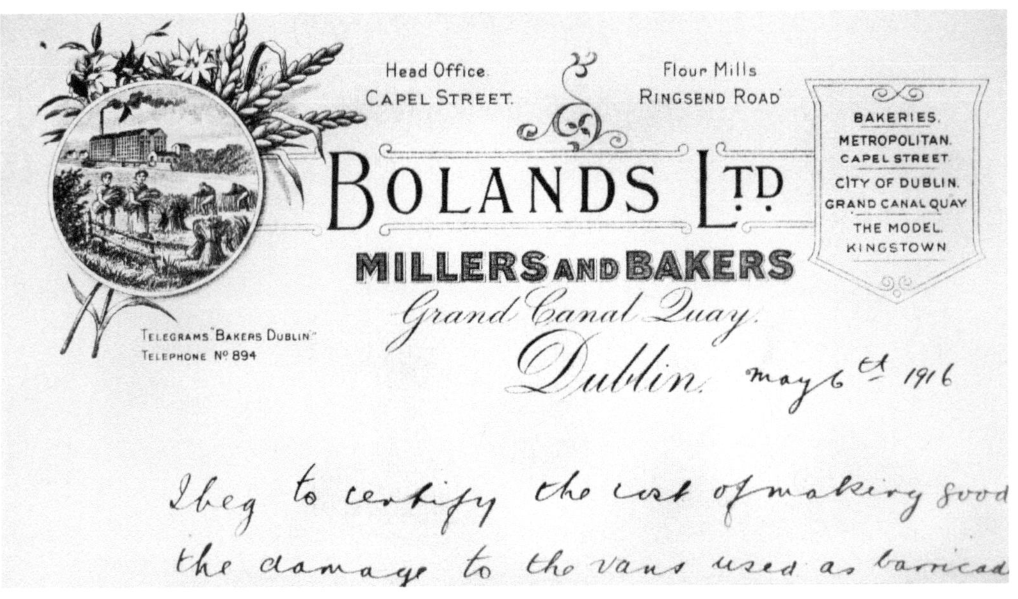

A compensation claim, on Bolands Ltd headed paper, in respect of minor damage after the 1916 Easter Rising. (Courtesy of the National Archives of Ireland)

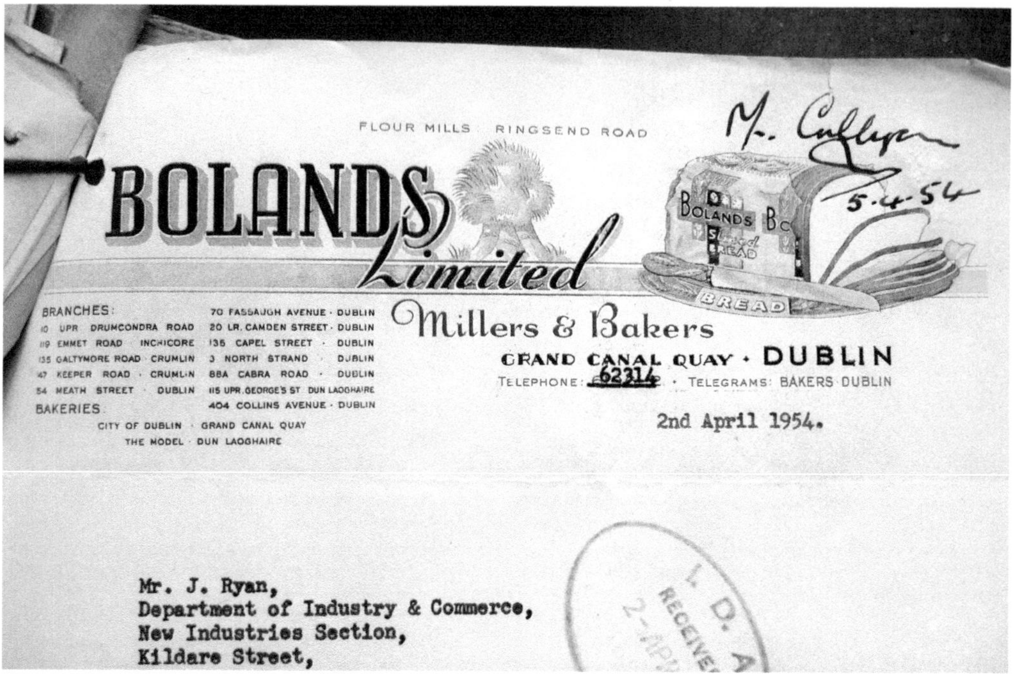

FLOUR MILLS · RINGSEND ROAD

BOLANDS *Limited*

Millers & Bakers

GRAND CANAL QUAY · DUBLIN

TELEPHONE: 62314 · TELEGRAMS: BAKERS DUBLIN

BRANCHES:
10 UPR DRUMCONDRA ROAD
119 EMMET ROAD · INCHICORE
135 GALTYMORE ROAD · CRUMLIN
47 KEEPER ROAD · CRUMLIN
54 MEATH STREET · DUBLIN
BAKERIES.

70 FASSAUGH AVENUE · DUBLIN
20 LR. CAMDEN STREET · DUBLIN
135 CAPEL STREET · DUBLIN
3 NORTH STRAND · DUBLIN
88A CABRA ROAD · DUBLIN
115 UPR. GEORGE'S ST · DUN LAOGHAIRE
404 COLLINS AVENUE · DUBLIN

CITY OF DUBLIN · GRAND CANAL QUAY
THE MODEL · DUN LAOGHAIRE

2nd April 1954.

Mr. J. Ryan,
Department of Industry & Commerce,
New Industries Section,
Kildare Street,

1954 headed paper of Bolands Ltd, now depicting sliced bread. (Courtesy of the National Archives of Ireland)

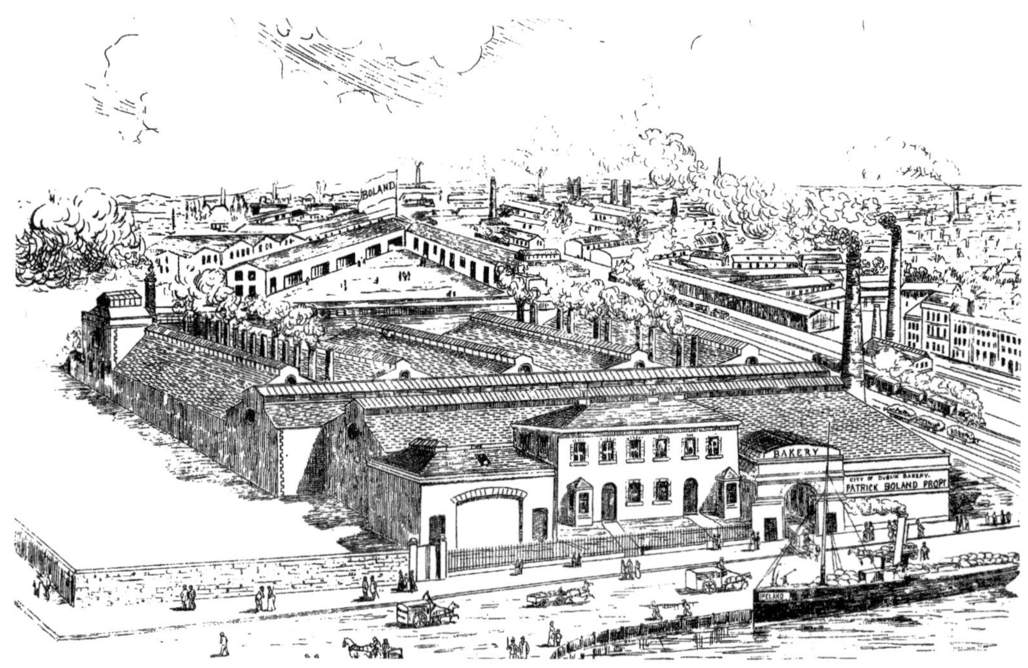

Bolands Bakery on Grand Canal Quay (corner of Grand Canal Street) in 1888. (Courtesy of Irish Architectural Archives)

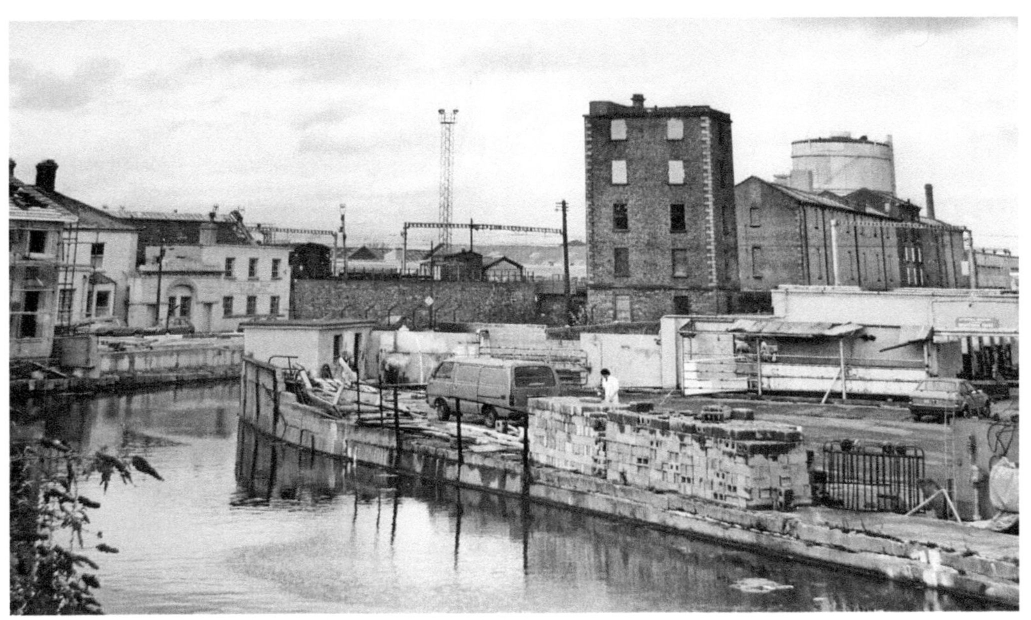

Grand Canal Quay, with Bolands Bakery on the left, and the tall Guinness Malthouse in the centre. (Courtesy of St Andrews Resource Centre)

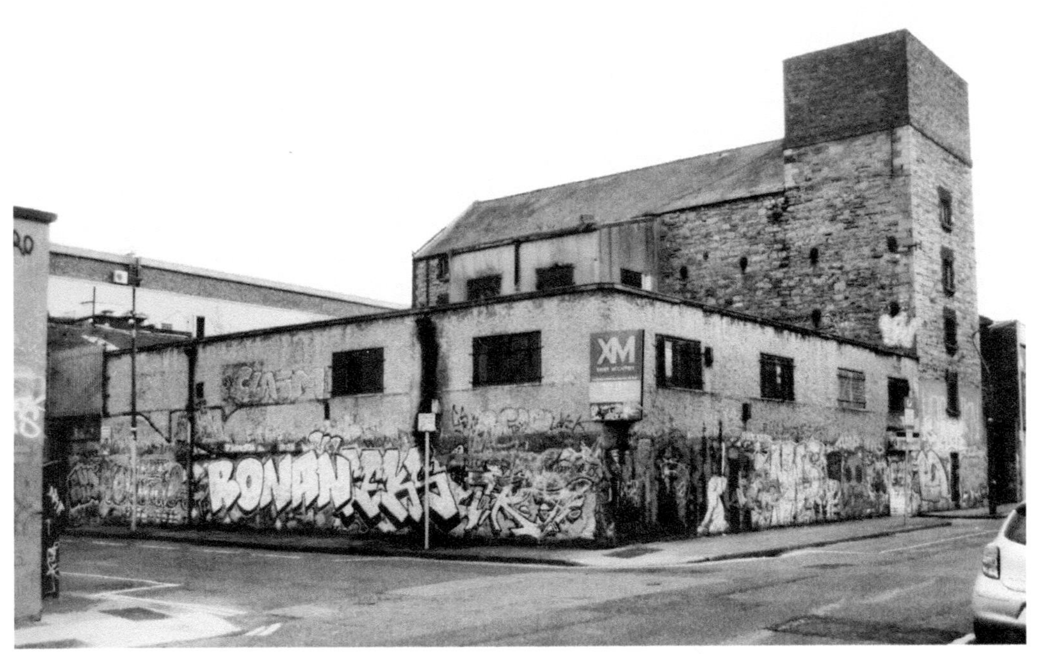

A recent photo of Windmill Lane/Creighton Street.

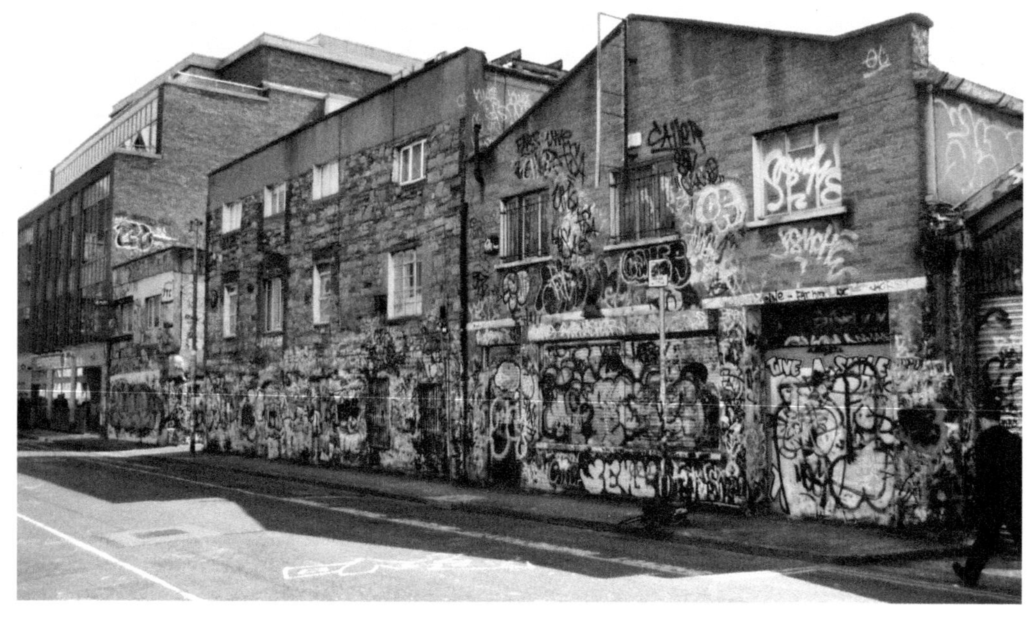

A recent photo of Windmill Lane, with colourful street art by U2 fans.

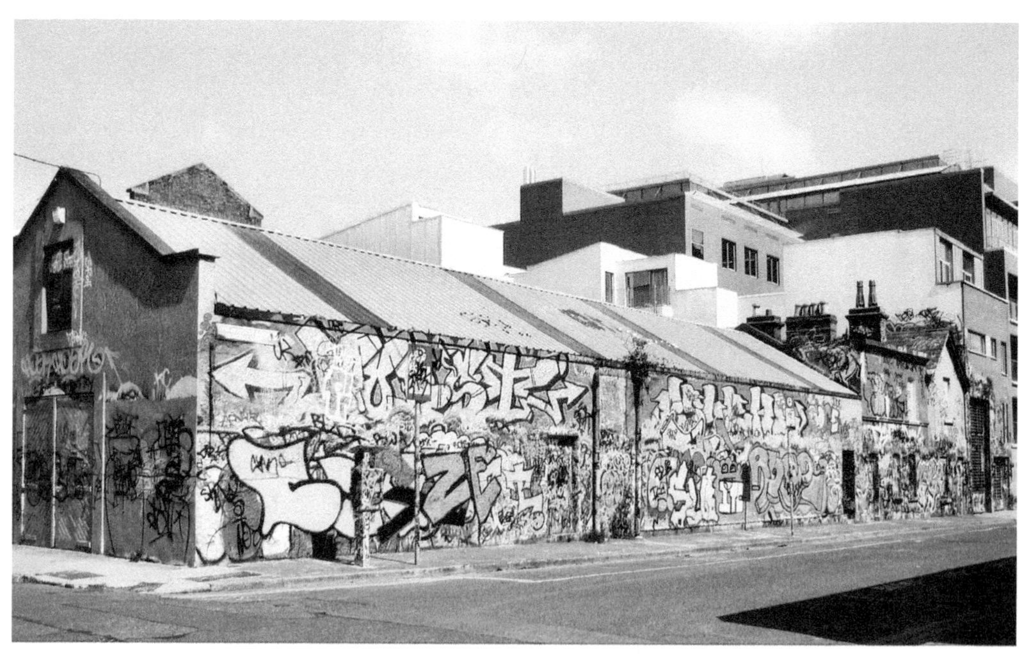

Recent colourful street art on the north corner of Windmill Lane/Creighton Street.

5

GENERAL BUSINESS

SALT MANUFACTURE, THORNCASTLE STREET

Ringsend had two salt factories for much of the nineteenth century, both at the north end of Thorncastle Street, one on each side of the road. Both probably used imported rock salt, as a newspaper reported in 1810 that Thomas Bray of Thorncastle Street had died, leaving 150 tons of rock salt, and 60 tons of coal. In 1834 Theophilus Page was a salt manufacturer, James Hill had a salt and lime works, and James Pommoret had a salt works in Fitzwilliam Street. Egan Irish Salt Works was recorded in 1859, run by Ellen Egan. Flower & McDonald had a salt works around 81 Thorncastle Street from about 1865 to 1905 – they were also coal merchants.

SUGAR REFINERY, PEARSE STREET

Bewley Moss & Co. built an eight-storey storage building in 1862, beside their sugar refinery on Pearse Street. The structure comprises stone external walls, wrought-iron floor beams supporting segmental brick arches, resting on cast-iron central columns. Dublin Sugar Refinery took over in 1880, but closed in 1886.

From 1890 to 1905, Dublin City & Banagher Distilleries Ltd (whiskey) were based here, with Alexander Findlater as chairman. The small former malthouse is now occupied by L. Connaughton & Sons (suppliers of beverages to ships and airlines), on adjoining Grand Canal Quay.

From 1911 to 1973, Hammond Lane Foundry operated from the premises.

The IDA built an enterprise centre for small businesses here in 1981, retaining the tower for craft workshops and a café. Now Trinity College own the business complex, which is still thriving.

HAMMOND LANE FOUNDRY, 111 PEARSE STREET

In 1902, 26-year-old David Frame, assisted by Thomas Buchanan, both from Scotland, acquired the long-established iron foundry of John G. Strong & Sons, 8-10 Hammond Lane (off Church Street near the Four Courts). The following year, the business is listed as Hammond Lane Foundry Company, with John Frame & Co. as proprietors (presumably his father). For a few years, David Frame was also involved in contracting, in partnership with another Scotsman named Crawford, based at 5 Talbot Place. The foundry business prospered, and within a short time, they bought the site of Robinson Saw Mills at 111A Great Brunswick Street (now called Pearse Street). In 1911 they acquired the adjoining premises at 111, which was previously a sugar refinery.

David Frame became a pillar of Irish industrial society, getting involved in such projects as the short-lived Beauparc Copper Mines in County Meath, Clondalkin Paper Mills, and even cinemas. He was instrumental in setting up Solas Teoranta (making light bulbs) in Bray, in 1934, and Irish Steel in Haulbowline Dockyard in Cork, in 1938. He donated part of Bray Head to Wicklow County Council, and was chairman of that body in 1928.

The company also dealt in scrap metal for their own needs and other companies (such as Irish Steel in Cork). When the Dublin & Blessington Steam Tramway ceased business in 1932, the foundry bought the tram tracks and carriages as scrap metal.

In 1937, the company bought the famous Matthew O'Byrne Bell Foundry, which later amalgamated with Fyffe Couplings, making 'Instantor' brass couplings for copper pipes.

The foundry made ranges, fire grates, gutters, downpipes, and cisterns, using cast iron. During the Second World War (1939-1945), the foundry made 20,000 landmines for the British War Department. In 1946 they set up a new subsidiary making domestic cookers for Dublin Gas – Parkham Crown D, retailing at £18 each. They were able to cast all the parts, and also had a vitreous enamelling plant for coating the cookers with a white hygienic finish. The business group later got involved in refrigerated rooms, and also set up Industrial Gases Ltd. In 1948 the directors were: D.D. Frame, J.J. Davy, G.T. Rowe, S.W. Aitken, and R.N. Eaton.

Besides the main premises in 111 Pearse Street, the company had a site at 77-81 Thorncastle Street (now the Ringsend Community Centre), in the period 1950s-'80s.

The foundry in Pearse Street closed in 1973, with the loss of 170 jobs, but the other subsidiaries continued, especially the scrap-metal business, which relocated to Sir John Rogersons Quay. In 1995 Hammond Lane Metals moved to the former Coal Distributors Ltd site on South Bank Quay (Pigeon House Road), where they continue to process all Ireland's scrapped cars.

TONGE & TAGGART FOUNDRY, 10 WINDMILL LANE

Lovers of cast-iron manhole covers will remember this famous company, also known as South City Foundry, which was founded in 1869 at 41 Bishop Street (previously used by George Craddock Foundry), and moved in 1902 to Windmill Lane. Their new premises, which included 5 Hanover Street East, had been occupied by the Brunswick Ironworks and Foundry (also known as M. Meade & Sons) since 1894. An additional foundry opened in 1938 at 1b East Wall Road (beside Masser). Tonge & Taggart teamed up with J. & C. McGloughlin (founded in 1875) of Pearse Street, who specialised in structural steelwork frames for buildings, and the Tonge McGloughlin group became a public company in 1954. McGloughlin moved to Jamestown Road in Inchicore in 1965. The Windmill Lane foundry of Tonge & Taggart moved to their other premises on East Wall Road in 1973. Within a few years the two companies were part of the TMG Group (Smurfit controlled), as were Hammond Lane Metal Company, Waterford Ironfoundry, and Pierce of Wexford. Tonge & Taggart went into liquidation in 1988, with the loss of 113 jobs, but the name and goodwill were bought by Cavanagh Foundry of Birr, County Offaly.

MINING COMPANY OF IRELAND/STRACHAN BROS, 11 FITZWILLIAM QUAY

Ringsend Ironworks was at 11 Fitzwilliam Quay for much of the nineteenth century, until the Mining Company of Ireland moved their lead-smelting works to Ringsend in 1887 from Ballycorus (Kilternan, County Dublin). Ballycorus was supplied with lead ore from their mine at Luganure in Glendalough, which they had mined since 1824. In 1890/91 the business went into voluntary liquidation and part of it was acquired by Strachan Bros, an old lead-manufacturing firm based in Loftus Lane. Strachan Bros continued to produce lead pipes (for domestic water supply) and lead sheet (for roofwork). In 1969, another old firm, Frys Metals Ltd, 197 Pearse Street, joined them at Fitzwilliam Quay. The Mining Company of Ireland moved to Clondalkin around 1990, where they still make lead sheet for roofing etc.

CHEMICAL MANURE AND FERTILISERS

From the 1880s to the 1930s there were a few fertiliser factories around the Charlotte Quay and Sir John Rogersons Quay areas, such as Richardson & Fletcher, Eckforts Ltd, and Hibernian Chemical Co. The Richardson & Fletcher site was later occupied by the sheet-glass division of the Irish Glass Bottle Company.

DUBLIN OIL & GREASE WORKS, RINGSEND ROAD

A Belgian by the name of Louis le Brocquy started a business in 1886 on Ringsend Road, at the corner of South Lotts Road, called the Dublin Oil and Grease Works, producing lubricating oils and greases. They stayed at Ringsend until 1896, when they moved to Harold's Cross and began trading as the Greenmount Oil Company. In July 1896, a few months before the lease expired, the Ringsend premises caught fire and was burnt to the ground.

The site was later used by Kennedy's bakery, then Heiton McFerran builders' providers, and now Watermarque office block.

COAL YARDS

In the twentieth century, Ringsend had no shortage of large coal yards, especially alongside Charlotte Quay, such as Wallace Bros, Heitons, and Tedcastle McCormick. Heitons had their own colliers – St Mungo, St Kenneth, St Eunan, and St Fintan.

Coal Distributors Ltd was set up in 1972/73 by various companies to provide one large coal depot (mostly Polish coal), based at South Quay Pier (now Hammond Lane Scrapyard). The consortium comprised M. Doherty & Co., P. Donnelly & Sons, Heiton Coals, MacKensie & Co., and Tedcastle McCormick.

ROPE MAKING

Being a maritime community, Ringsend had a few rope-making factories in the nineteenth century, with names such as Todhunter as far back as 1826, and Thomas Crosby & Sons in 1870. Ropes comprise many strands of hemp twisted together into various thicknesses. Usually the strands were laid out along a long lane or shed, and then twisted together. Hence, old maps show various Ropewalks in Ringsend, including near Caroline Row.

REGAL CINEMA, FITZWILLIAM STREET

Cities Cinemas Ltd demolished some old cottages in Fitzwilliam Street and opened the Rinn Cinema in November 1925, with a capacity of 950 seats. The name was changed to the Regal in 1933. The widespread use of television in the 1960s resulted in falling numbers of patrons and the cinema closed in 1965. It was converted for a variety of businesses in 1986, and since 2013 its main use is by the Abundant Grace Christian Assembly (Pentecostal), which also runs a café and charity shop behind the library.

'THE PRODUCTS', 83 THORNCASTLE STREET

In the 1950s and '60s, Irish Products and Avondale Products processed cattle by-products to make pet food. In the 1970s, Robert Wilson & Sons were in the same business. From 1983 to 1999, Premier By-Products Ltd continued to produce pet food. Now the smells are just a memory and Portview apartments/offices were built on the corner site – the original 'Point'.

BUTLERS CHOCOLATES, 77 SIR JOHN ROGERSONS QUAY

The sweet aromas emanating from Butlers Chocolates would melt your heart. The company started in a small mews building in Lad Lane in 1932, and was sold to Seamus Sorensen in 1959. 1988 saw a move to the IDA Enterprise Centre on Pearse Street, and then to the quays in 1996. Finally, in 2003, the business relocated to Clonshaugh Industrial Estate, near the airport, where they continue to thrive, and have opened specialist cafés in Ireland and around the world. The site of their former factory on Sir John Rogersons Quay is now a modern block of apartments called Butlers Court.

REG ARMSTRONG MOTORS, 9-19 RINGSEND ROAD

Reg Armstrong was a legend in the motoring world. In 1952, as a young man, he won the Isle of Man TT race on a Norton motorcycle. The following year, the German company NSU, gave him the contract to assemble their motorcycles at 23/24 Halston Street (near the Four Courts). In 1958, he was appointed to assemble their 24 bhp NSU Prinz car, and he acquired the Ringsend Road premises, which was formerly occupied by James Beckett & Co., the famous building contractors, renaming it South Dock Works. With fellow director Cedric Machesney, the car assembly business thrived in the 1960s, taking on the German/USA-designed Opel Rekord, Opel Kadett, and the Japanese Honda. Halston Street continued with the assembly of motorcycles, including Honda machines from 1963, but later moved to Thorncastle Street in Ringsend.

In the 1970s, the company was assembling Mini cars for British Leyland, but soon the Government was forced to allow the importation of fully assembled cars, thus ending the Irish assembly line, and resulting in the loss of many good skilled jobs.

The 1-acre site was eventually sold to Zoe Developments in 1991, and Shelbourne Village (apartments) was built shortly afterwards, while still retaining the petrol station. The original Ringsend Road façade comprised a two-storey building with many windows and a fancy arched entrance door – the latter is now preserved on the west side of the present Maxol petrol station. The motorcycle site on Thorncastle Street was acquired by Zoe Developments in 1989, who built Fisherman's Wharf apartments and townhouses.

RALEIGH BICYCLES, 8-11 HANOVER QUAY

Raleigh bicycles were assembled in a single-storey former grain-store in Hanover Quay from the 1950s until it closed in 1980, with the loss of 135 skilled jobs. Recently the old building, dating from the 1860s, was remodelled for Airbnb (an online accommodation agency).

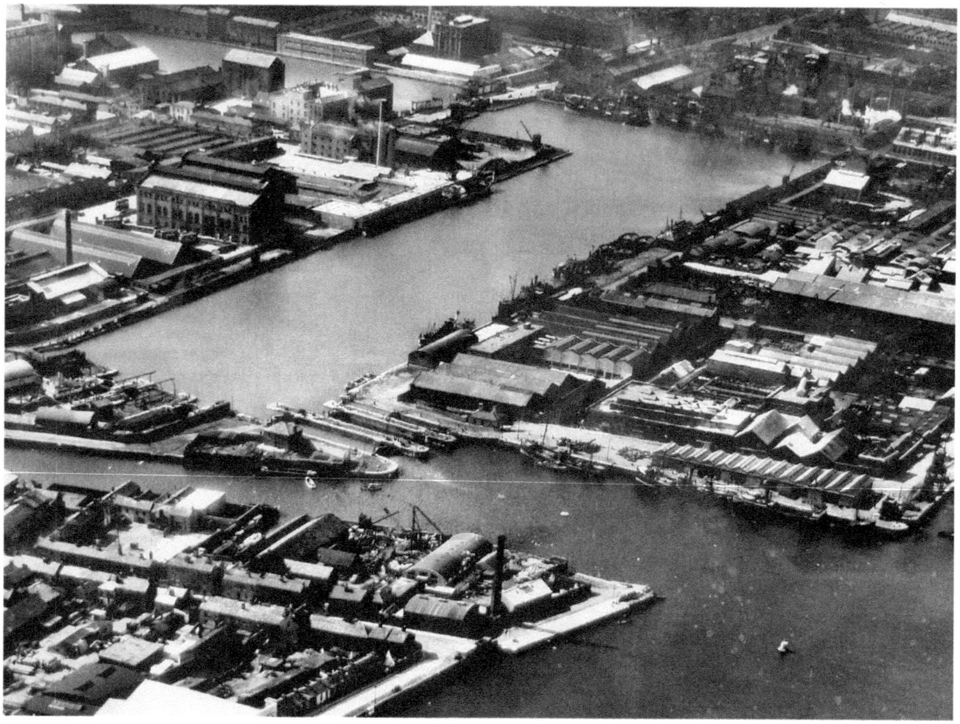

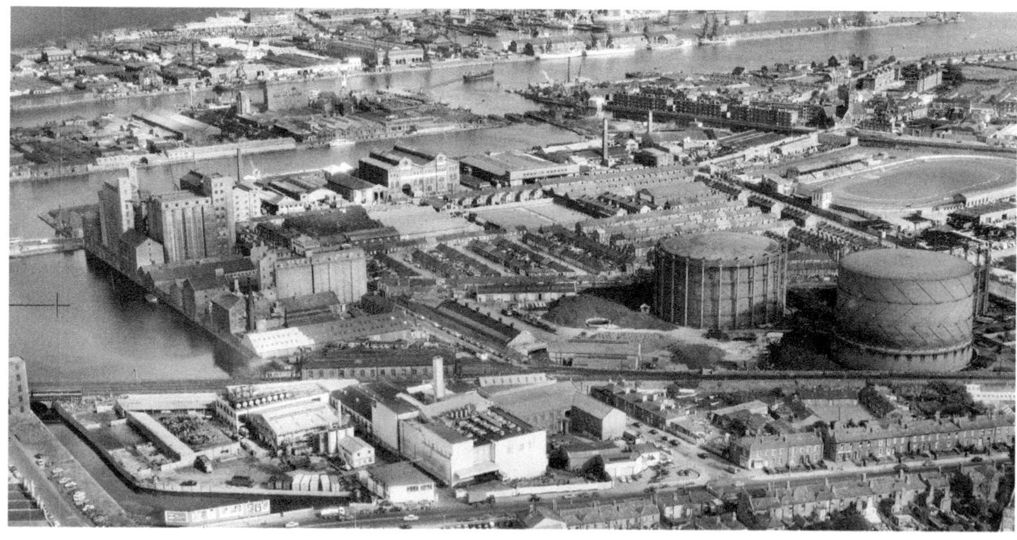

Ringsend Basin in the 1940s from the east. (Courtesy of Christy Mullen)

Ringsend in the early 1970s, with International Meats (slaughterhouse) on the left in the foreground. (Courtesy of the National Library of Ireland)

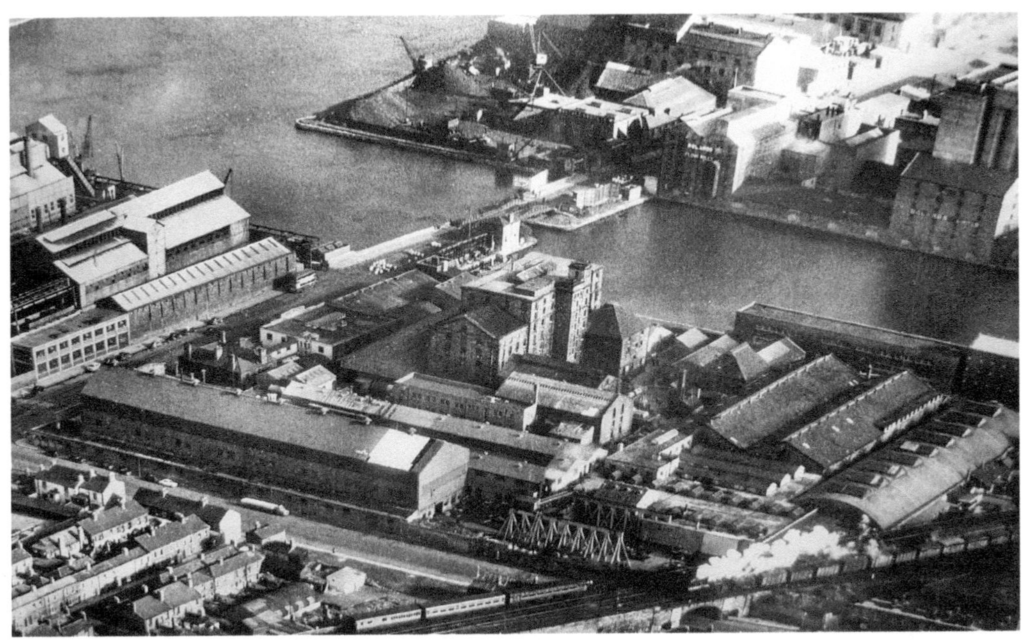

Grand Canal Quay, *c.* 1950s. Dublin Gas Company is on the left. (Courtesy of St Andrews Resource Centre)

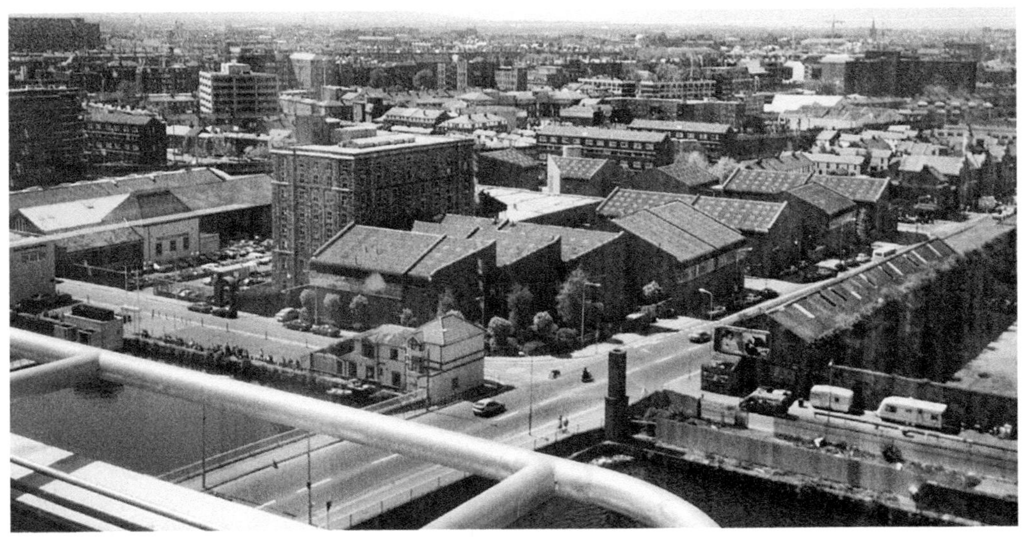

The IDA Enterprise Centre on Pearse Street in 2000. The tall central building was a sugar refinery, and then occupied by Hammond Lane Foundry. Dublin Gas Company, on the right, has since been substantially demolished.

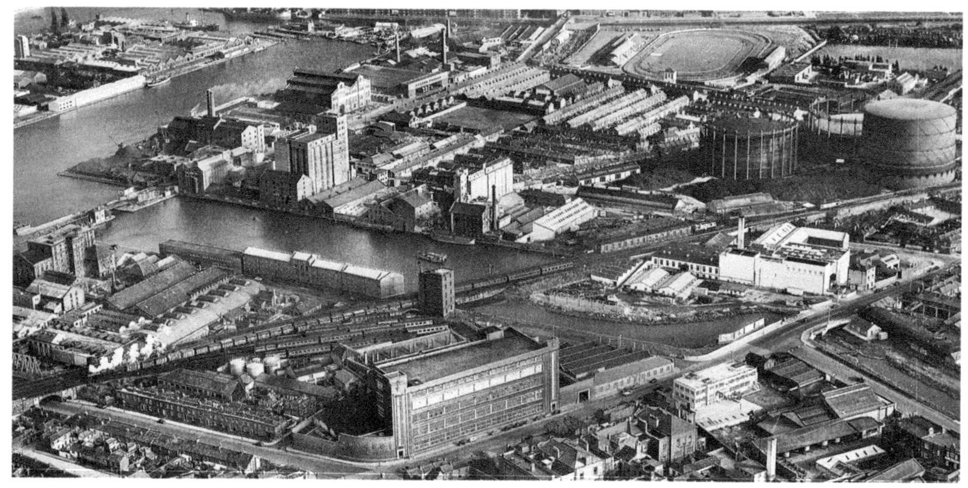

A 1950s view of Grand Canal Basin, with Bolands Bakery in the foreground. (Courtesy of the National Library of Ireland)

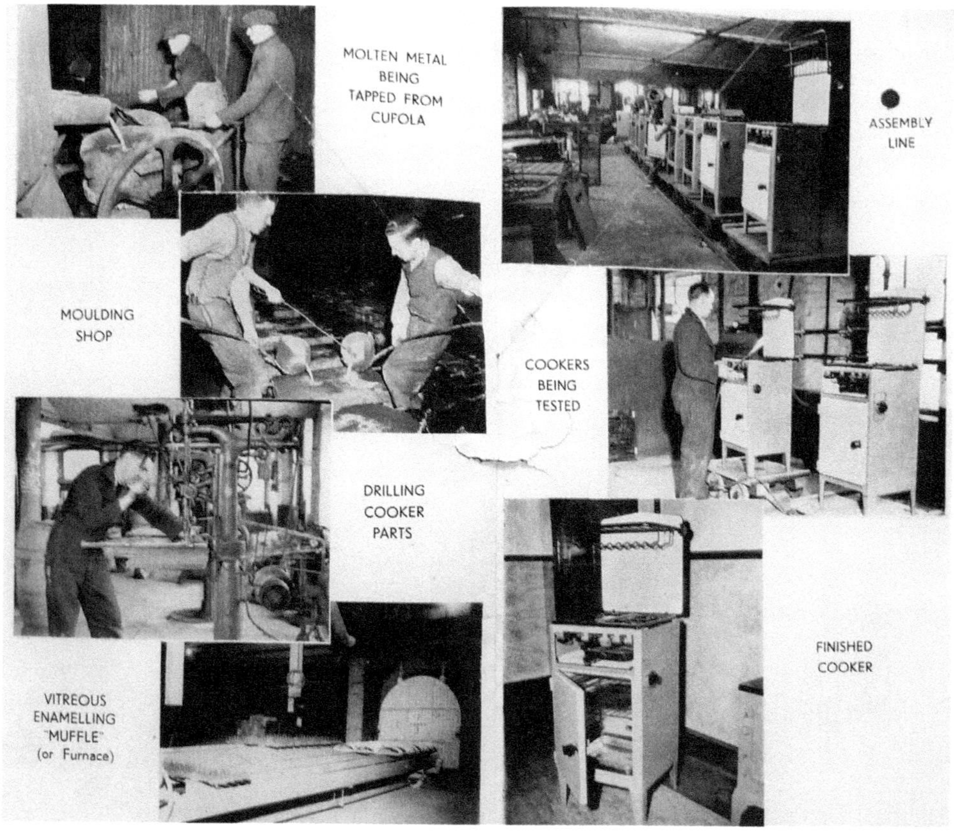

Hammond Lane brochure of 1949, showing the casting and assembly of domestic gas cookers. (Courtesy of the National Archives of Ireland)

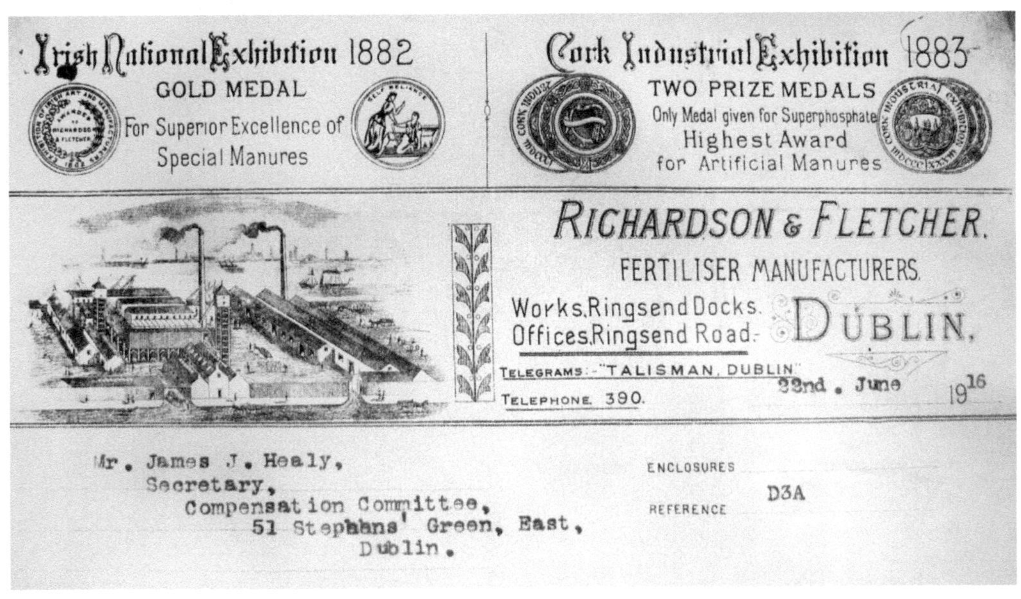

Elaborate headed paper for Richardson & Fletcher in 1916. The Irish Glass Bottle Company later used this Ringsend Road site for their sheet glass division. (Courtesy of the National Archives of Ireland)

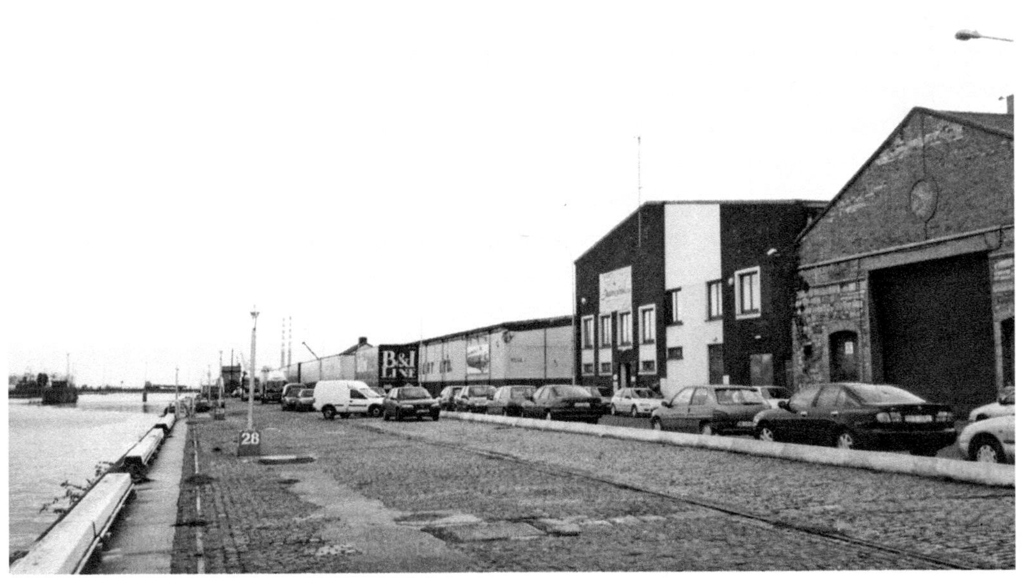

A 1999 photo of Butlers Chocolates factory (brown and cream coloured) at the corner of Sir John Rogersons Quay and Benson Street.

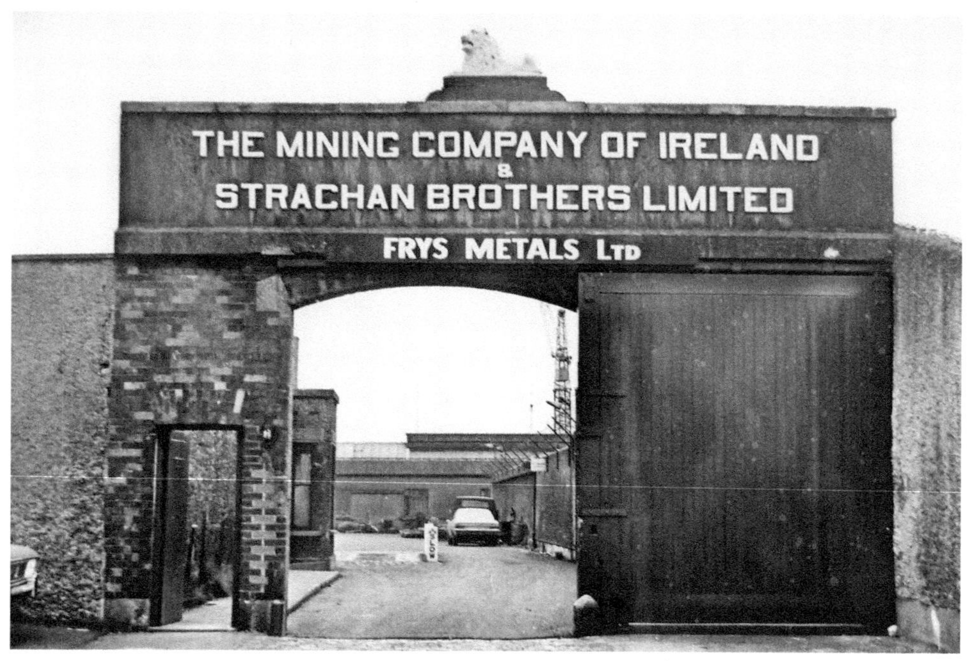

Early 1970s photo of this famous lead factory on Fitzwilliam Quay. Note the lion over the entrance. (Courtesy of the Mining Company of Ireland)

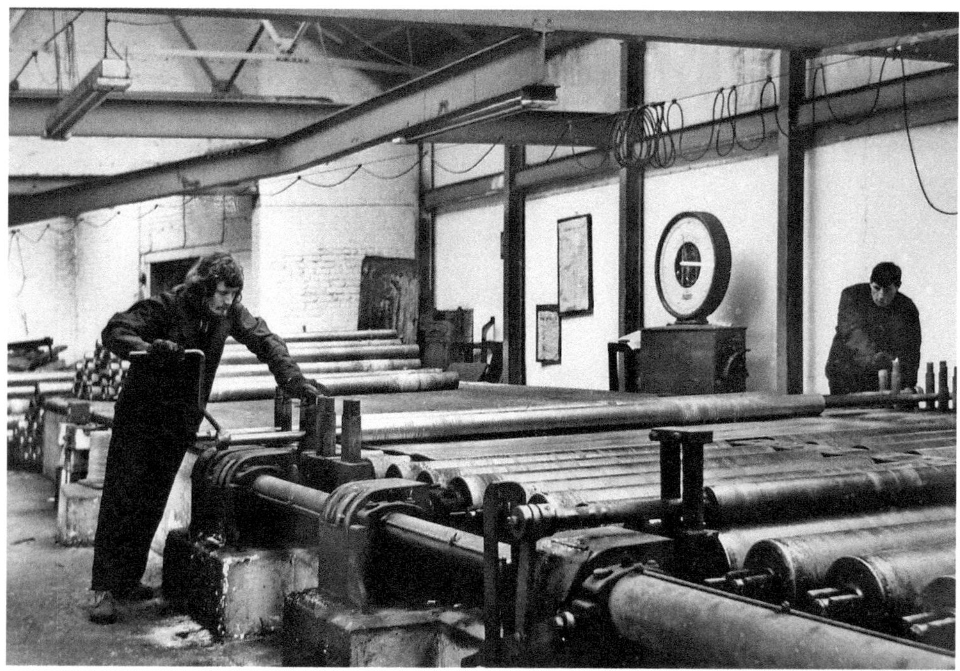

Rolling sheet lead inside the factory on Fitzwilliam Quay. (Courtesy of the Mining Company of Ireland)

6

EDUCATION & RELIGION

RINGSEND SECOND-LEVEL COLLEGE, CAMBRIDGE ROAD

The Pembroke Technical School (the title in a terracotta panel over the original entrance) opened in October 1893, as a night school for men and women, boys and girls. The Earl of Pembroke provided the site, and paid for most of the building cost – thereafter the Vocational Education Committee funded the school. Designed by William Kaye-Parry, and built by Collen Bros of Portadown, the fine building included a large two-storey rear hall. Another terracotta plaque proclaimed '*PER MARE VIVIMUS*', Latin for 'By the Sea we Live', since the establishment incorporated a Fishery School (although this section closed in 1897).

The report for the year 1894/95 noted that although there were 245 pupils on the roll book, the average daily attendance was forty-nine. Most of the pupils had no primary education, since there was no compulsory attendance at school. Subjects taught included navigation and seamanship, net making, boat building, metalwork, mechanics, maths, chemistry, drawing, shorthand, book-keeping, typewriting, reading, writing, arithmetic, cookery, laundry work, dress making, machine knitting, ambulance, and swimming.

Throughout the following decades, its primary function was as a mixed secondary school, with adult evening classes. From 1916 until recent years, car mechanics was an important subject. However, from time to time, students, both young and older, have built small boats in the school, especially in the 1960s.

Rising attendances in the 1970s necessitated building a larger school. The charming old building was demolished in 1978, but not before RTÉ used it to make a controversial television serial called *The Spike*, employing some local lads as 'extras'. The real students were accommodated in the vacant Boys National School in Thorncastle Street for two years, and the present school, founded on precast concrete piles, was opened in September 1980.

Ballsbridge College in Shelbourne Road was established as a branch of Ringsend Technical School in 1903 (initially in a prefab), and the present building dates from 1948.

The Pembroke Town Hall was another branch of Ringsend Technical School from 1930-51, before becoming the headquarters of the Vocational Education Committee (VEC), bearing in mind that the Township was taken over by Dublin Corporation in 1930.

CATHOLIC PRIMARY SCHOOLS

In 1839, there was a Parochial School in a small house in Chapel Avenue, Irishtown, near the Catholic Chapel.

A new school was built in Thorncastle Street in 1844, comprising two rooms, each 36ft by 20ft, probably with the boys on the ground floor and the girls on the first floor. The total cost was £500, comprising a Government grant of £178, and local contribution (mostly the Pembroke Estate) of £322. The teachers lived in the school and also in a small rear cottage until 1884, when a teacher's residence was built on the site of the cottage, at a cost of £250 (with grant of £100). An evening school operated until 1889.

In 1899, a very attractive single-storey girls school was built on Cambridge Road, leaving more space for boys in the old school. In the 1970s, a mixed primary school was built on the site of the girls school, with boys in the east wing and girls in the west wing.

The old National School on Thorncastle Street became a youth centre after it closed, and was also used by the Technical School from 1978 to 1980 (while their own new building was under construction), but was demolished in recent years to make way for council housing.

ANGLICAN PRIMARY SCHOOLS

St Matthew's Mixed National School opened in 1832, just outside the walls of St Matthew's graveyard in Irishtown. It was listed in 1840 as schools, widow's almshouse, poor shop, and dispensary, with John Reed as physician, and Mr and Mrs Betts as master and mistress. Generally, an almshouse was a sort of retirement home for poor widows, but in Irishtown must have comprised only one or two small rooms, and it continued to be listed until around 1900.

In 1903/04, the school accommodation is described as one classroom on each floor, boys on the ground floor, and girls and infants on the first floor, plus the caretaker in the basement. There were 54 boys on the rolls, and 130 girls and infants.

A new girls school cum parochial hall opened across the road on 8 October 1904, having been built by B.B. Pemberton, to a design by J.F. Fuller. The boys remained in the old building beside the church, until 1951, when they moved across the road to join the girls, after which the old school became St Matthew's Mission Hall.

A new two-teacher mixed primary school opened in 1959 off Cranfield Place, and in 1969 St Stephen's (from Northumberland Road) joined with St Matthew's. Many extensions were built over the following years, and now St Matthew's is a busy hub of education.

The original school beside the church was demolished in the 1960s, leaving a grass patch beside the traffic lights. Irishtown Gospel Hall (Plymouth Brethren) occupied the old girls school in 1988, to be replaced in recent years by the Abundant Grace Christian Assembly, although the lovely granite building (with Portmarnock redbrick dressings) now lies empty.

HIBERNIAN MARINE SCHOOL, 28 SIR JOHN ROGERSONS QUAY

Hibernian Marine School was a Protestant orphanage for the sons of sailors, established by Royal Charter in 1775. A Government report in 1810 recorded 110 boys, aged from 9-16, who were apprenticed to the Royal Navy and the merchant navy. The building had two dormitories, each 48ft by 18ft, two more of 25ft by 22ft, and one of 25ft by 7½ft, plus apartments for the chaplain, master, usher, housekeeper, and five servants. There was also an infirmary, 25ft by 22ft. One rear wing, 51ft by 26ft, held the chapel, with laundry underneath, while the other rear wing was the schoolroom, with dining room underneath.

The school was in 1 Upper Merrion Street in the 1880s, a private house, with accommodation for about thirty-five boys, before moving in 1904 to Clontarf (now a housing estate called Seacourt off St Gabriels Road). After amalgamation with Mountjoy School and Bertrand & Russell School in 1972, it became Mount Temple Comprehensive School, often linked with the members of rock band U2, and author, Christy Nolan.

ST PATRICK'S CATHOLIC CHURCH

During the eighteenth century, Irishtown had a Catholic chapel, as shown on the 1762 Barker map for the Pembroke Estate. On the 1837 Ordnance Survey map the chapel is shown on Chapel Lane (now the site of Hamilton roofing salvage company).

In 1853, the Star of the Sea church was built, at a cost of £6,000, to serve the people of Ringsend, Irishtown and Sandymount, but the walk proved too much for Ringsend parishioners, so six years later, another church was built beside Ringsend Bridge on the site of the church presbytery (which was also used as a Sunday school for girls, run by the Sisters of Charity from Sandymount). Another building on the site was used as an evening school, run by the Society of St Vincent de Paul.

The Ringsend rectangular church, designed by J.F. Fuller and costing £800, was capable of holding 300 people, and was opened on 14 July 1859. A bell was blessed on 25 March 1860. One wall of the old presbytery remains, beside the bridge abutment.

A new redbrick presbytery was built on Cambridge Road by W.H. Beardwood in 1890, and later extended to the rear. The nearby curate's house was built in 1921 on the site of St Patrick's Parochial Hall, and the extended premises is now a women's refuge. The prefabricated timber hall opened in 1885 and housed St Patrick's Literary Institute, with reading room and lending library.

The present granite church was built in three phases, with the sanctuary opening on 27 July 1913, and the third section on 21 November 1916, all on the same site as the 1859 church. William Byrne & Son was the architect, and Thomas Connolly & Son of Upper Dominick Street was the building contractor, at a cost of £15,000. It has some nice stained-glass windows by Earley of Camden Street behind the altar, and features lovely marbles and mosaics. The carved marble pulpit is in honour of Canon Mooney, who died in 1917, leaving £25,184 (a fortune in those days) in his will to Maynooth Seminary – the Ringsend people also presented an Illuminated Address dedicated to him that same year, with scenes from Ringsend, which now hangs in the sacristy.

The four-faced chiming turret clock was installed in 1916 by Ganter Bros of South Great Georges Street, although may have been supplied by John Smith of Derby in England. This clock was paid for by the workers of the Irish Glass Bottle Company. The three driving weights had to be hand-wound twice a week. It was a very strenuous job and these days the clock has electric winding. The bells, cast by Matthew O'Byrne of Dublin, vary from 7 to 23 cwt and have names inscribed: B.V. Maria, Santa Bridgida, Santo Laurentius O'Toole (patron saint of Dublin), Santo Josepheus, and the large tenor bell proclaims – *Érin go Brath* (Long Live Ireland). Sadly, the old St Patrick's bell from the 1859 church was not included. The clock is nicknamed the 'Four Faced Liar', and is the subject of a famous Wolfe Tones song, 'There's Quare Things in Dublin'.

The Irish Glass Bottle Company had a little oratory on their premises, where weekly mass was held.

ROYAL CHAPEL OF ST MATTHEW'S, CHURCH AVENUE, IRISHTOWN

The Royal Chapel of St Matthew's Anglican church was commenced in 1704 (the tower a few years later), with support from the Board of Works, and was enlarged in 1879, with new transepts and sanctuary designed by J.F. Fuller. The nave was reduced in size in the 1970s, by building a cross-wall, with two-storey meeting rooms in the rear part. There are three pairs of 1880s stained-glass windows in the apse, by Earley and Powell of Dublin. There is another pair of windows on the south side of the chancel, reputed to be by Mayer of Munich in 1899, depicting St Mark and St Matthew – St Matthew appears to have only one leg!

The tower houses a collection of eight tubular bells, dated 1878, cast by Harrington of Coventry. They are of different lengths, and represent a musical scale. From a chiming frame on a lower storey, a collection of ropes operate timber-tipped hammers, which strike the tops of the bronze tubes, and therefore various sweet tunes can be played by one person.

The foundation stone for the two-storey rectory opposite the church was laid on 8 September 1928, and the redbrick building was sold to the Garda Síochána in the mid-1970s. The original police barracks was a three-storey yellow-brick building across the road, abutting Barrack Lane. In the 1911 Census, two sergeants, and seventeen constables, mostly Catholics, are listed. The present Irishtown Garda Station, with impressive design and bulk, was opened in 2008 on the site of the former rectory/Garda station.

CHURCH OF IRELAND LABOUR HOME AND YARD

This noble charitable endeavour was established in October 1899 at 43 Thorncastle Street (former University Boat Club) by the Church Army, which was founded around this time in London by Revd William Carlisle. Poor men were given employment chopping timber into firewood, and were paid 10*d* plus a meal for a nine-hour day. A small number of men were also given accommodation. Captain Robert Pryce Griffith and his wife managed the charity.

In 1907 they transferred to a newly built premises at York Road (east side of YMCA Mission Hall), designed by Robert J. Stirling, comprising a house for the Griffiths and their family, plus a house for about twenty-five men, and a large dining hall. At that time, 100 men were employed. The 1911 Census lists thirteen occupants (Mr and Mrs Griffith, their young son, manager, and nine boarders).

In 1933, Captain J. Savage was running the yard. The fruit of the men's labour could be bought for the following prices: firewood – 4*s* 9*d* per 100 bundles, logs – 2*s* per cwt, chips – 1*s* 9*d* per sack.

By the late 1960s the yard was closed and was redeveloped by Zoe Developments in 1990 into Alexandra Quay apartments.

RINGSEND YMCA MISSION HALL

The Young Men's Christian Association was founded in 1844 in London by George Williams, as a quasi-religious social club, and an Irish branch was formed in 1849.

Sarah Elizabeth Bewley was born in Willow Park, Booterstown, and she married Charles Pease in County Durham, England. Her husband died shortly afterwards and she returned to Dublin, devoting herself to charitable causes, especially Methodist projects (despite the fact that the Bewley name is mostly associated with the Society of Friends or Quakers).

Charles E. Stewart persuaded Mrs Pease to fund a new hall on a vacant site at York Road, designed by George P. Beater, and the Ringsend YMCA Mission Hall opened on 14 March 1896, including a rear tearoom, catering for the various Protestant denominations in the district. The 1895 lease with the Pembroke Estate was signed by Mrs Pease, Dr H.T. Bewley (her brother), and William Fry Junior (her solicitor). William Fry was the first president, and Charles E. Stewart was the honorary secretary. Members paid a small annual subscription. By 1911, the club had its own brass band, which received payment for public performances. Also in 1911, a cricket ground was acquired in Claremont Road in Sandymount, and a football club was started. In 1913, Mrs Pease paid for a rear extension to accommodate the Young Women's Christian Association. In due course, there was also a Boys Section.

Activities included evangelistic service every Sunday at 4 p.m., Bible classes, public lectures (for example, on exotic travel topics), Band of Hope meetings (temperance movement), indoor games, and annual excursions. During the Second World War, the Protestants from Sandymount, Irishtown, and Ringsend organised the Community Kitchen in the YMCA Mission Hall for poor people.

Mrs Pease died in 1924 and left an estate valued at £29,833, with her brother, Dr H.T. Bewley, and her solicitor, William Fry, appointed as executors and trustees. She left £2,000 to the Mission to Lepers, £1,000 to the Methodist church in Dublin, and the Ringsend Mission Hall (including £1,000 support) to her trustees. Willow Park was subsequently sold to the Holy Ghost Fathers in the adjoining Blackrock College for use as their junior school.

Charles E. Stewart had been active for many decades in the Ringsend YMCA. He had given up his business in 1899 to become a Port Missionary, visiting the numerous ships, and hosting (with his wife) the annual Christmas party in the Sailors Rest, 63 North Wall.

In the 1970s, the Mission Hall was partly rented out to different groups, to provide additional income. Since 1996, the Fair Play Community Café, under the auspices of the Mission Hall trustees, has been in occupation.

METHODIST CHURCH, IRISHTOWN ROAD

The original Methodist church, built in 1830 in Thomas Street, was in the heart of Ringsend, and a small school was added to the rear in 1855.

In 1904, they moved to a new church at the corner of Irishtown Road and Watery Lane (Dermot O'Hurley Avenue), designed by George Francis Beckett, and built by James Beckett (these Becketts were related to the famous playwright, Samuel Beckett). The two side aisles were partitioned off from the church and used as a National School (consisting of three interconnected classrooms on both sides). In 1932 a rear parish hall was added. The manse was at 4 Newgrove Avenue.

The church closed in June 1961 and parishioners joined their fellow Methodists in Christchurch, Sandymount (an 1864 church designed by Alfred Jones). The site of the former Irishtown church is now a block of apartments.

The original Ringsend church was sold in 1914 for £70 to the Catholic Church, to become St Patrick's Hall, and then the Catholic Young Men's Society in 1936. The original front of the building is hidden behind a shallow two-storey extension while the rear school has been replaced by a single-storey hall. In its heyday, the CYMS was a very active social club, with its own football team, not unlike the rival YMCA, but nowadays, the premises welcomes senior citizens to snooker and bowls.

PRESBYTERIAN CHURCH, SANDYMOUNT ROAD

Built in 1858 (opposite the new Star of the Sea church) by S.H. Bolton of Dublin, to a design by Hay of Liverpool (born in Scotland), with a National School by William Stirling added in 1868.

The congregation merged with the Methodists in Christchurch, Sandymount, in 1975, and their old church was demolished in 1996, with the site being used for sheltered housing.

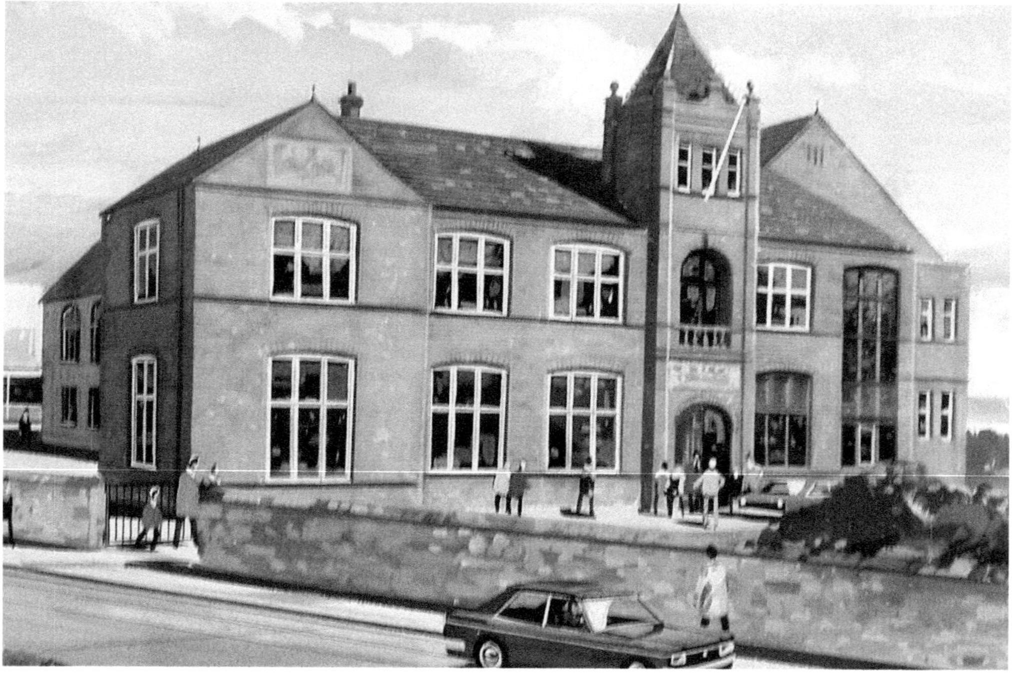

Alan Armitage painting of Ringsend Technical School, presented to the principal, Tony Carney, in 1980, by Gleeson Byrne Whelan Associates. (Courtesy of Ringsend College)

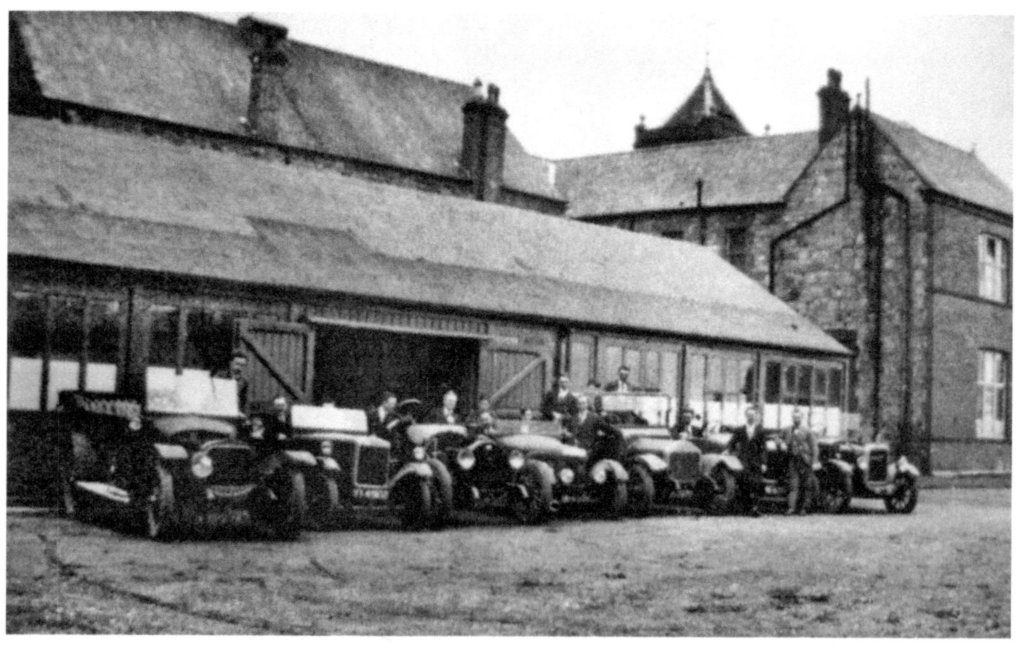

Ringsend Technical School was famous for training car mechanics. (Courtesy of Ringsend College)

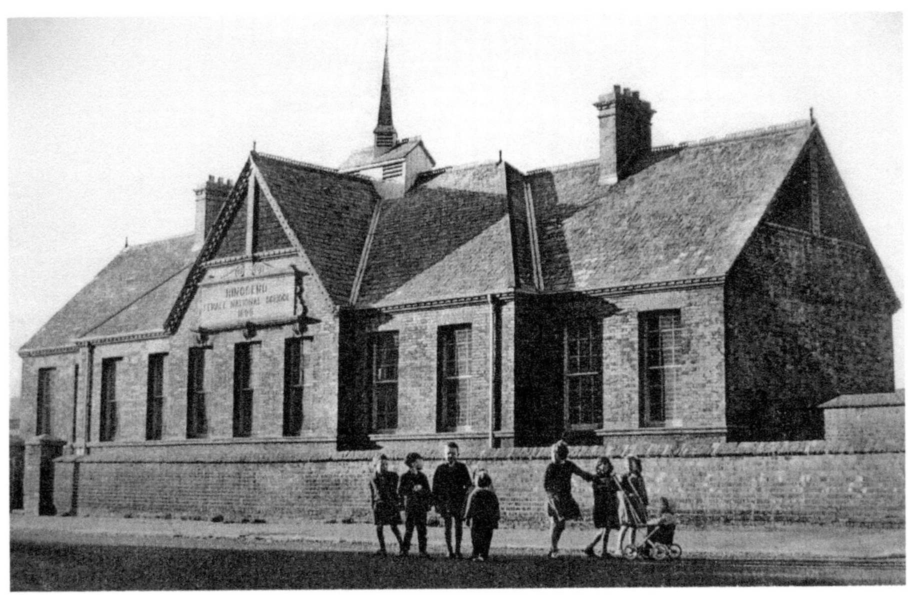

Ringsend Girls National School on Cambridge Road, on the site of the present mixed school. (Courtesy of Ringsend Boys School)

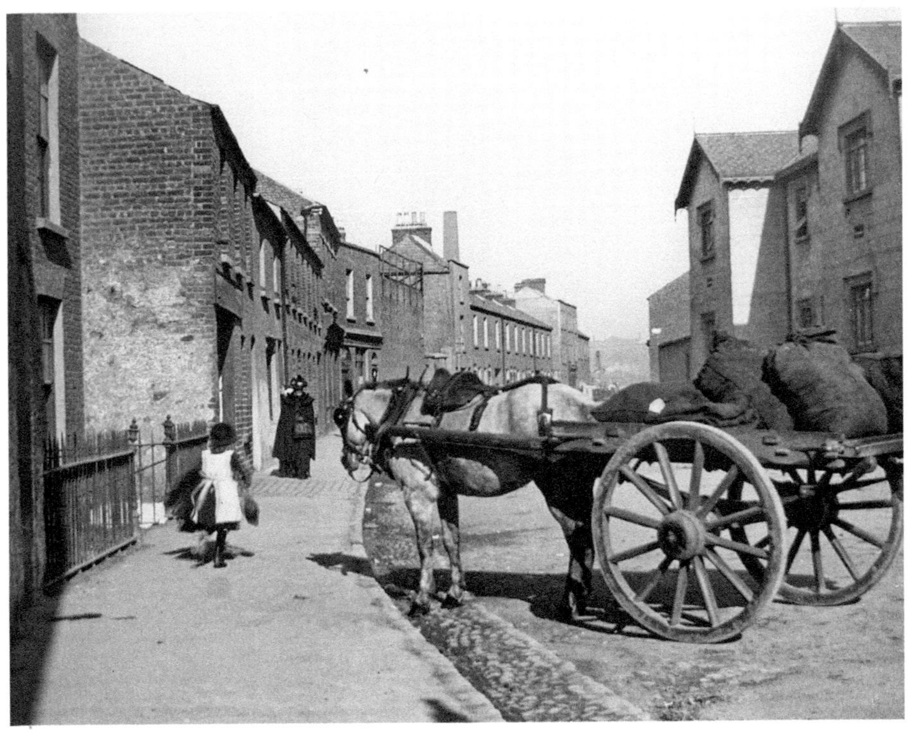

Thorncastle Street looking north, with the Boys National School on the right. (Courtesy of South Dublin County Council Libraries)

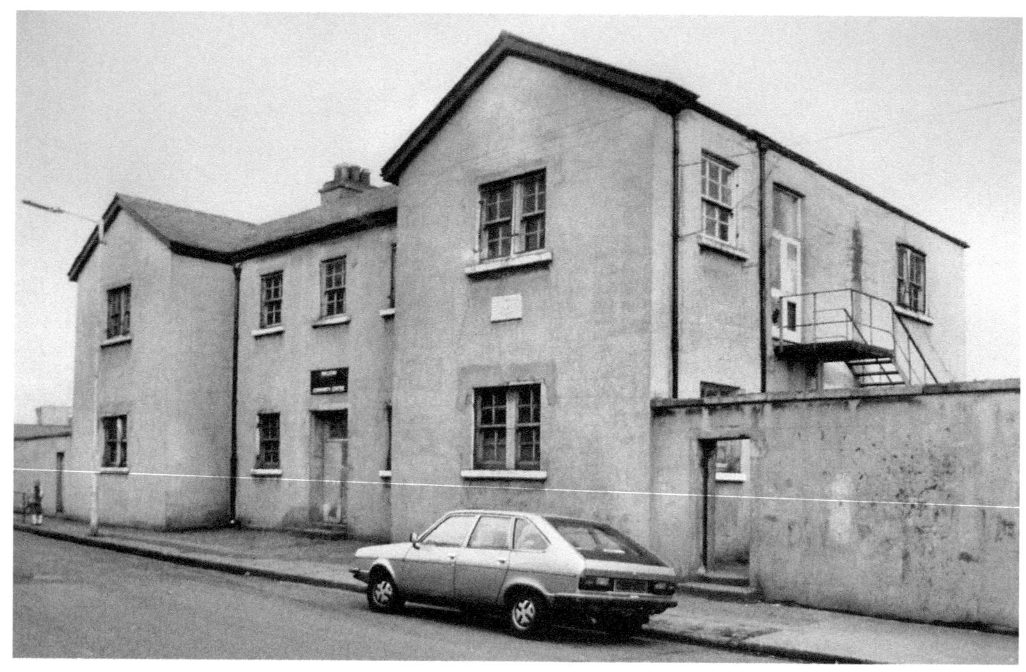

Ringsend Boys National School on Thorncastle Street. (Courtesy of Jim Cooke)

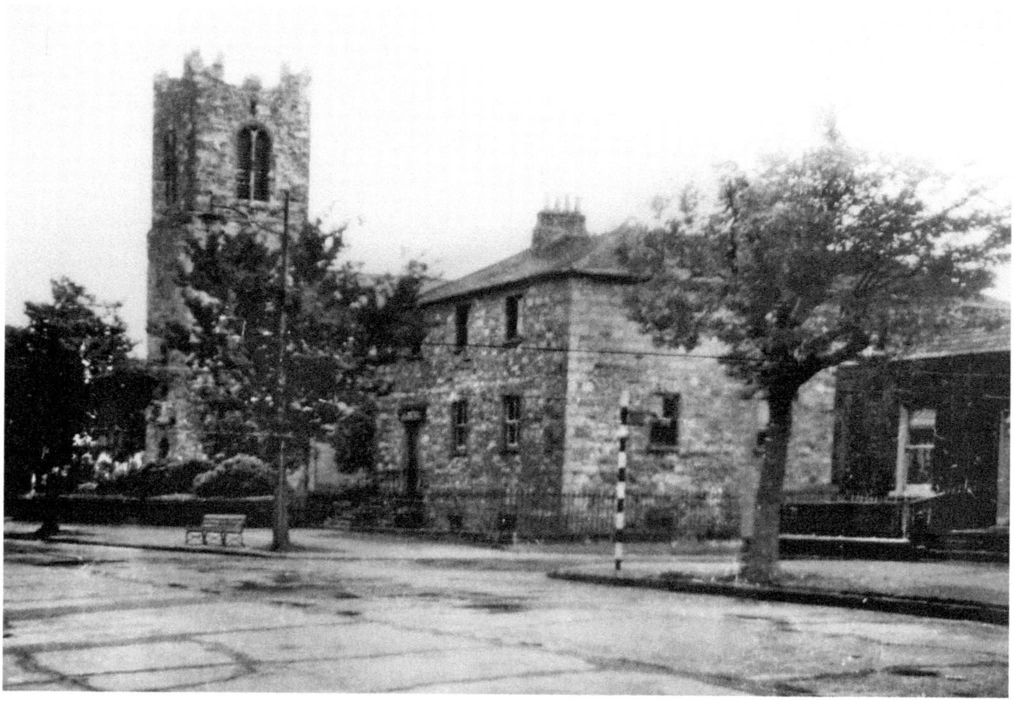

St Matthew's National School before demolition. (Courtesy of St Matthew's church)

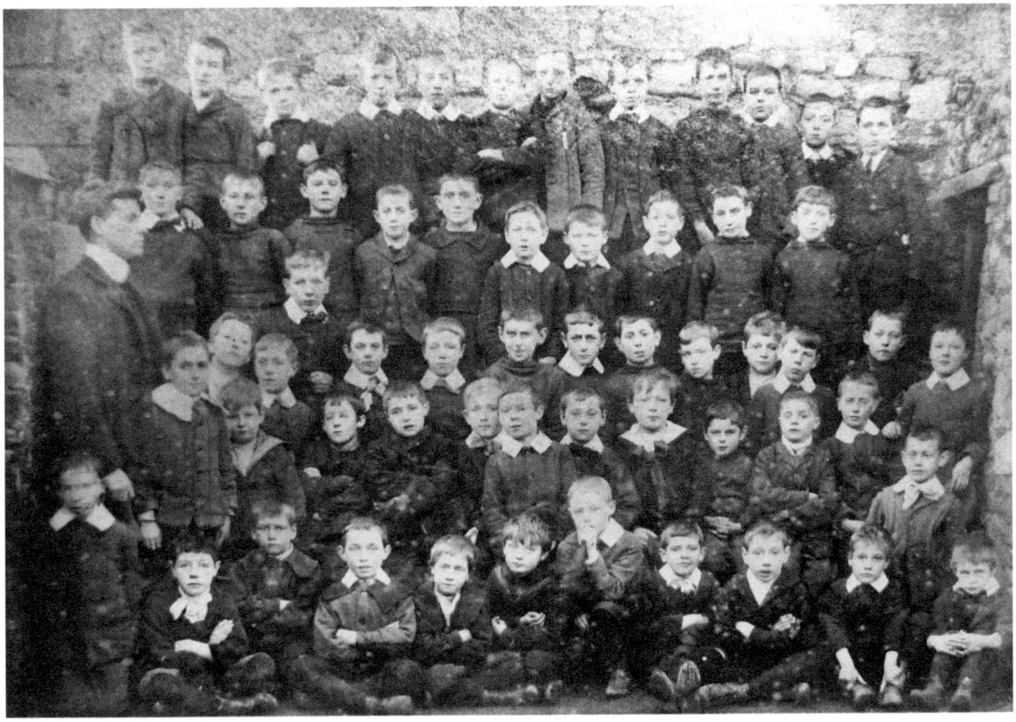

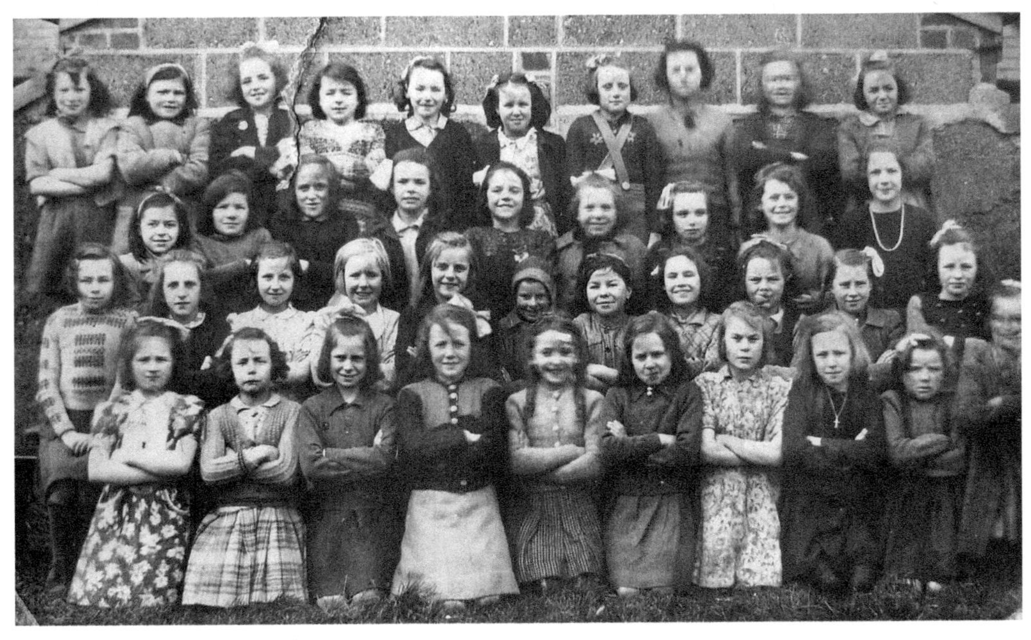

St Matthew's National School. (Courtesy of St Matthew's church)

Ringsend Girls National School in 1945. (Courtesy of NewsFour)

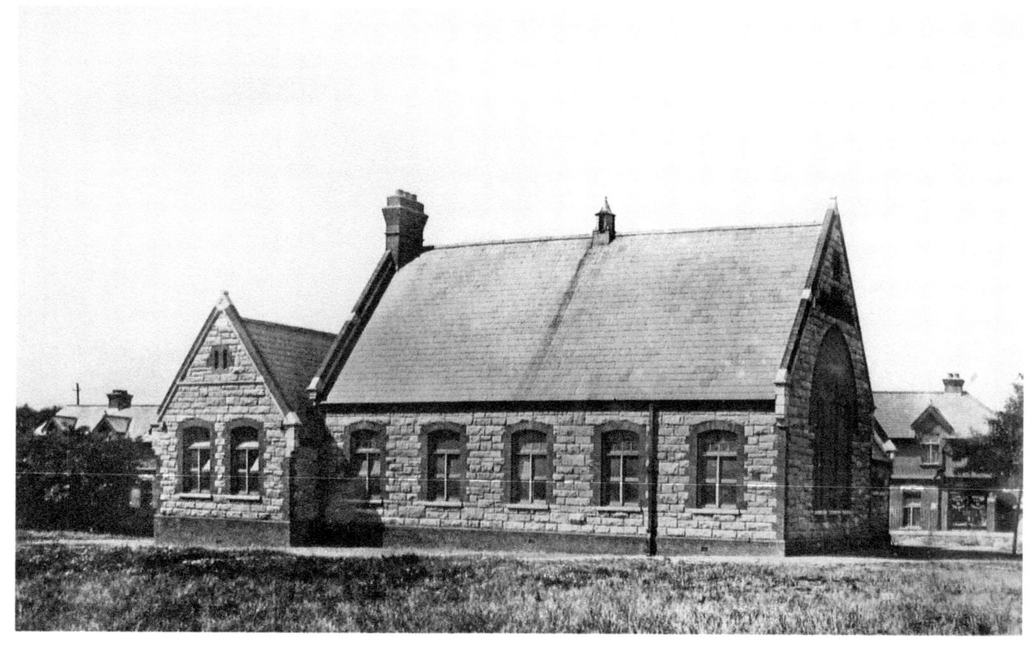

St Matthew's Girls National School cum parochial hall, dating from 1904, was later used as Irishtown Gospel Hall. (Courtesy of NewsFour)

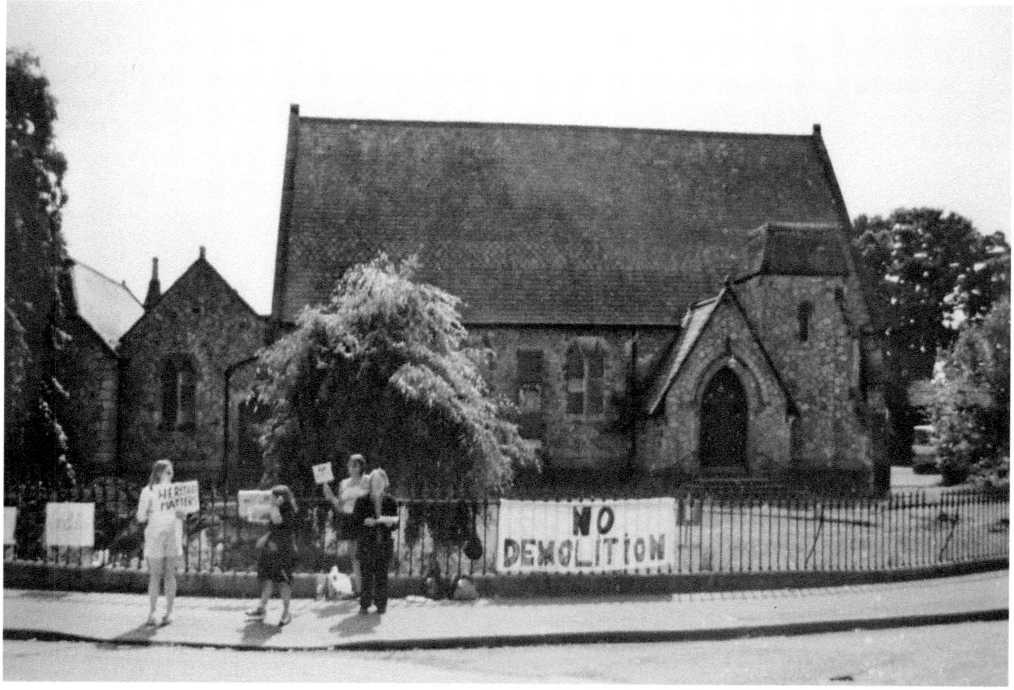

Irishtown Presbyterian church before demolition in 1996. (Courtesy of NewsFour)

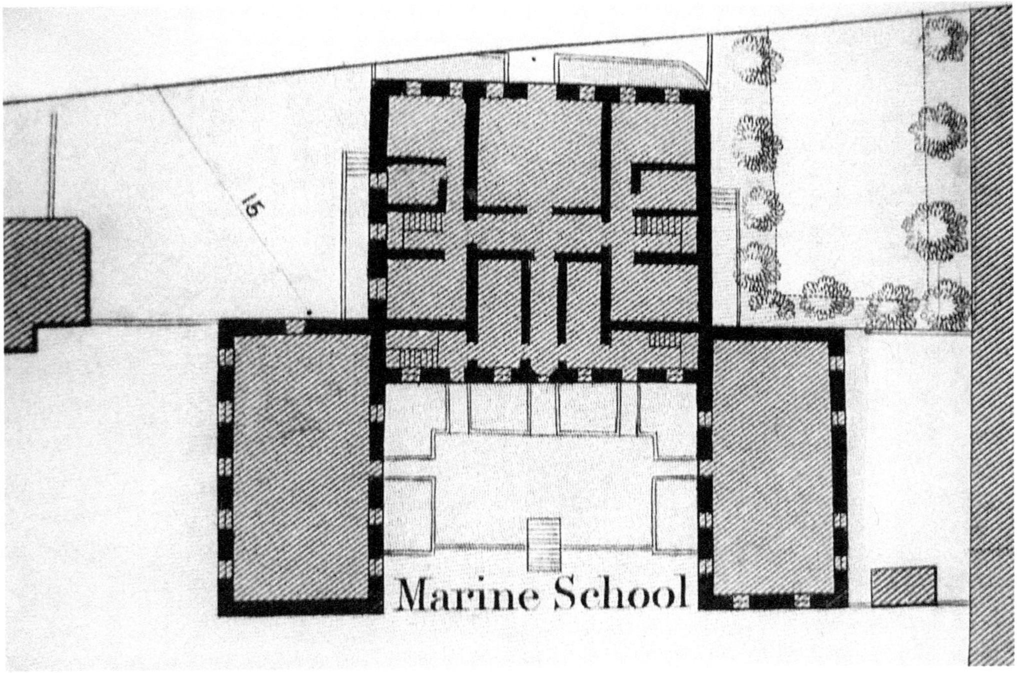

The Hibernian Marine School at 28 Sir John Rogersons Quay. (Courtesy of Valuation Office)

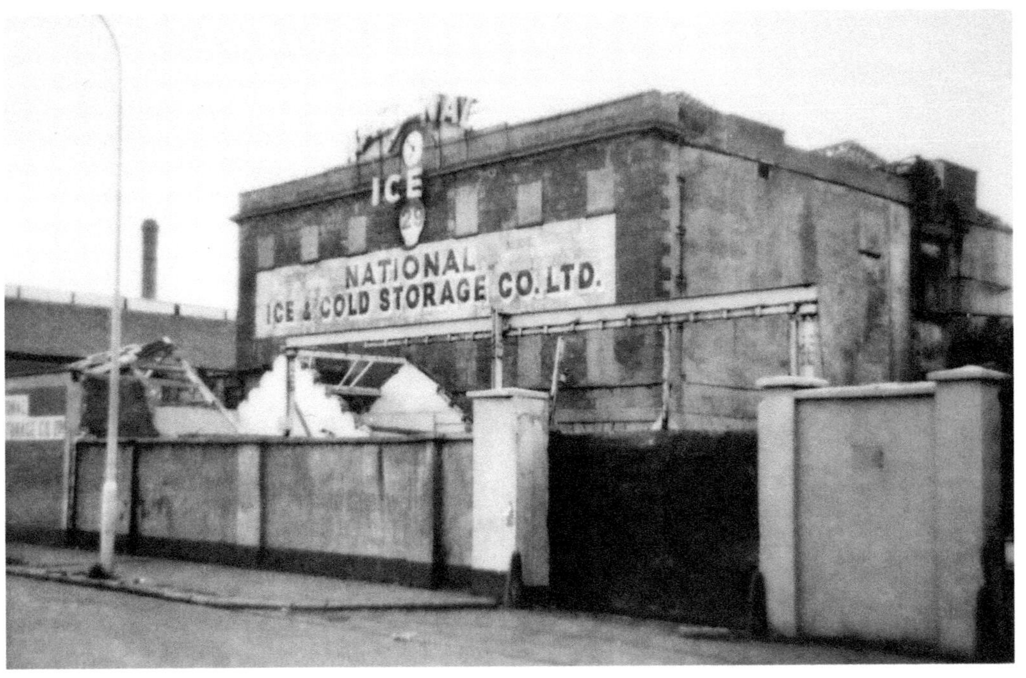

The Hibernian Marine School was later used for business purposes. (Courtesy of Irish Architectural Archive)

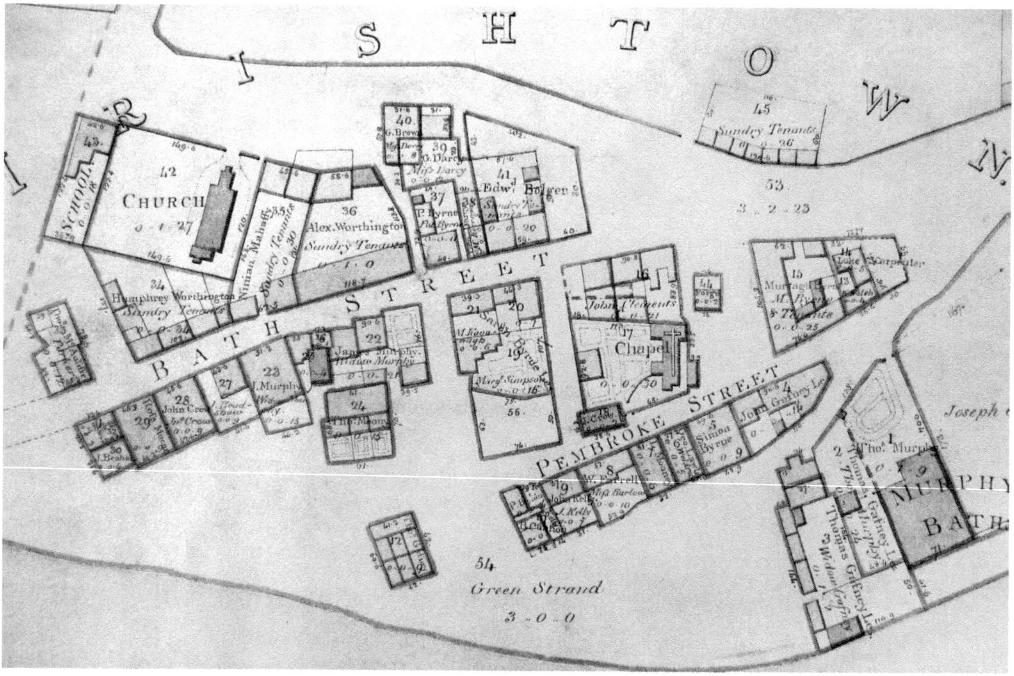

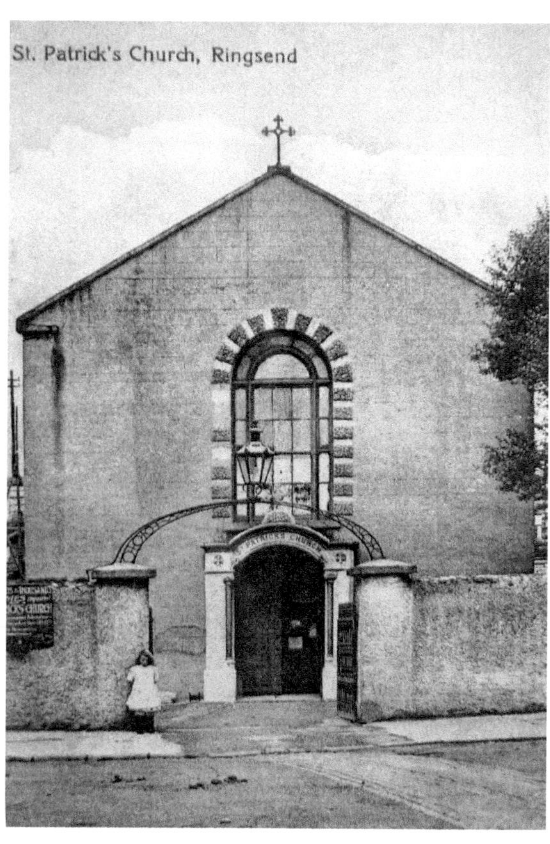

Map of Irishtown in the 1830s, showing the Catholic chapel and the Protestant church. (Courtesy of the National Archives of Ireland)

Postcard of St Patrick's church, *c.* 1900. (Courtesy of Brian Siggins)

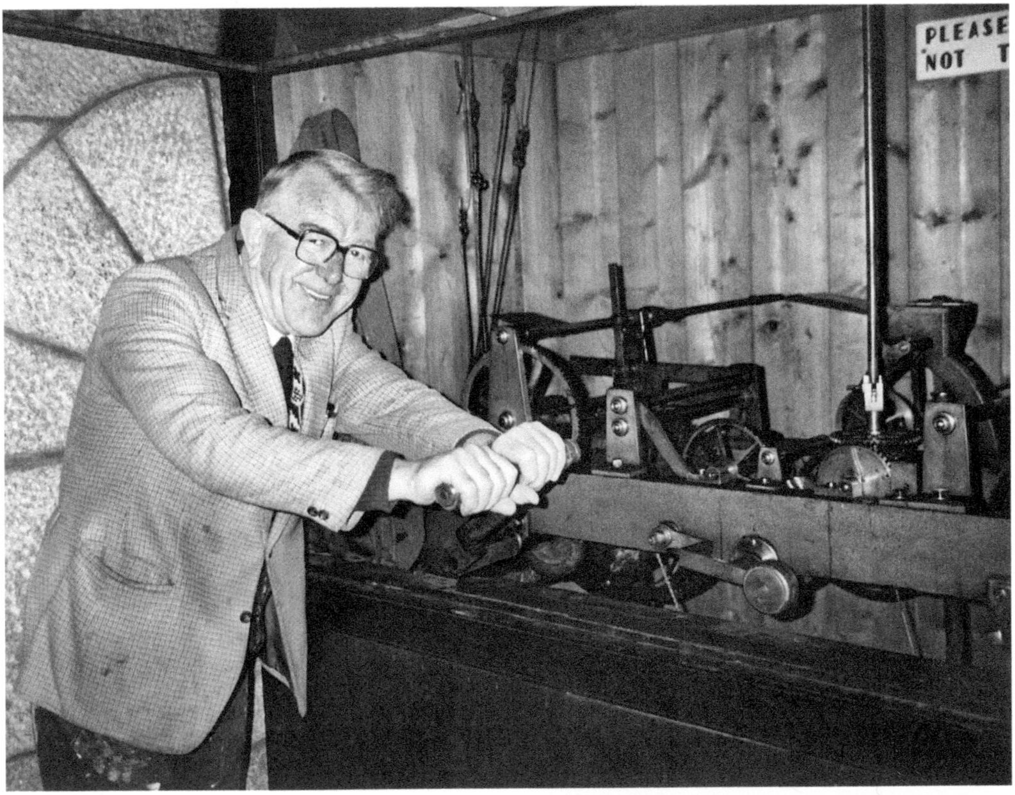

Michael McDonald hand-wound (with great
effort) the clock in St Patrick's church for
many years prior to the 1990s, after which
an electric winder was installed. (*Times,
Chimes & Charms of Dublin*)

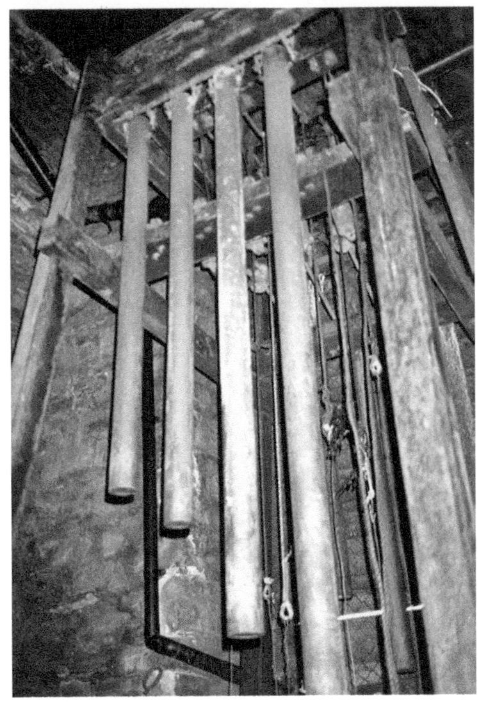

The sweet-sounding tubular bells in St
Matthew's church, ranging from 6-8ft long,
deserve to be reactivated.

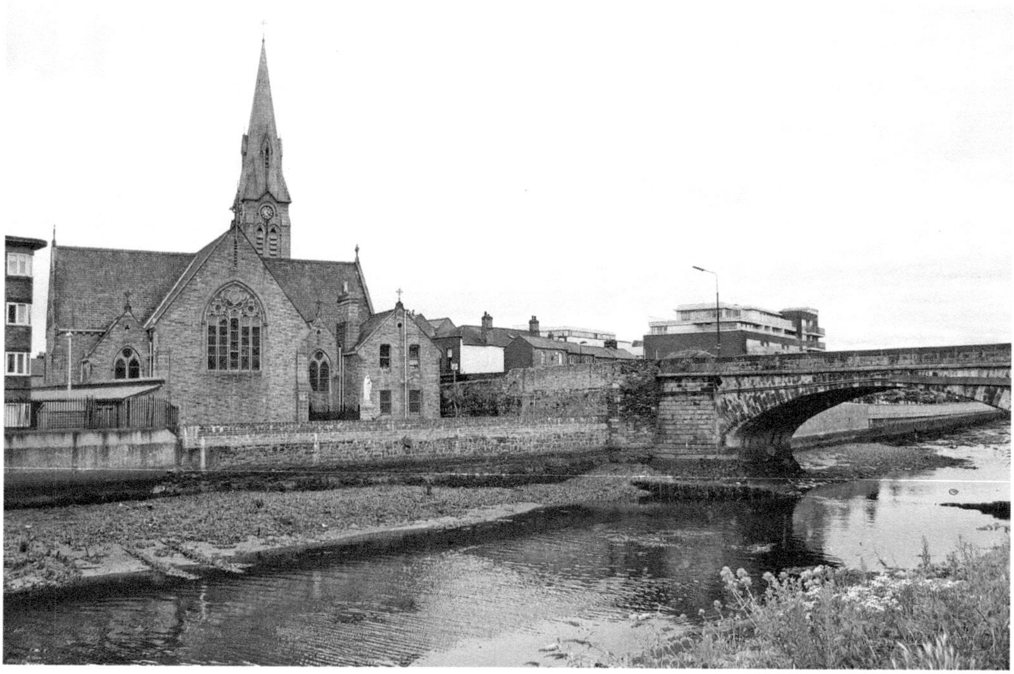

St Patrick's church and single-arch bridge are Ringsend landmarks.

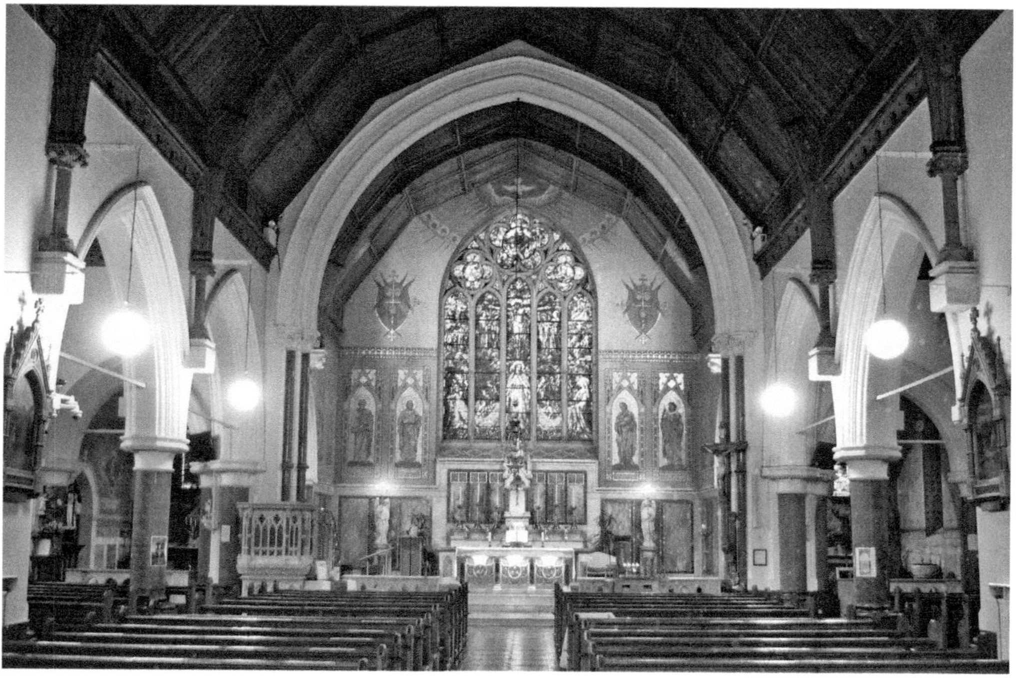

The attractive interior of St Patrick's church.

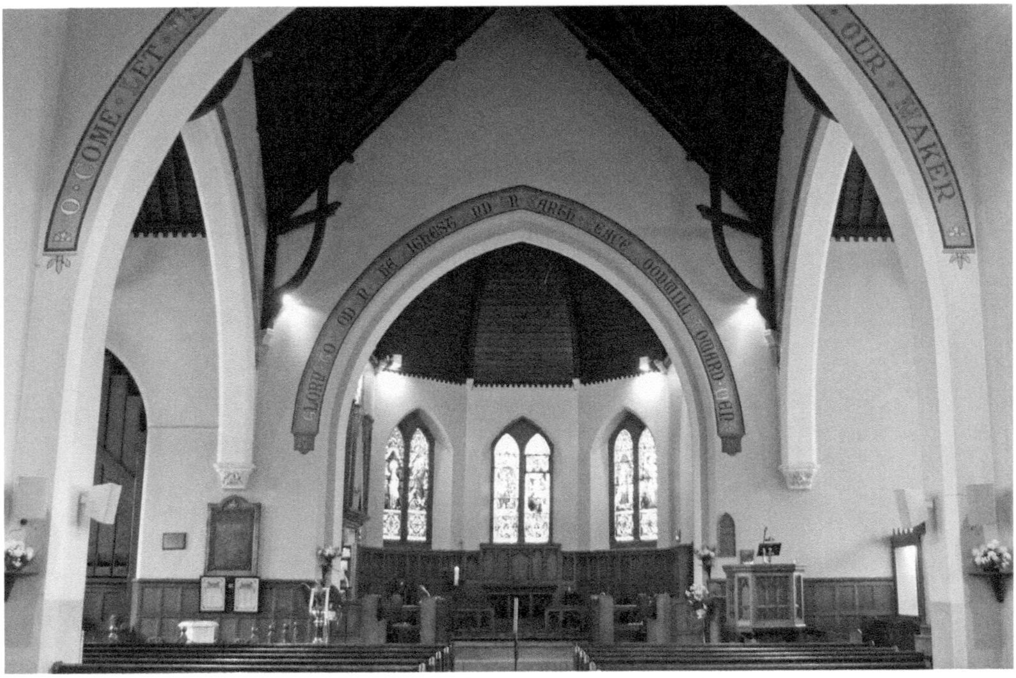

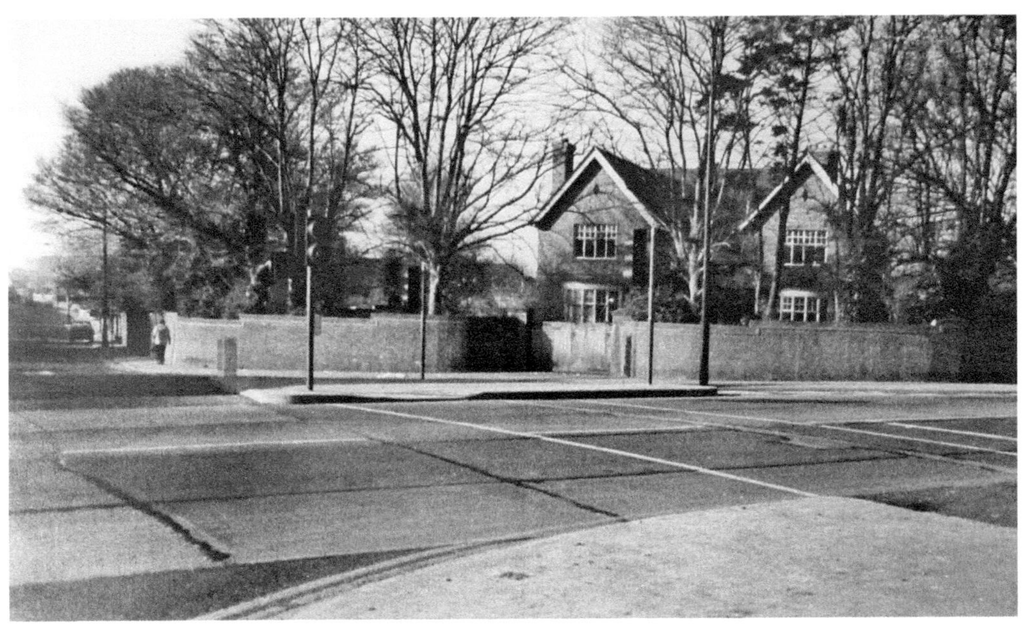

St Matthew's church has a homely interior.

St Matthew's Rectory was converted into the local Garda station in the 1970s, and only demolished in recent years, to make way for the present impressive Irishtown Garda Station. (Courtesy of Gladys Rathorne)

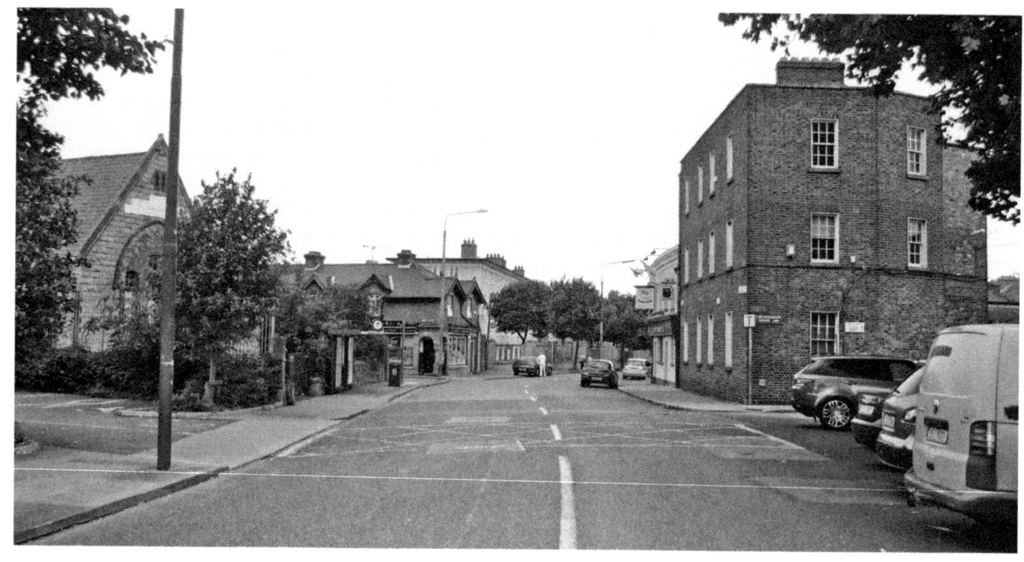

Irishtown Road, with the former police barracks on the right and former St Matthew's Girls National School on the left.

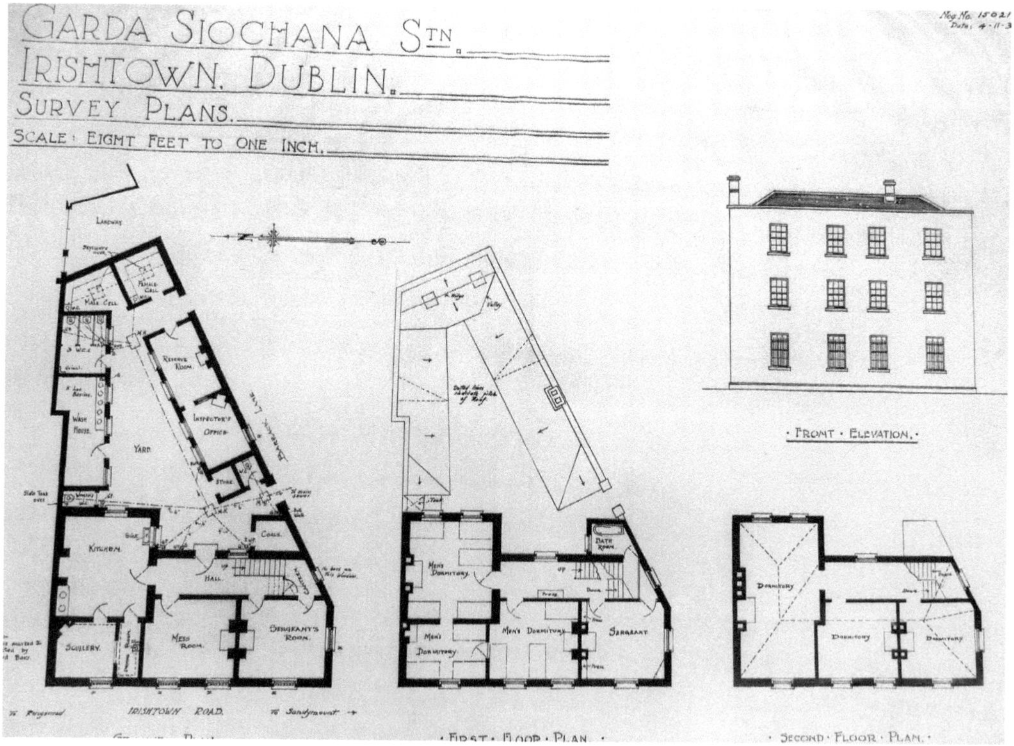

1931 plan of Irishtown Garda Station (originally a police barracks), mostly comprising dormitories for the guards. (Courtesy of the Office of Public Works)

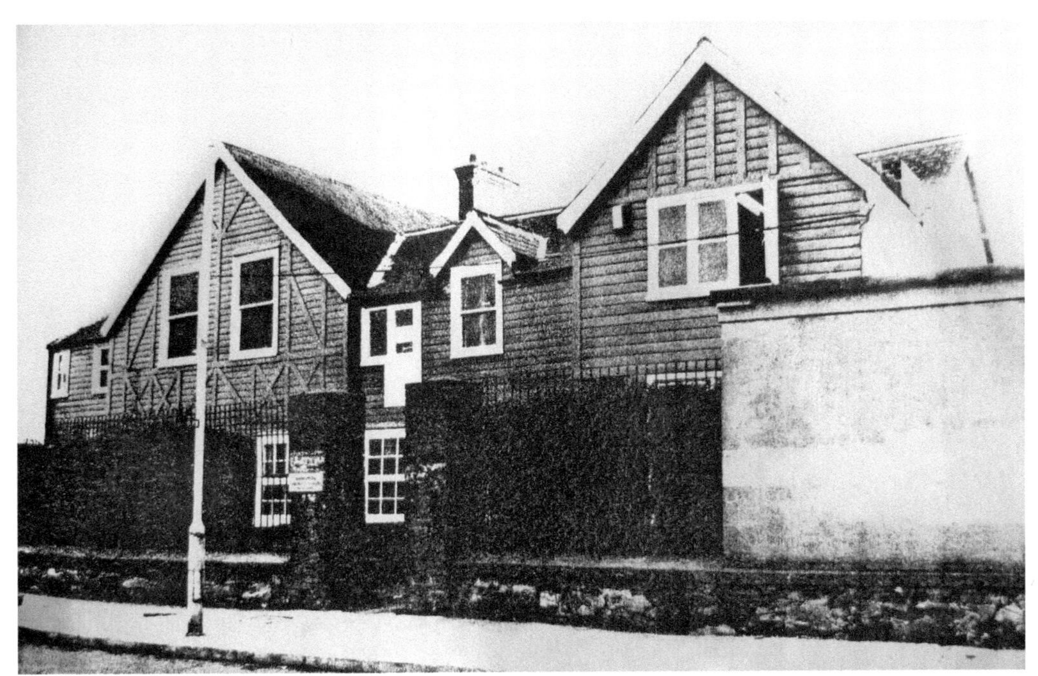

The Church Army Labour Yard
& Home was on York Road beside
the YMCA Mission Hall. (Courtesy
of Jim Cooke)

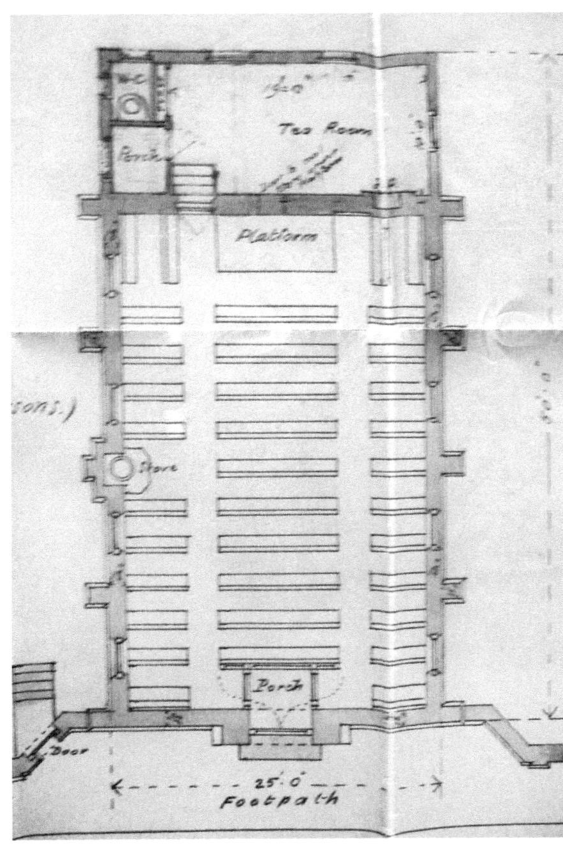

1895 plan of the YMCA Mission
Hall on York Road for Mrs Pease.
(Courtesy of the National Archives
of Ireland)

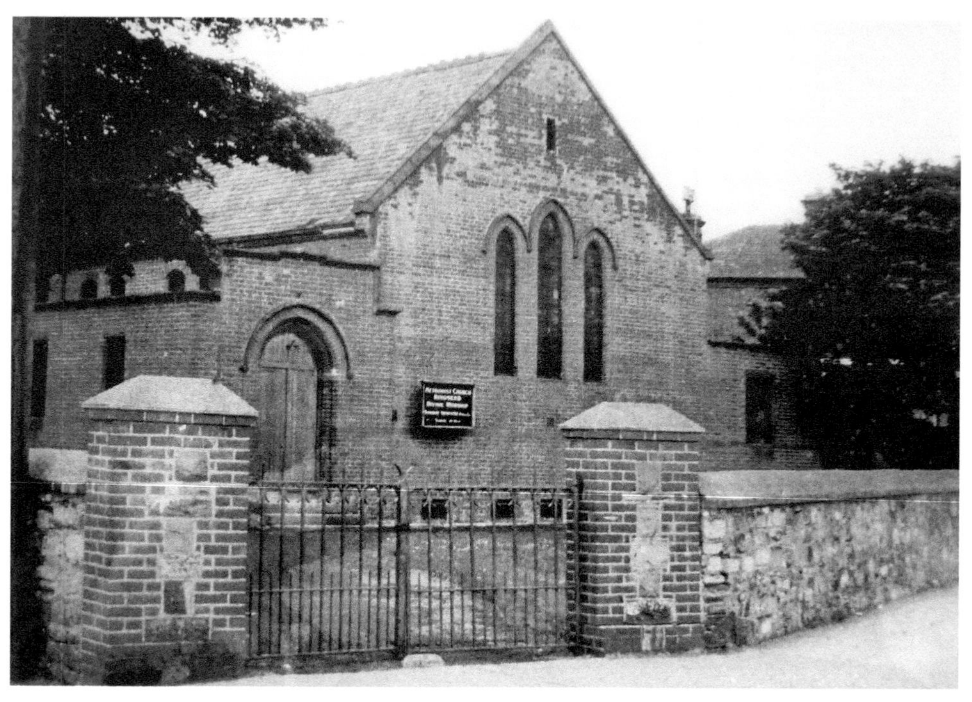

The former Methodist church on Irishtown Road. (Courtesy of Brian Siggins)

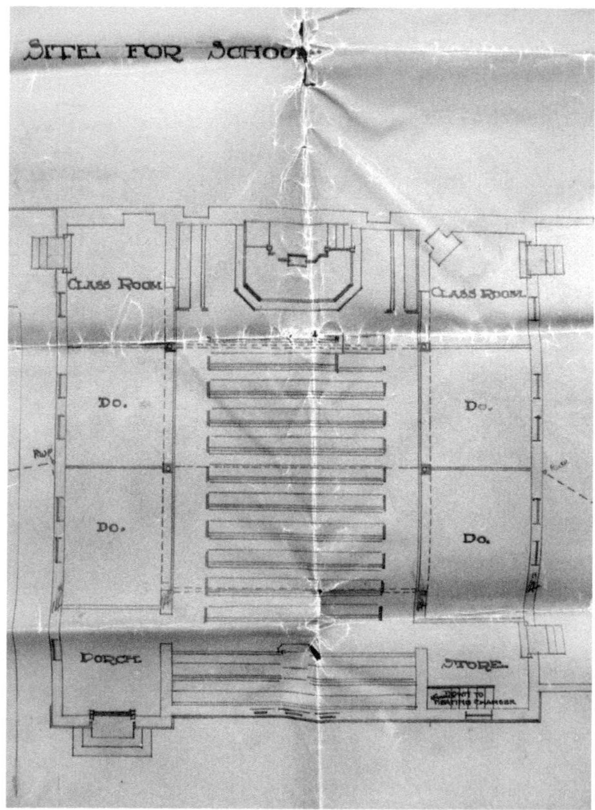

Plan of the Methodist church on Irishtown Road. Both side aisles were partitioned off to create a National School with six classrooms in total. (Courtesy of the National Archives of Ireland)

7

HOUSING & HEALTH

Ringsend was very fortunate to be administered by the Pembroke Township until 1930, since the wealthy ratepayers in Ballsbridge could subsidise good council housing around the turn of the twentieth century, many built by G. & T. Crampton, including Pembroke Cottages and Pigeon House Road (mid-1890s and 1903), Stella Gardens and The Square (1916). In the 1920s, semi-detached two-storey houses were favoured, such as O'Connell Gardens, Derrynane Gardens, and Ringsend Park.

Dublin Corporation stripped away the heart of the village when they demolished the west side of Thorncastle Street (the River Dodder side), and built monotonous four-storey blocks of flats, first Whelan House (in fact two blocks) in the late 1930s, and then O'Rahilly (four blocks) in the mid-1950s. Canon Mooney Gardens repeated the mistake on Cambridge Road around this time. In 1948, George Reynolds Flats were built on Irishtown Road.

When it came to building housing in Irishtown in the late 1970s (Bremen Road etc), the Corporation opted for 300 three-storey houses, naming the various new streets after famous ships. From the 1930s, the Corporation had reclaimed the foreshore here by dumping refuse, so special foundations were needed for the new houses. Sean Moore Road was built in 1980 to link Pigeon House Road and Beach Road.

Cambridge Court, courtyard-style two-storey blocks of apartments for senior citizens, was built by the Corporation in 1986, showing what could have been done decades earlier in nearby Thorncastle Street.

Nowadays, many council-built houses are in private ownership, having been sold to the former tenants.

PRIMARY CARE CENTRE, IRISHTOWN ROAD

This state-of-the-art mini public hospital opened in 2009, on the site of the former St Patrick's Dispensary, which had been built in 1908 for the South Dublin Union.

The William Ashford Memorial on Irishtown Green (a stone obelisk dated 1894) commemorates a popular dispensary doctor.

DUBLIN CORPORATION ISOLATION HOSPITAL, 85 PIGEON HOUSE ROAD

Near the south-west corner of the former Pigeon House Fort, but on the opposite side of the road, a redundant Royal Engineers Submarine Mining Station was adapted in early 1903 by Dublin Corporation as an isolation hospital, catering for a smallpox outbreak in Dublin at that time. Patients were 'isolated' from the general public to prevent spread of the disease. A large prefab (timber framed with corrugated-steel sheeting) was erected in the space of twenty-one days by McManus & Co. of London, at a cost of £939, and comprised a male ward for thirty patients, and a female ward for twenty patients. The existing buildings were adapted at a cost of £664. There was no internal staircase, but instead the first-floor verandah on the south side was accessed via an open staircase on the west gable wall. Cork Street Fever Hospital (founded by Quakers) was contracted to run the isolation hospital. The hospital opened in March 1903 and dealt with 243 patients that year. This smallpox outbreak originated on ships from Liverpool and Glasgow, and was generally concentrated in the poor areas around the North Dublin Union and Hardwicke Hospital. Dublin Corporation quickly and efficiently contained the outbreak, and anyone found hiding the disease was fined in the Police Courts – even a few people who pawned infected clothing were traced and fined. There were 360 cases in Dublin in 1903, of which thirty-three people died. For the next seven years, the hospital was empty and unused.

Tuberculosis (TB, and also known as 'consumption') was another serious health issue around this time, and in 1910, Dublin Corporation granted the use of the isolation hospital to the Women's National Health Association of Ireland, with funding of £1,000 per year by an Irish-American philanthropist, and it was re-named the Allan A. Ryan Home in his honour. Ryan had been approached by Lady Aberdeen, the wife of the Lord Lieutenant of Ireland, John Hamilton-Gordon. Lord Lonsdale in England donated the four open-air shelters (small summerhouses), where some patients had to sleep, as part of their treatment. The Home centred around the two-storey building, using the ground floor for two male wards, a day room, a kitchen, matron's room, and the first floor had three female wards (two large, one small). The large prefab in the centre of the site was used as a recreation room. The laundry and boilerhouse were located to the west of the two-storey building, and also a toilet block. The nurses' quarters were in the centre of the complex. Eighteen beds were provided in 1910, and the 1911 Census recorded twenty-two patients, both male and female. Patient numbers increased, but most were transferred to Peamount Sanatorium in Newcastle, County Dublin, which was founded in 1912. TB is a disease of the lungs and fresh air is the usual requirement for recovery, so the Pigeon House Road, beside Dublin Corporation's new sewerage works, which opened in 1906, was a very poor choice of site. In 1914, the Alan A. Ryan funding ceased, and Dublin Corporation took back the premises on 20 January of that year.

The Daughters of Charity acquired the property in 1918, calling the facility St Catherine's Hospital, and stayed until 1955, at which stage the remaining patients were transferred to another hospital. The nuns re-activated the large central prefab, using it for separate male and female wards, a recreation room, and a maid's room. The ground floor of the two-storey old building had a kitchen, matron's room (with WC in the north circular annex), and nurses' dining room, while there were five rooms on the first floor. The single-storey wing had separate male and female dining rooms, one small ward and a bathroom. The east entrance lodge became their chaplain's house, near which was a detached mortuary chapel. The nuns added a convent at the north-west corner and a chapel at the south-west corner, 49ft by 20ft, plus sacristy of 20ft by 20ft. All the buildings were single-storey, except the old red-bricked building – the convent was part single-storey and part two-storey.

The urological department of the Meath Hospital was in occupation after 1955, until at least 1990, and was listed as a convalescent home for the Meath Hospital. Nowadays the site is home to a number of small businesses, and thankfully the original redbrick buildings alongside the road still survive.

CATS AND DOGS HOME

This charity started in 1840, as the Dublin branch of the Society for the Prevention of Cruelty to Animals (DSPCA), with initial offices at 36 Westmoreland Street, and then at 29 South Frederick Street. In 1885 they leased a half-acre site in Grand Canal Quay, which was part of the sugar refinery site. The location was beside the railway bridge, opposite the Guinness malt stores, and simple buildings were immediately erected, including a caretaker's lodge. This site was initially known as the Dublin Home for Starving and Foresaken Cats, and when dogs were admitted it became known as the Cats and Dogs Home. Part of the work of the DSPCA was arranging for horse drinking troughs to be provided around the city.

During the 1916 Easter Rising, Eamon de Valera was based in nearby Bolands Bakery, and he took over the Home, because it was beside the main railway bridge, releasing all the animals. He also released the horses stabled in the bakery, when their supplies of hay ran out.

Initially the Home used a tricycle with a large box to rescue animals, and a van was acquired in 1929.

Effectively the Dogs Home (grant-aided by the Government) was being run on behalf of the Garda Síochána, who would collect many stray dogs. During 1940, the authorities feared that the stray dogs would spread Foot and Mouth Disease, and it seems that many dogs were 'put down'.

In 1990, the Home moved to Potterton Restfields (for retired horses) in Stocking Lane, Rathfarnham, and then in 2003 moved to a wonderful purpose-built 32-acre campus in nearby Mount Venus Road, including a veterinary hospital, dogs hotel, cats hotel, and charming open space and pond for the goats and geese.

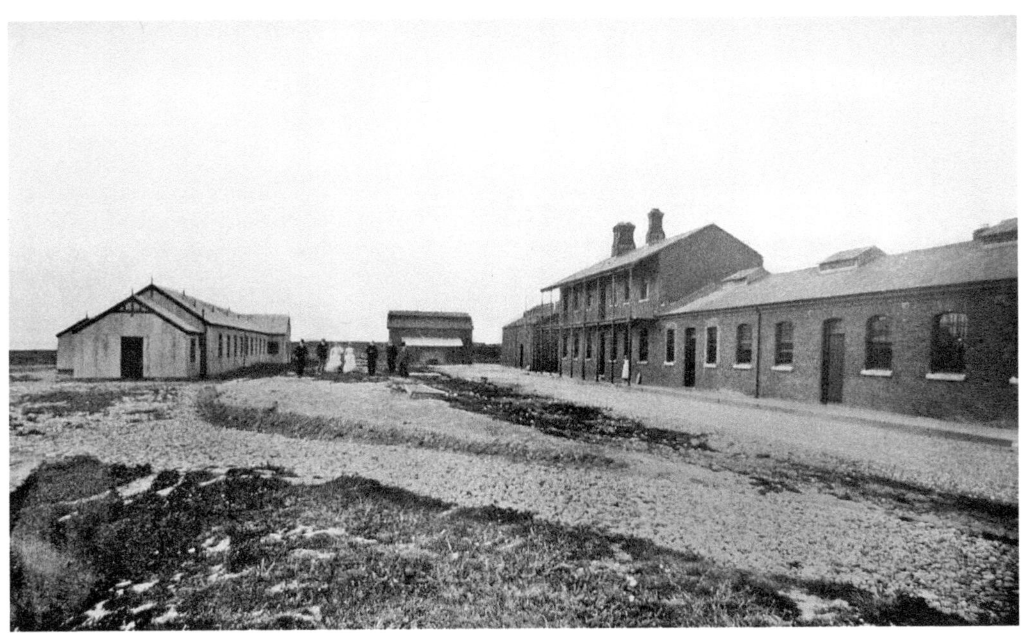

A 1903 view of Dublin Corporation's Isolation Hospital on Pigeon House Road, looking west. (Courtesy of the National Archives of Ireland)

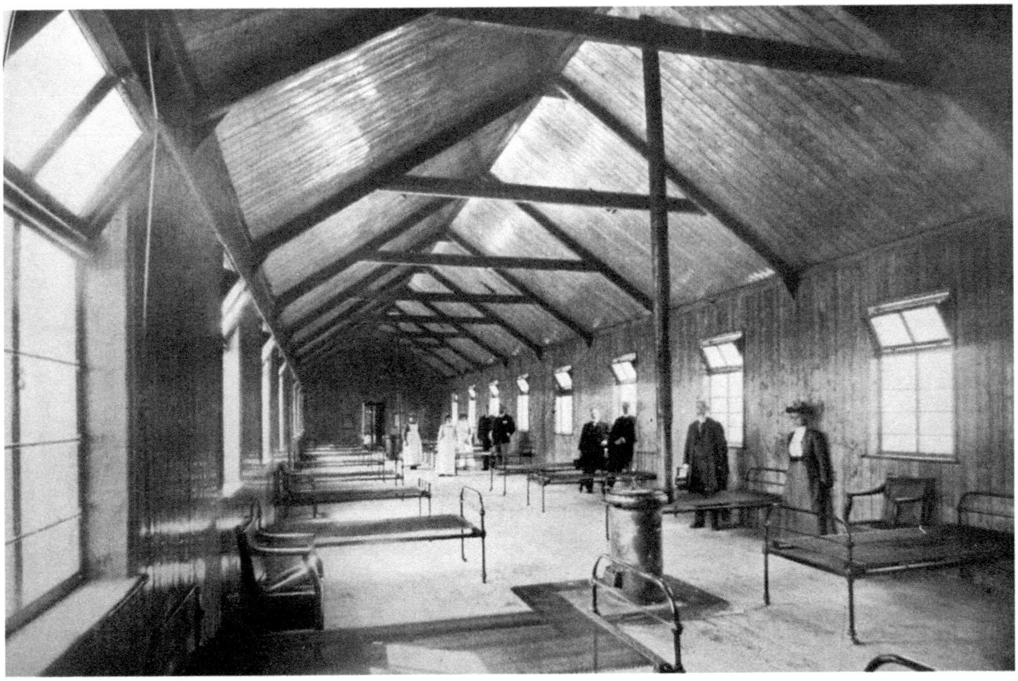

The male ward in the Isolation Hospital, 1903. (Courtesy of the National Archives of Ireland)

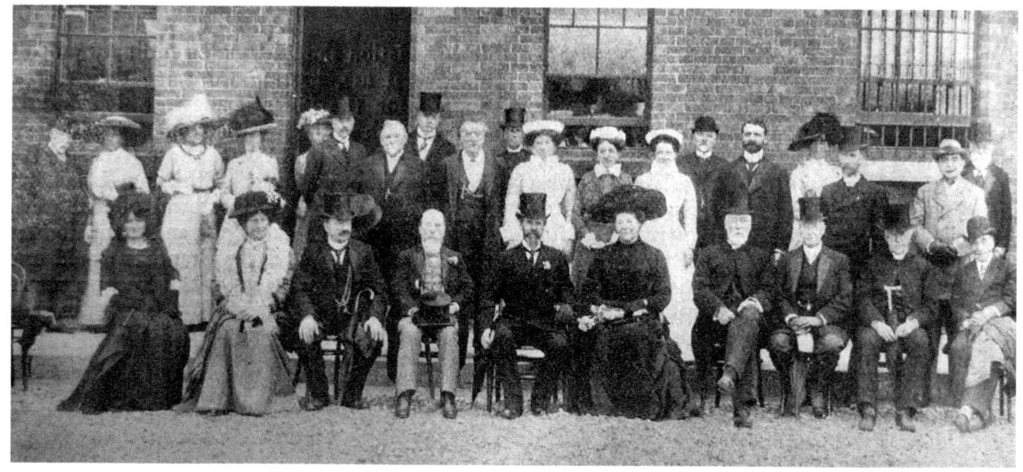

The opening of the Tuberculosis Hospital in the former Isolation Hospital on Pigeon House Road in 1910, with the Lord Lieutenant of Ireland and his wife, Lady Aberdeen, in the centre front. (Courtesy of Trinity College Dublin)

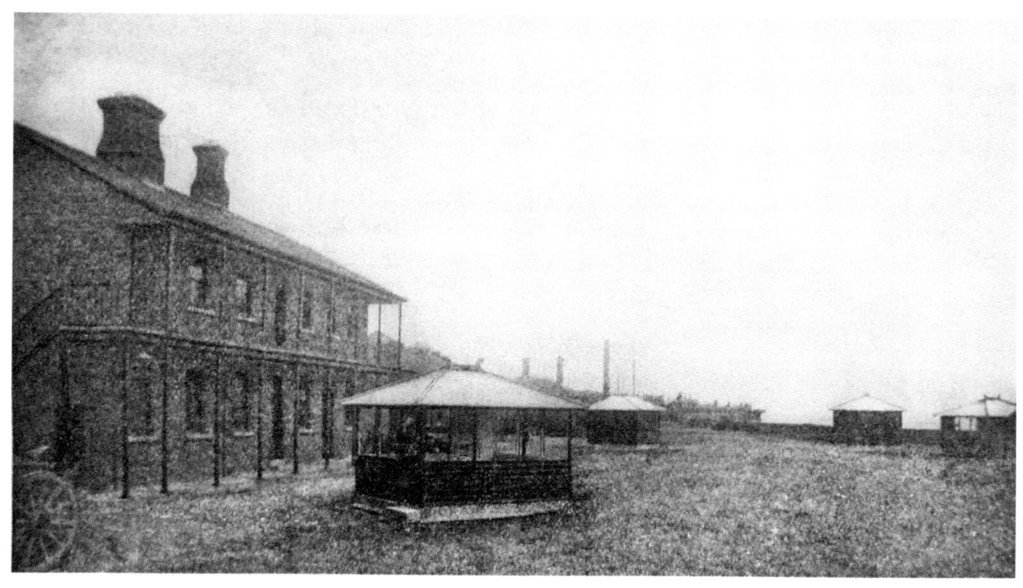

The Tuberculosis Hospital looking east, 1910. The open-air huts were sometimes used as sleeping quarters, in order for the patient to get plenty of fresh air. (Courtesy of Trinity College Dublin)

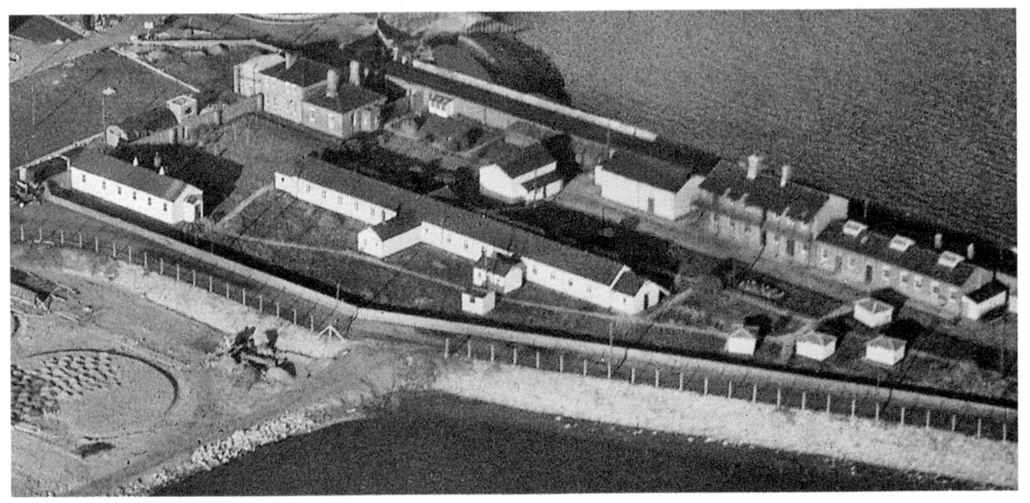

A 1950s aerial view of St Catherine's Hospital on Pigeon House Road. This was formerly a tuberculosis and isolation hospital, and before that, a submarine establishment. (Courtesy of the National Library of Ireland)

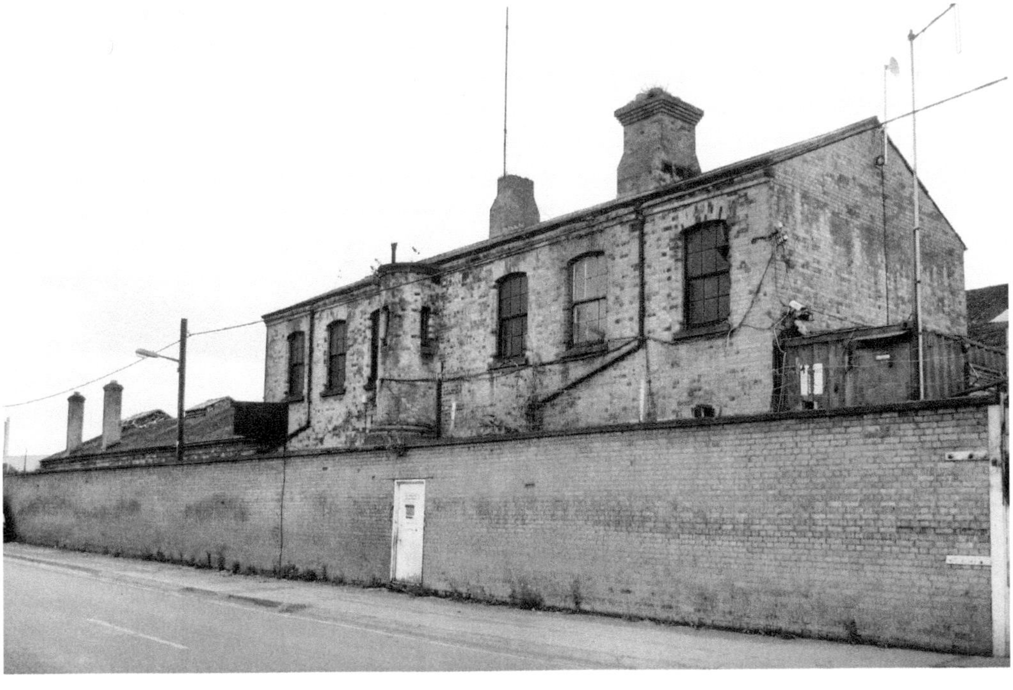

Part of the former St Catherine's Hospital is still in use for business purposes.

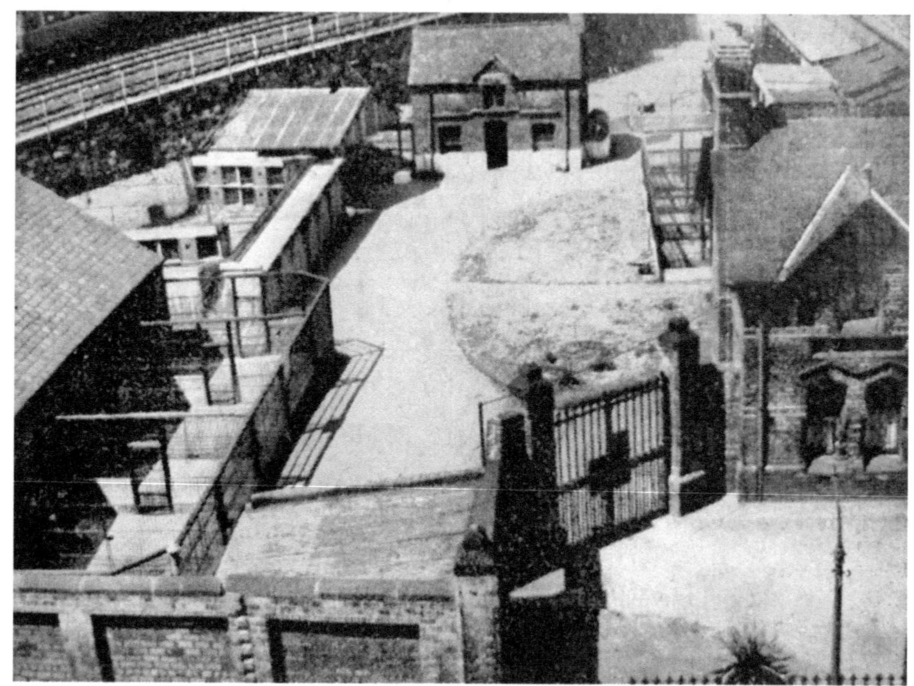

Mid-twentieth-century aerial view of the Cats and Dogs Home on Grand Canal Quay, alongside the railway bridge. (Courtesy of ISPCA)

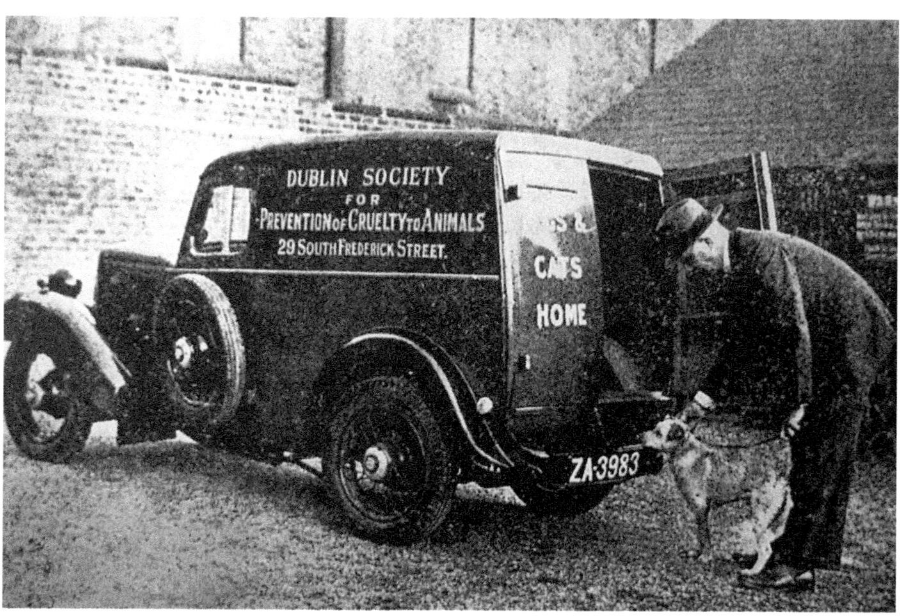

A 1937 photo of the van used by the Cats and Dogs Home. Prior to acquiring a van, they used a bicycle with a big basket in front to collect stray dogs and cats. (Courtesy of ISPCA)

8

ROWING & RECREATION

Ringsend was the mecca for the sport of rowing for much of the nineteenth century, before the various clubs moved to the calmer waters (non-tidal) of the River Liffey at Islandbridge. Rowing for the fishermen of Ringsend was part of their tough daily routine, but then university students and young shop/office workers saw it as a pleasant hobby and various clubs sprang up.

The Dublin Metropolitan Regatta is still a famous sporting and social event, having been founded in Ringsend in 1869 before moving to Blessington in the 1950s.

The 1886 Ordnance Survey map and *Thoms Street Directory* shows seven rowing clubs on the River Dodder-side of Thorncastle Street, with Neptune RC (No. 56) nearest the Point, then University Boat Club, Dolphin RC, Pembroke RC (the three sharing No. 47), Commercial RC (No. 39), University RC (No. 33), and finally Tyro RC (also No. 33 – with P.J. Kenny as honorary secretary).

DUBLIN UNIVERSITY BOAT CLUB (TRINITY COLLEGE)

The Pembroke Club was founded in 1836 by Trinity students and their boathouse was built in Thorncastle Street the following year. In 1843, the University Rowing Club was founded and four years later, in 1847, the clubs amalgamated to create the Dublin University Rowing Club.

In 1867, Dublin University Boat Club was formed by a splinter group, with their own clubhouse nearby.

Dublin University Rowing Club and Dublin University Boat Club amalgamated in 1898, under the latter name, and moved to a newly built clubhouse and grandstand on the south bank of the River Liffey at Islandbridge, where the first Trinity Regatta was held that same year. Today, the club is still thriving.

John Kells Ingram had a long-standing connection with the club – he wrote 'The Memory of the Dead', otherwise known as 'Who Fears to Speak of '98'.

COMMERCIAL ROWING CLUB

The Commercial Rowing Club was founded by shop workers and office workers because they were excluded from the Trinity College clubs, which catered only for students. It was founded in 1856 in Ringsend on the site of present-day O'Rahilly Flats – in 1905 its address was No. 4 Commercial Court. In 1942, they moved to Islandbridge, on the north bank of the River Liffey, nearly opposite the Trinity College Club, taking over the former Dublin Rowing Club premises. Women were admitted in the 1960s. At Christmas 1993, vandals burned down the clubhouse, but it was rebuilt shortly afterwards. Now the club has about 160 members and they use low lightweight fibreglass boats fitted with sliding seats, competing with sculls, fours and eights.

DUBLIN ROWING CLUB

This club was in Ringsend in 1839 and then moved to Islandbridge in 1906, before closing in 1942 and passing on their clubhouse to the Commercial Rowing Club.

DOLPHIN ROWING CLUB

This club was beside the Commercial Rowing Club in Ringsend from around 1876. They closed in 1941, and their premises was sold to Sandymount Boxing Club. By 1953 the boxing club was based in 42e Pearse Street as the Sandymount Athletic & Boxing Club.

NEPTUNE ROWING CLUB

The Neptune was part of Lot 8 of the James Martin Estate sold in 1883 by the Landed Estates Court, and this lot was called the Quay of Ringsend, and now known as 'Flower's Salt Works, the Neptune Rowing Club, and Flanagan's Coal Yard', held under lease dated 1822 from Richard Verschoyle (agent for the Pembroke Estate) to James Hill. The Neptune sub-lease was for twenty-seven years from 1876, between James Martin and the trustees, Frederick William Hammond and Thomas McGovern. This was not the original lease, since newspapers reported in 1861 that a new ballcourt (racket) was being provided by the Neptune. Upon lease expiry in 1903, the club folded. A new club, with the same name, was founded in February 1908, presumably including some of the old club's members, and made their Junior debut at the Metropolitan Regatta in June, wearing light green and black. A new clubhouse at Islandbridge was approved by Dublin Corporation in 1909. Neptune were closely associated with the adjoining Dublin Rowing Club, since F.B. O'Rourke was a prominent member of both in the early years.

UNIVERSITY COLLEGE DUBLIN (UCD) ROWING CLUB

The UCD Rowing Club was founded in 1917, and became tenants of the Commercial Rowing Club in Ringsend. In 1919, they moved next door to share premises with the Dolphin Rowing Club. In 1928, they moved to Islandbridge, sharing premises with the Dublin Rowing Club, until their own premises was built in 1932.

SMALLER OLD ROWING CLUBS IN THORNCASTLE STREET

Victoria Rowing Club was founded in 1840, with Arthur Bennett as treasurer. Liffey Rowing Club and Phoenix Clubs both came into existence in 1845 with the Irish Rowing Club formed in 1850 and the Brunswick Rowing Club in 1855. Fitzwilliam Rowing Club and another Liffey Rowing Club were both founded in 1870 and Tyro Rowing Club was in existence from 1883 to 1888. In 1895 Warrington Club was listed at No. 41 Thorncastle Street. In 1870, Pembroke Rowing Club was founded in Ringsend, although not connected to the 1836 Pembroke Club – the former closed in 1909.

CURRENT RINGSEND ROWING CLUBS

St Patrick's Rowing Club, located beside the East-Link Toll Bridge, started in 1936. Their lovely new clubhouse on York Road was built in 1986 (extended in 2004) at the same time as the new Toll Bridge, on land that was reclaimed for the new access road to/from the bridge. Their traditional heavy timber boats (called skiffs) are manned by four rowers and a cox, and they do not use sliding seats. Because of the tides and winds around the mouth of the River Liffey, rowers have to be tough.

Stella Maris started in 1937, after they broke away from St Patrick's RC. Their clubhouse is beside the Poolbeg Yacht Club

The Poolbeg Yacht & Boat Club was founded in 1971, and they met in the YMCA Mission Hall, and CYMS Hall. They bought the old trawler, *Rospico*, in 1974, for use as their clubhouse, but it was wrecked in a storm, and instead they used the tiny wheelhouse of the trawler as their premises, positioned to the west of the former Coastguard Station. The upmarket clubhouse opened in 1987, and the Marina followed in 2004.

The Plurabelle Paddlers was set up in 2011 by breast-cancer survivors, as a great way to keep fit and meet like-minded women. Their clubhouse is on Hanover Quay, beside the derelict lock-keeper's lodge. They organise the Dublin Dragonboat Regatta every September in Grand Canal Harbour. Each boat holds about sixteen women sitting two abreast, in addition to a cox at one end and a drummer at the other end.

SEA BATHING

Rocques' map of 1760 shows baths for men in Ringsend, and baths for women in Irishtown, complete with a very small building at each coastal location.

As early as 1809, Thomas Murphy had a public baths at the north-east end of Irishtown, while Richard Cranfield had a more substantial establishment, with indoor pool, at the south-east end of Irishtown. Both businesses were gone by 1890, and Tritonville Avenue houses were built on the site of Cranfield Baths.

SHELBOURNE PARK GREYHOUND STADIUM, SOUTH LOTTS ROAD

Greyhound racing nowadays is much more glamorous that in bygone days, when it was regarded as foolish gambling indulged in by men only. The year 1927 is given as the year when Ireland's first greyhound track opened in Shelbourne Park, but in fact whippet racing was very popular in Ireland long before that date. A whippet looked similar to a greyhound, but relied on smell instead of sight. The whippet ran in a straight line following a scented rag held by his owner some distance away, whereas the greyhound spotted a hare and ran after it. Newspapers in 1917 reported whippet racing at Jones Road and the Royal Hospital in Kilmainham, and at Shelbourne Park in 1919. Pathé News showed whippet racing in Shelbourne Park in 1921.

Shelbourne Park in those days was also popular for horse racing, or trotting (harness racing) to be more exact – a two-wheeled buggy (sulky) being pulled by a horse, still popular with Travellers today. In 1914, the Shelbourne Sports Co. Ltd, South Lotts Road, organised horse racing in Ringsend Park (which may in fact have been Shelbourne Park). In 1919, trotting was held in Shelbourne Park, including the Six-Furlong Dash, and the Mile Open Handicap.

By 1921, a stadium grandstand had been built in Shelbourne Park, erected by Smith & Pearson, and both whippet racing and horse trotting were regular events.

In 1926, greyhound racing officially started in Manchester (Belle Vue), when the first oval track was built, with an artificial hare mounted on a guide rail. Celtic Park opened in Belfast on 18 April 1927 (closed 1983). Shelbourne Park in Dublin opened a few weeks later on 14 May 1927, after installing a 500-yard oval track in their existing stadium. Harold's Cross Greyhound Stadium opened in 1928. Thereafter, the poor whippet faded away.

In 1953 and other years, speedway events were held in Shelbourne Park, where motorcycles raced around the dirt track.

In 1968, Bord na gCon, a state body set up in 1958, purchased the Shelbourne Park stadium. During the 'Celtic Tiger' years, major upgrading work was undertaken, and these days, Shelbourne Park is a destination for parties and corporate events.

IRISHTOWN STADIUM

Ringsend is well known as the birthplace of Shelbourne Football Club and Shamrock Rovers FC, as well as Clanna Gael/Fontenoy Gaelic Football and Hurling Club.

In 1951, a football pitch was opened on reclaimed land (in fact, partly a Corporation dump) by Shelbourne FC, called Shelbourne Stadium or Ringsend Stadium, including a cinder athletic track laid by En Tout Cas.

Dublin City Council provided a new building in 2004, with changing rooms on the ground floor, and extensive gym on the first floor, in addition to an athletic track, all-weather football pitches, etc. Crusaders Athletic Club and Dundrum AC are based here now.

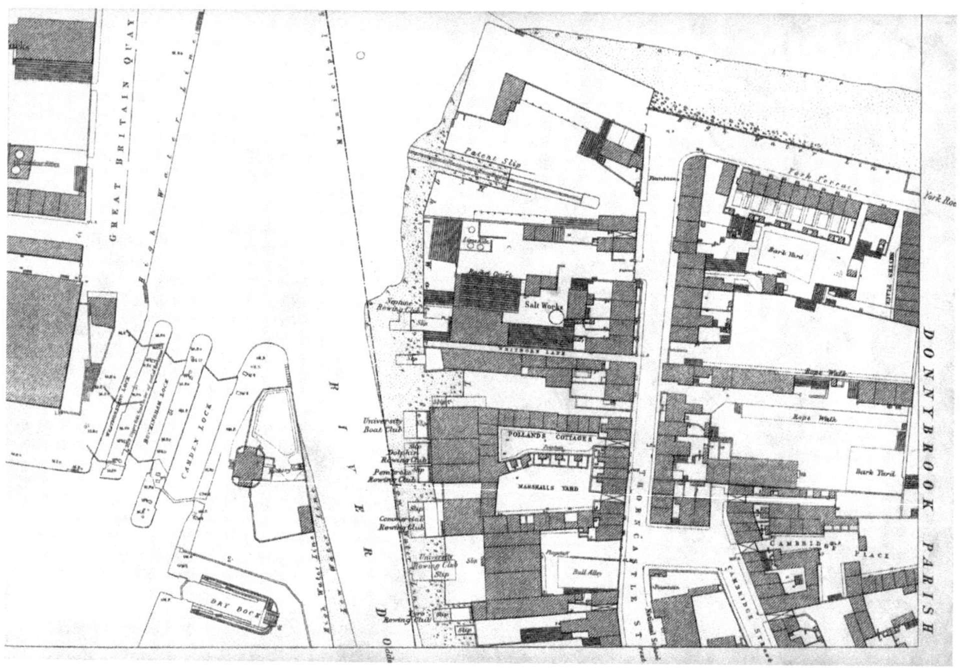

1886 Ordnance Survey map of the River Dodder alongside Thorncastle Street, showing many rowing clubs. (Courtesy of Dublin City Council)

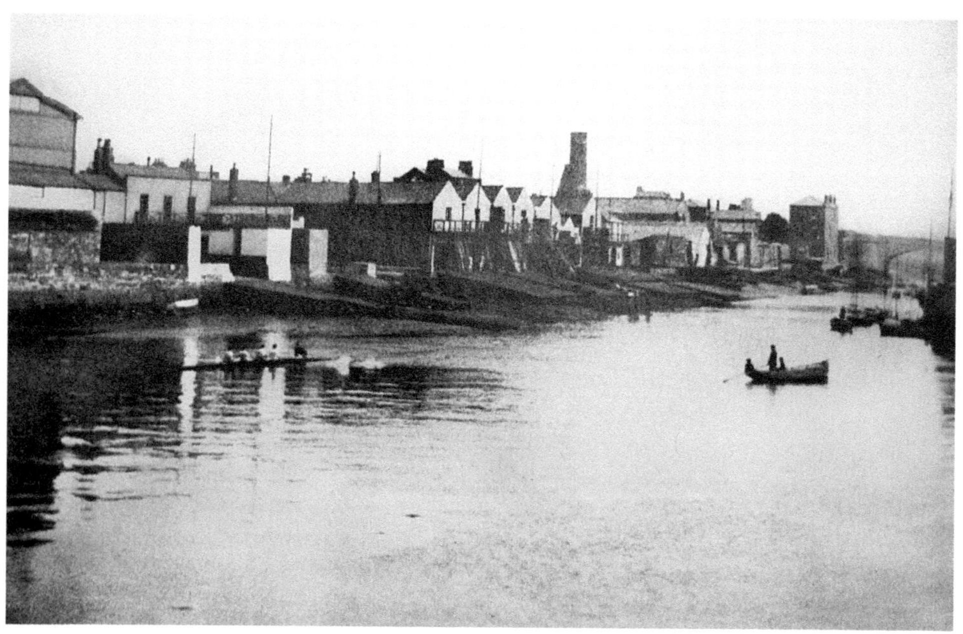

Looking south along the River Dodder behind Thorncastle Street, in the early twentieth century – the new St Patrick's church has not yet been built beside Ringsend Bridge. (Courtesy of the Commercial Rowing Club)

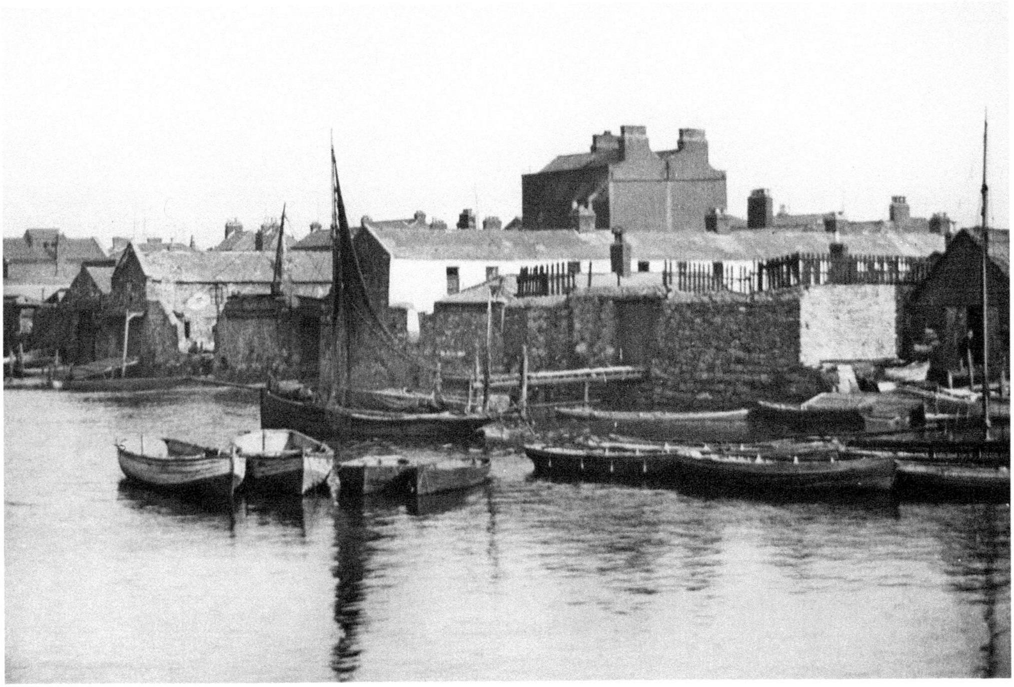

Old view of River Dodder behind Thorncastle Street, looking north-east. (Courtesy of South Dublin County Council Library)

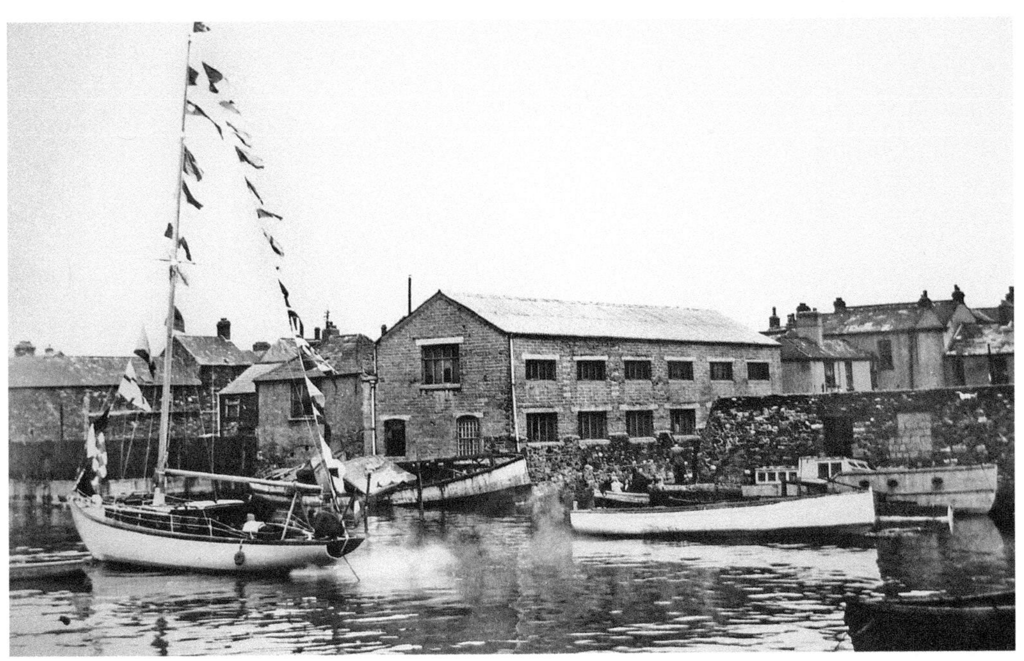

Early twentieth-century view of the River Dodder behind Thorncastle Street. (Courtesy of NewsFour)

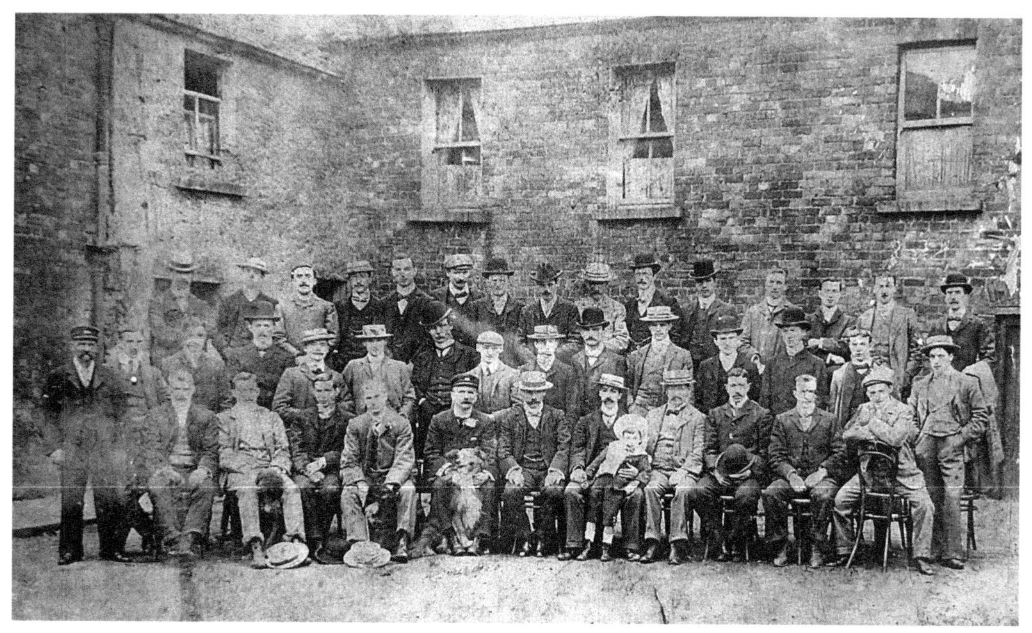

Commercial Rowing Club in 1901, in Thorncastle Street. (Courtesy of the Commercial Rowing Club)

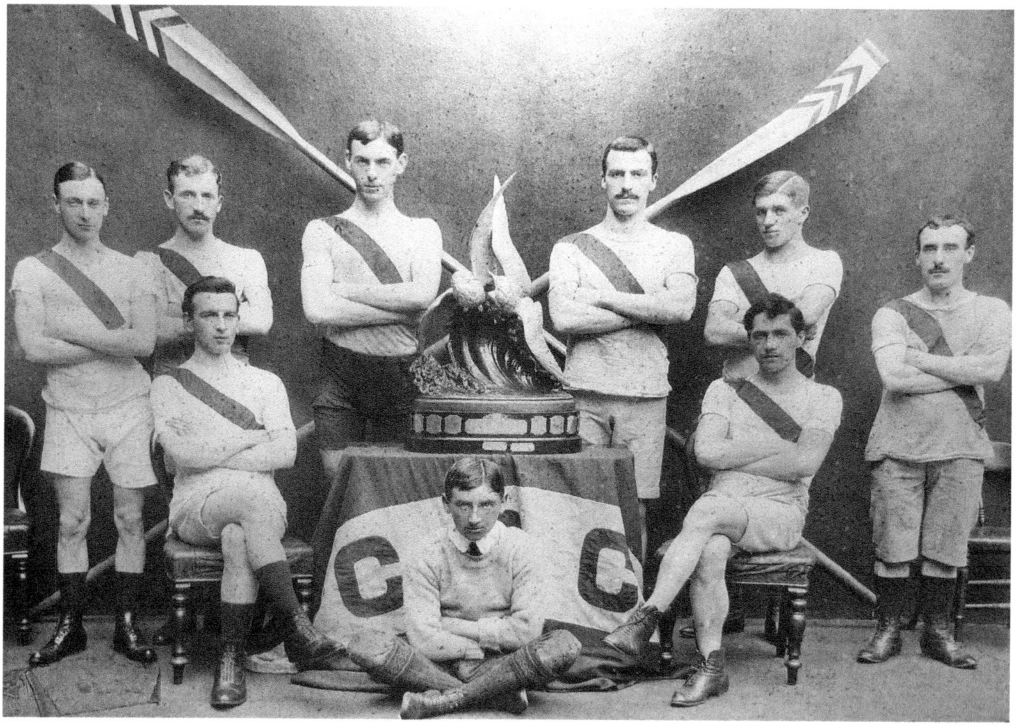

Commercial Rowing Club. Junior Eight, winner of the Grey Cup in 1903/04. (Courtesy of the Commercial Rowing Club)

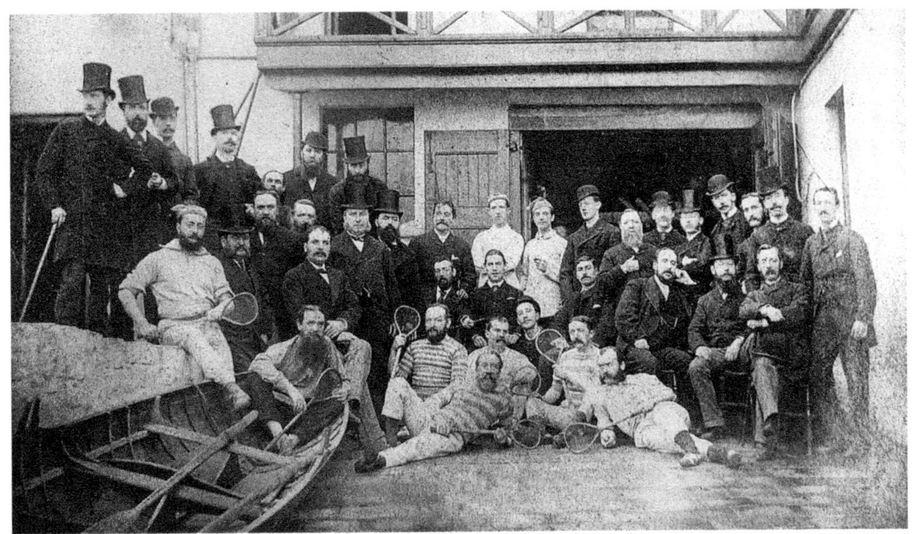

Original Neptune Rowing Club in Ringsend in 1879. Note some members holding rackets (the forerunner of squash). (Courtesy of Neptune Rowing Club)

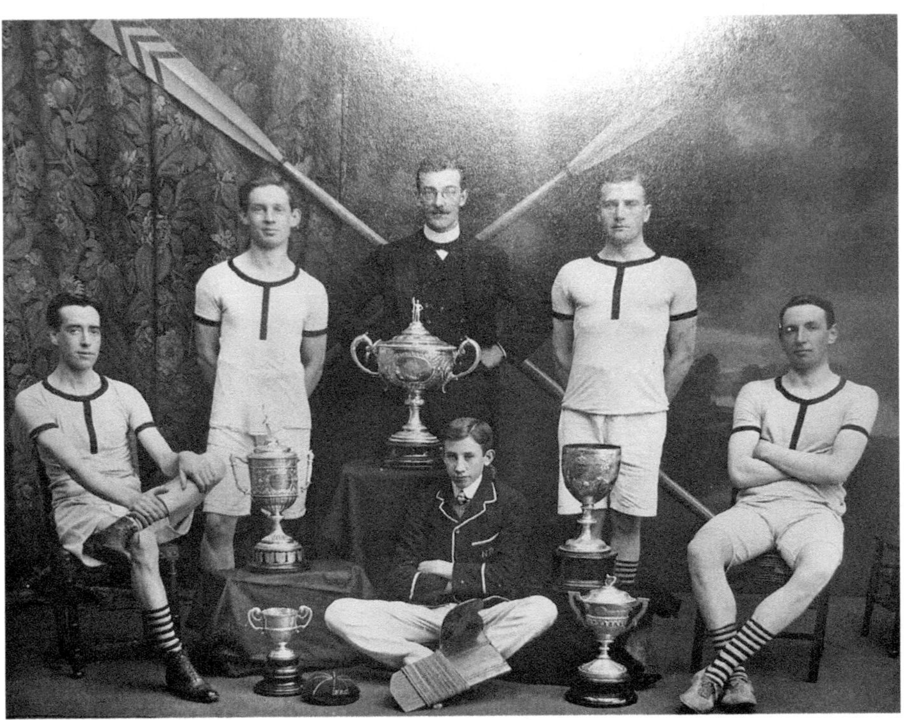

The newly re-established Neptune Rowing Club, 1908. Standing, from left to right: N.A. Hand (stroke), F.B. O'Rourke (captain), R.H. Magill (2). Seated: E.V. Farrell (bow), R. Quinn (cox), M.V. Hennessy (3). Junior Four, unbeaten: Liffey Cup in Metropolitan Regatta, Chapelizod Cup in Dublin University Boat Club Regatta, Boyne Cup in Boyne, Marina Cup in Cork, Murphy Cup in Limerick. (Courtesy of Neptune Rowing Club)

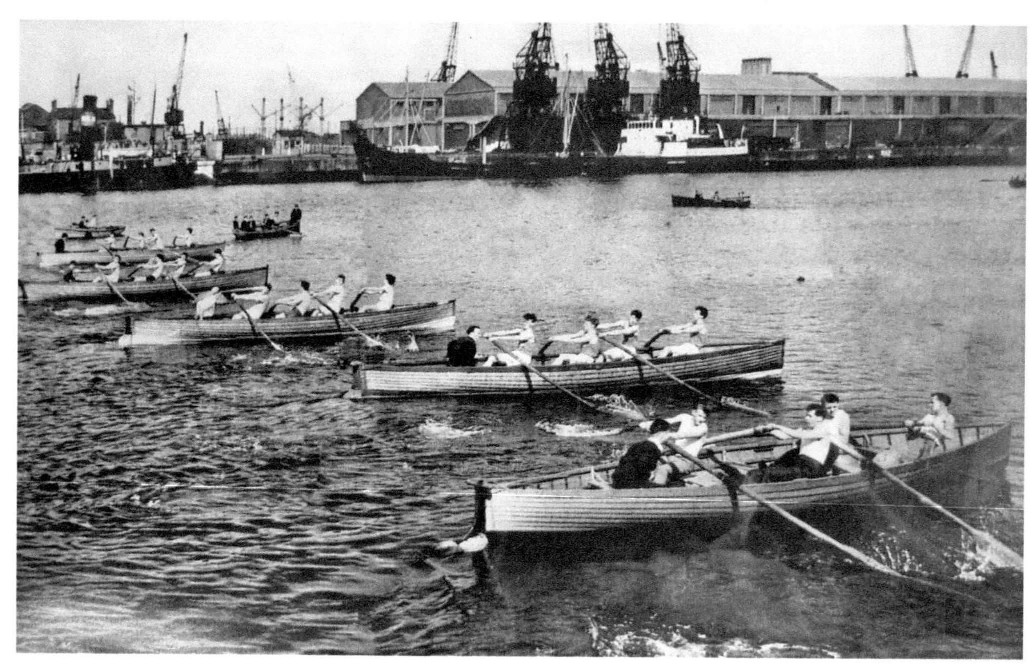

St Patrick's Annual Regatta, 1957. (Courtesy of St Patrick's Rowing Club)

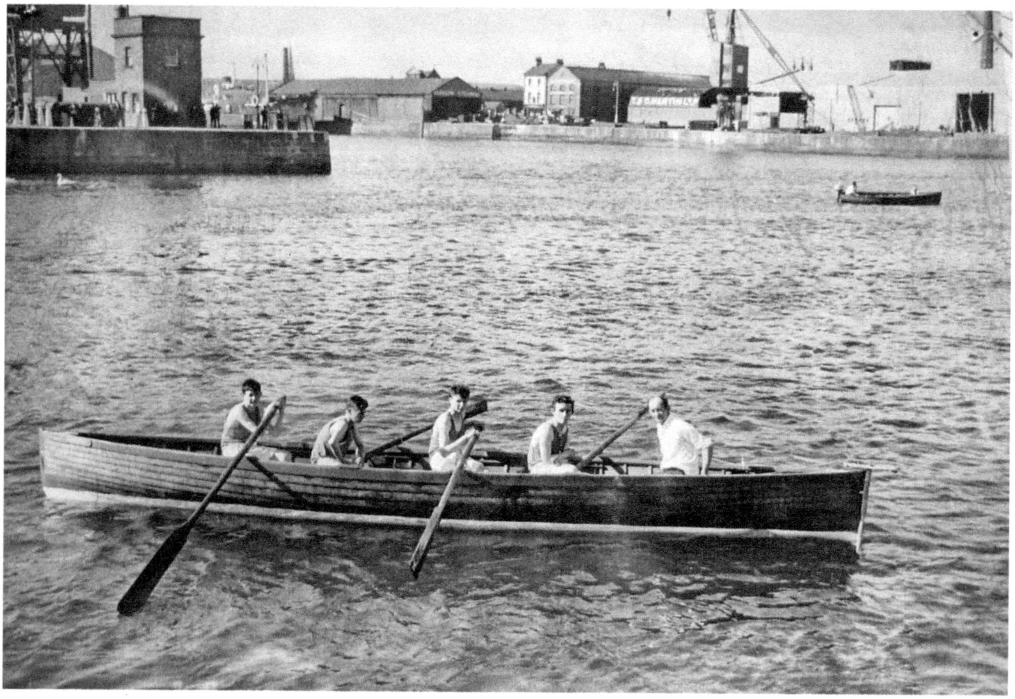

Sir John Rogersons Quay and Great Brittain Quay; note the Hailing Station at the corner, *c.* 1960s. (Courtesy of NewsFour)

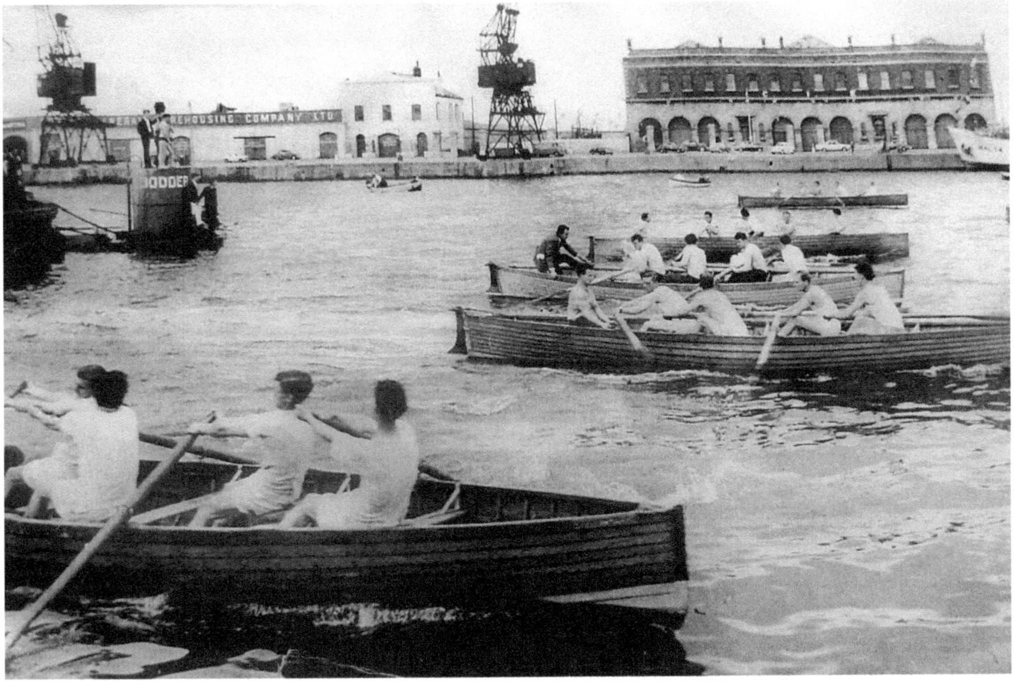

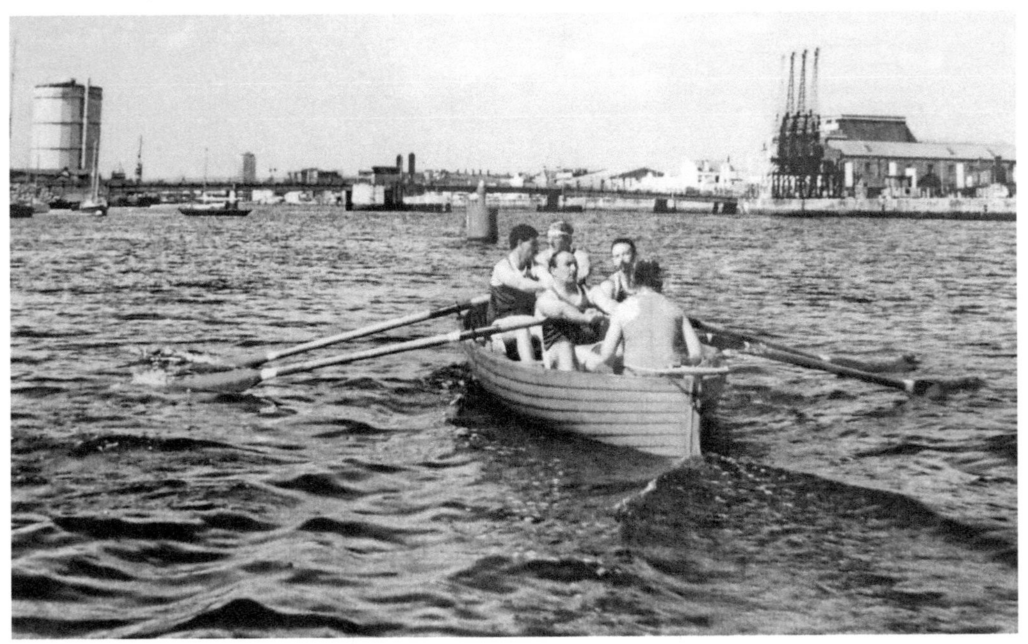

Regatta, at the mouth of the River Dodder, *c.* 1960s. (Courtesy of Stella Maris Rowing Club)

St Patrick's crew in the 1980s, in much tougher conditions than the tranquil waters of Islandbridge. (Courtesy of St Patrick's Rowing Club)

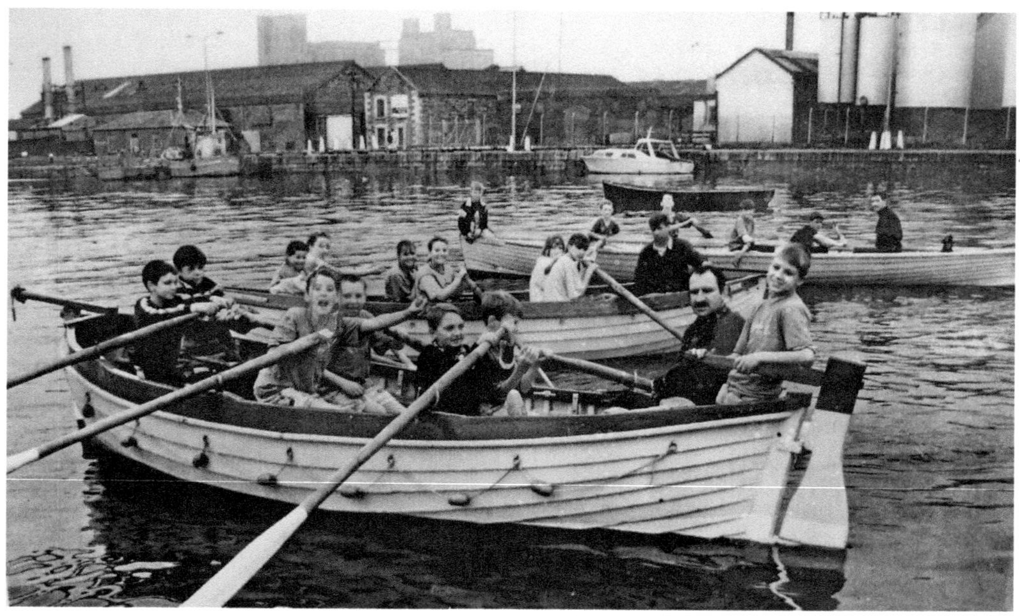

Ringsend youngsters know how to have fun and exercise on the River Dodder, with Great Brittain Quay in the background, 1990s. (Courtesy of St Patrick's Rowing Club)

TRITONVILLE
BATHS,
NEAR IRISHTOWN CHURCH,
BUILT BY THE LATE RICHARD CRANFIELD,
And generally known by the name of
CRANFIELD'S BATHS.

COLD BATH.

THIS Bath is forty feet long, by twenty-two broad, and four feet deep, supplied by a Reservoir as large as itself, into which the Sea flows every Tide.

The Public are respectfully informed the price of the Cold Bath is as follows:—

Single Bath,	...	...	£0 0	5
Monthly Subscription,	...	...	0 8	4
Per Quarter,	...	..	1 0	0
Per Year,	...	...	2 10	0

THE COLD SHOWER BATH

Is on the very best construction, being supplied by a tube from an erected Reservoir containing upwards of fifty tons of water, the pressure of which can be given to any degree of weight and strength the Patient requires

Ladies' and Childrens' private Cold Bath, as usual
Terms as above

A Car attends in College-green for the convenience of Bathers every Morning

TEPID BATHS.

The Tepid Baths of this Establishment are so much superior for neatness, cleanliness, attendance, and purity of WATER to every other in this Kingdom, that one view would convince any person, who will take the trouble to inspect them, and examine others, that there is none equal, or can stand in competition with them

THOMAS DIXON (acting Proprietor for these last ten years, since the death of his Father-in-law, the late Mr. Cranfield) thinks it his duty to remark, that the Water once made use of, is never returned into the Cauldrons, or made use of in any manner a second time in those Baths.

☞ The same Attendants that has given such general satisfaction for these eleven years past are still continued.

An 1819 advertisement in the *Freeman's Journal* for Cranfield Baths. (Courtesy of Irish Newspapers Archive)

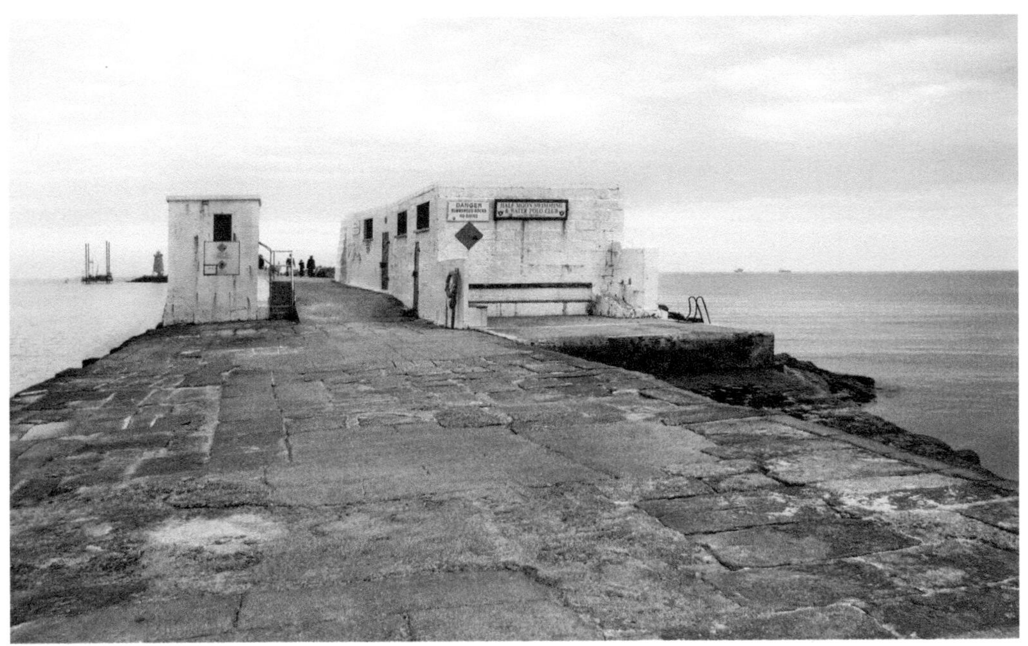

The former Half Moon Battery on the South Bull Wall was an outpost of the Pigeon House Fort, but is now occupied by the Half Moon Swimming Club.

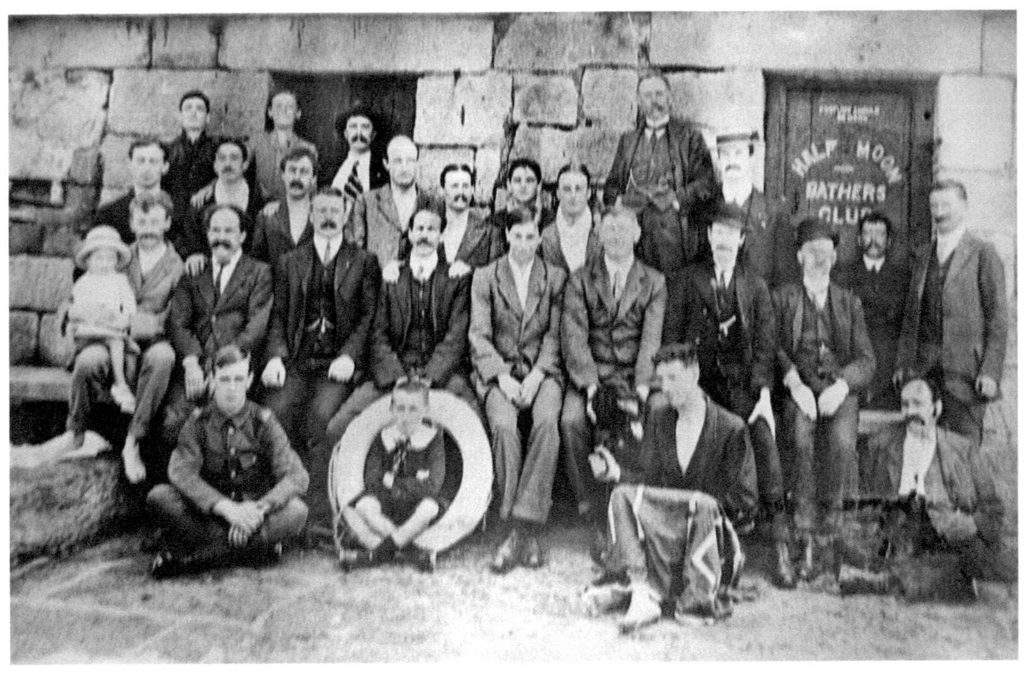

Members of the Half Moon Bathers Club, at the Half Moon Battery (also known as the Five Gun Battery) on the South Bull Wall, 1911. (Courtesy of NewsFour)

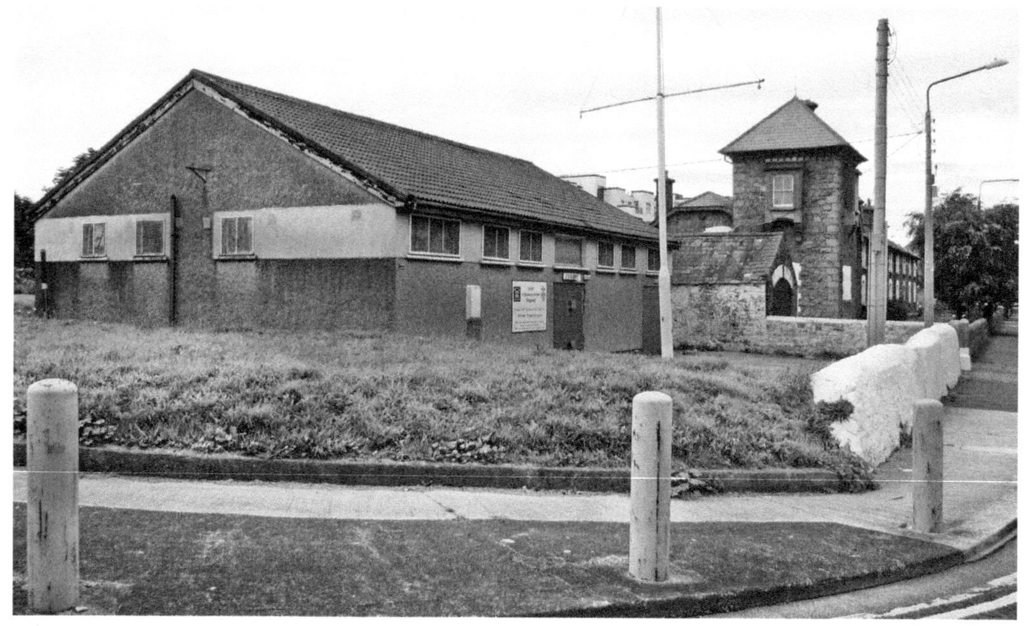

The 1st Port of Dublin Sea Scouts beside the former Coastguard Station. The club was founded in 1908, and originally had a slip directly into the adjoining sea.

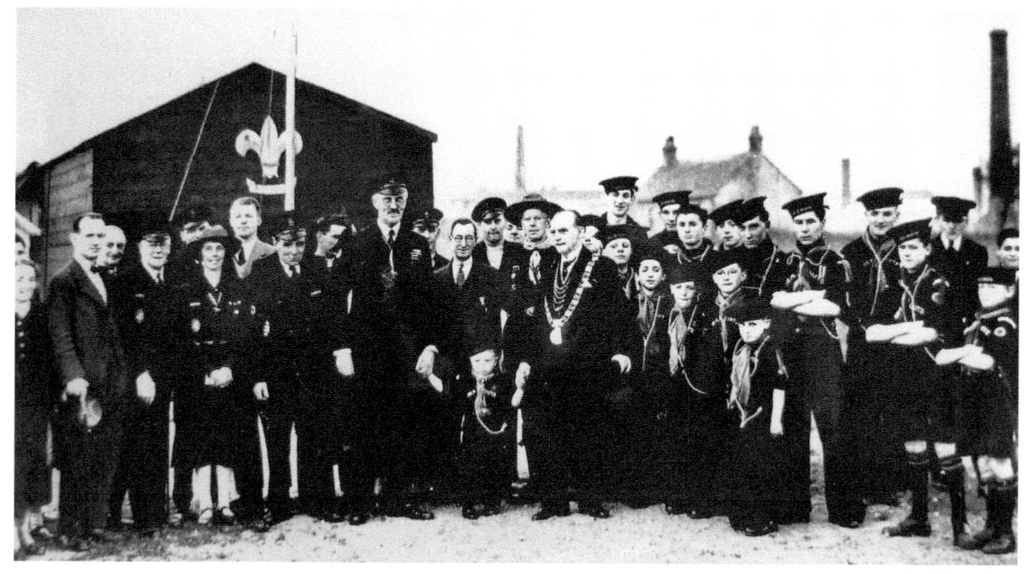

4th Port Dodder Sea Scouts was founded in 1934 at 97 Lower Gardiner Street, by Skipper Perrin and used Alexandra Basin for boating. In 1938, they moved to a strip of land alongside the River Dodder in Ringsend, behind Derrynane Gardens. This photo, dated 1945, shows Skipper Perrin and Lord Mayor Alfie Byrne, with the Pembroke Sewage Pumping Station in the background. (Courtesy of 4th Port Dodder Sea Scouts)

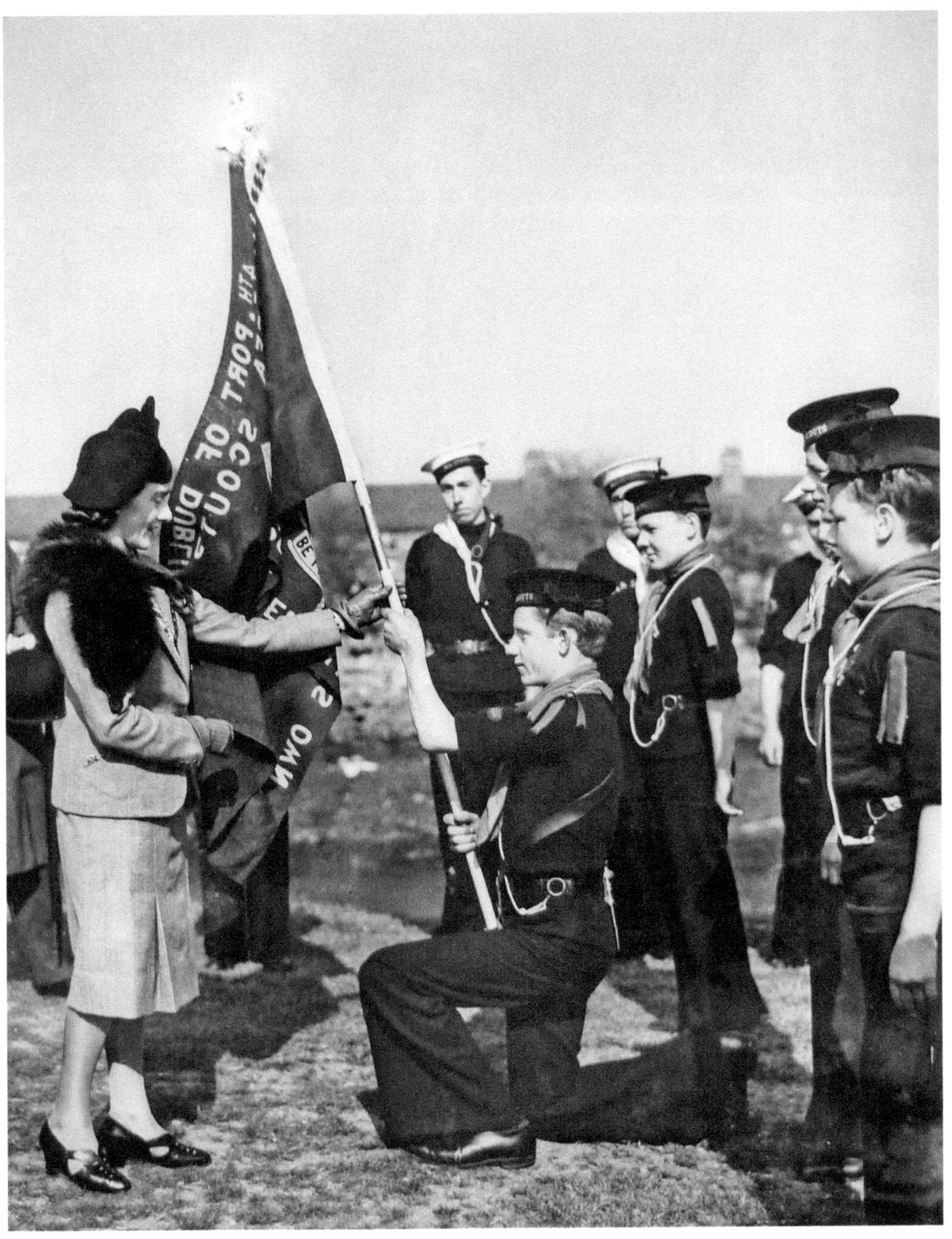

Presentation of 'Colours' to the 4th Port Dodder Sea Scouts by Mrs G.S. Childs, on 29 April 1939. (Courtesy of 4th Port Dodder Sea Scouts)

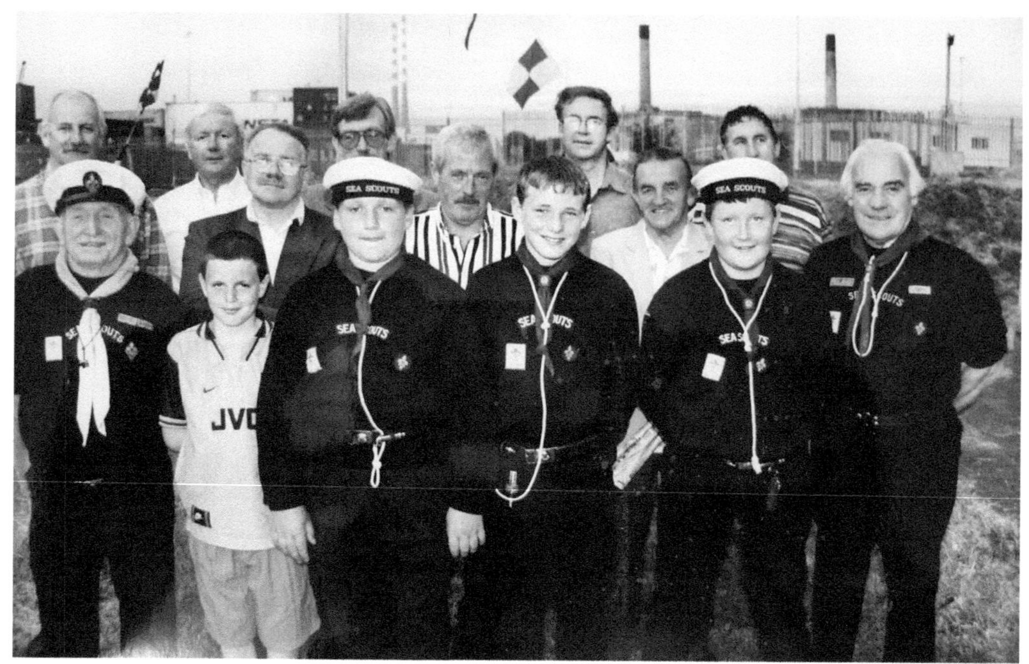

Proud Sea Scouts in Ringsend. (Courtesy of NewsFour)

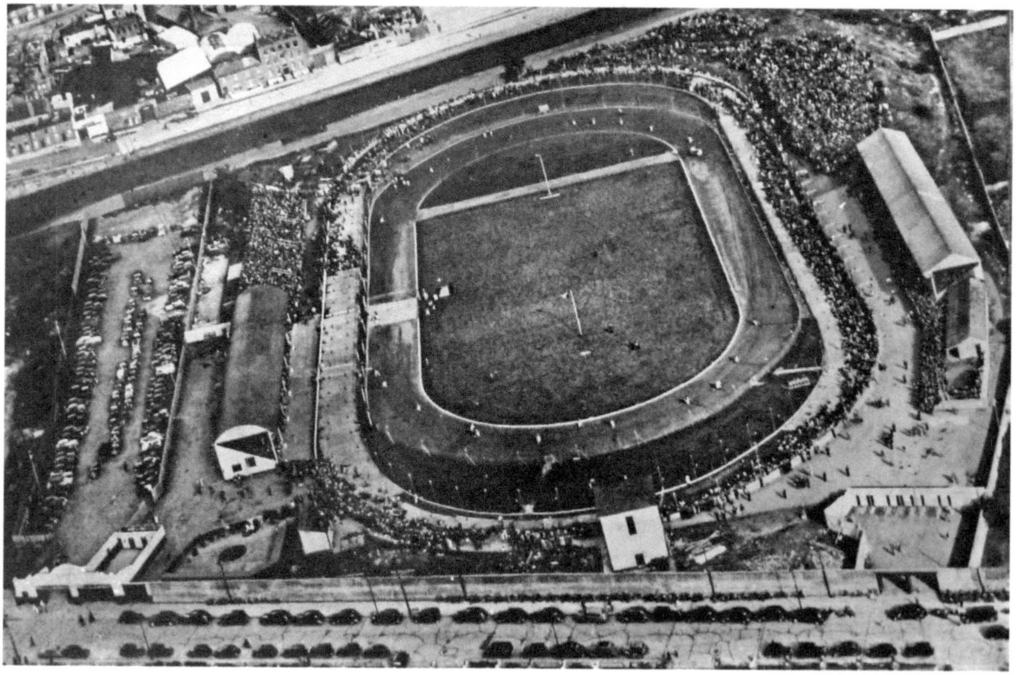

Mid-twentieth century aerial photo of Shelbourne Park Greyhound Stadium, in the days when it had two grandstands. (Courtesy of Bord na gCon)

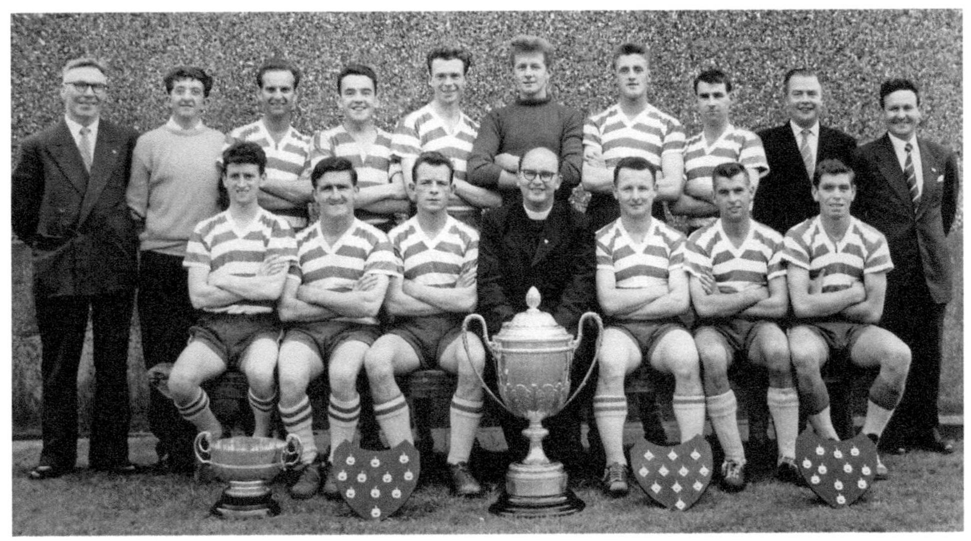

St Patrick's CYMS, 1958/59. From left to right, back row: W. Byrne, P. Carroll, J. Stafford, J. Kelly, N. Mullen, M. Smyth, M. Keegan, L. Joyce, P. Mullen, P. Moran. Front row: E. Morley, B. Lester, J. Gregg, Father Kenny, J. Moran, G. Joyce, M. Caulfield. (Courtesy of St Patricks' CYMS)

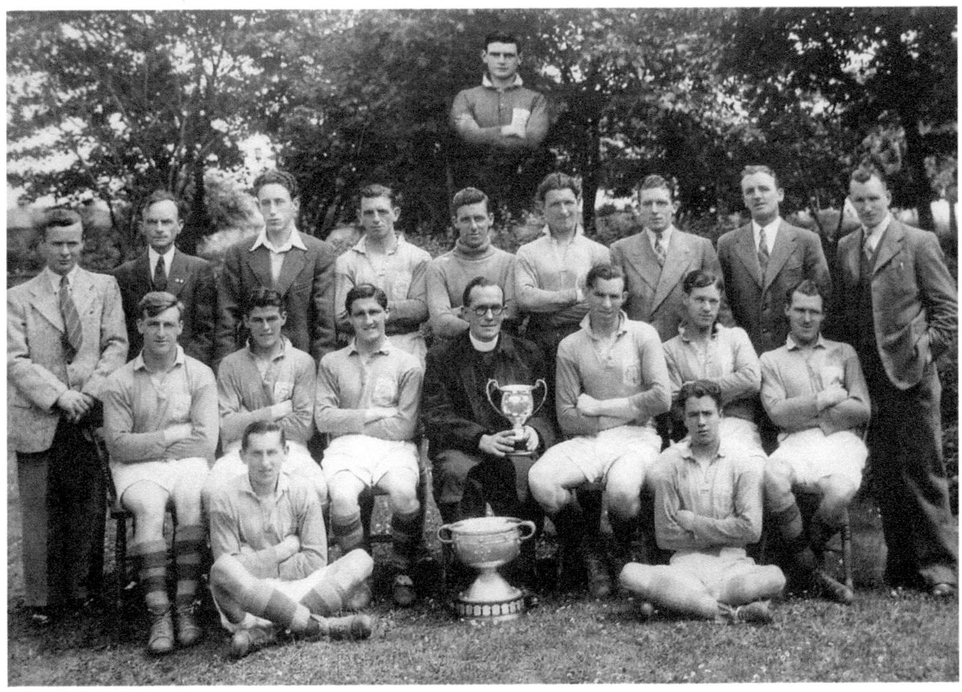

St Patrick's CYMS, 1945-46. From left to right, standing: S. Moran, J. Stanley, T. Dunne, J. Barry, T. Lester, P. Barry, G. Wogan, A. O'Byrne. Seated: M. Lester, J. Cleary, B. Lester (Captain), Fr J. Patterson (Spiritual Director), J. Behan, A. Dunne, J. Wogan. On the ground: D. Burtenshaw, J. Brennan. Inset: L. O'Byrne. (Courtesy of St Patrick's CYMS)

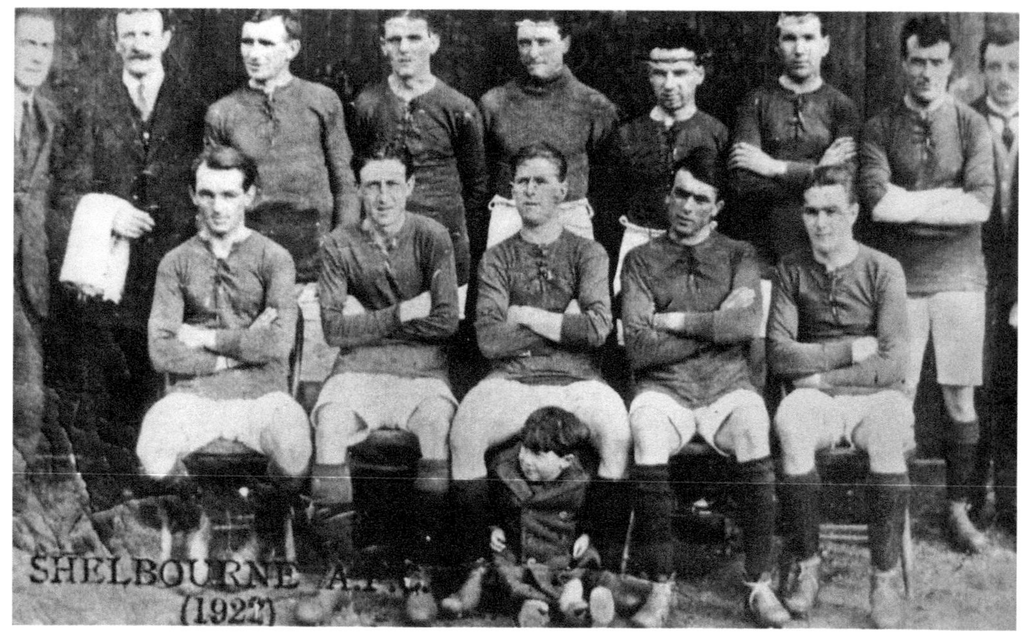

Shelbourne Associated Football Club in 1922. (Courtesy of NewsFour)

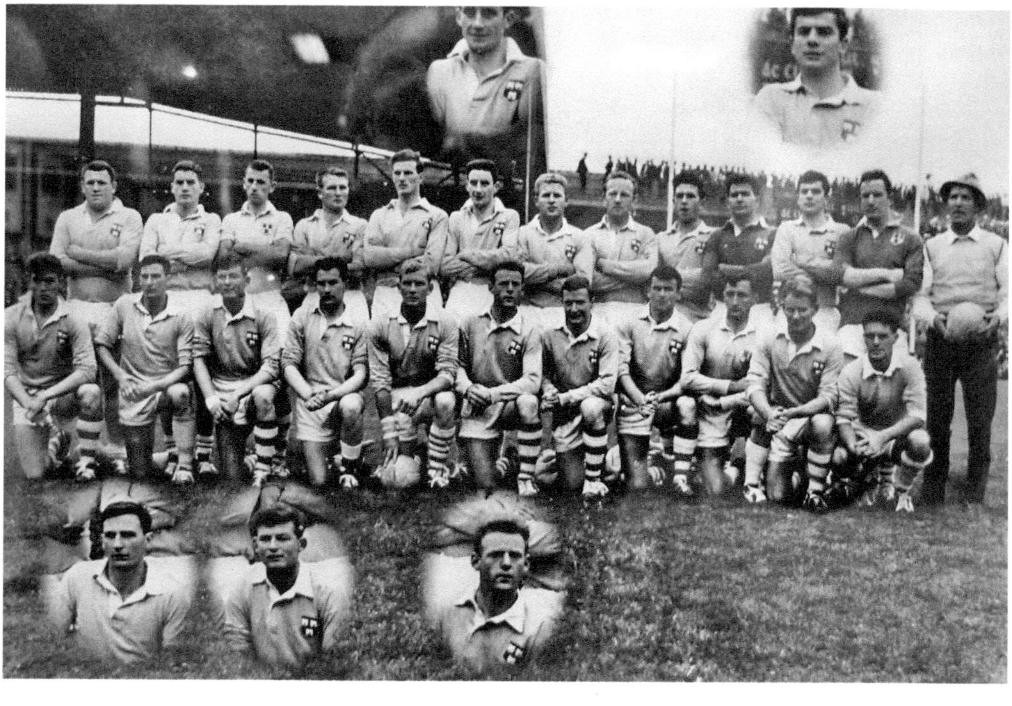

Clanna Gael Gaelic Football Club, 1963. They were founded in 1929 by teachers from St Patrick's Training College in Drumcondra. They merged with Fontenoy in 1968, which was founded in 1887 in Bath Avenue. (Courtesy of Clanna/Fontenoy Club)

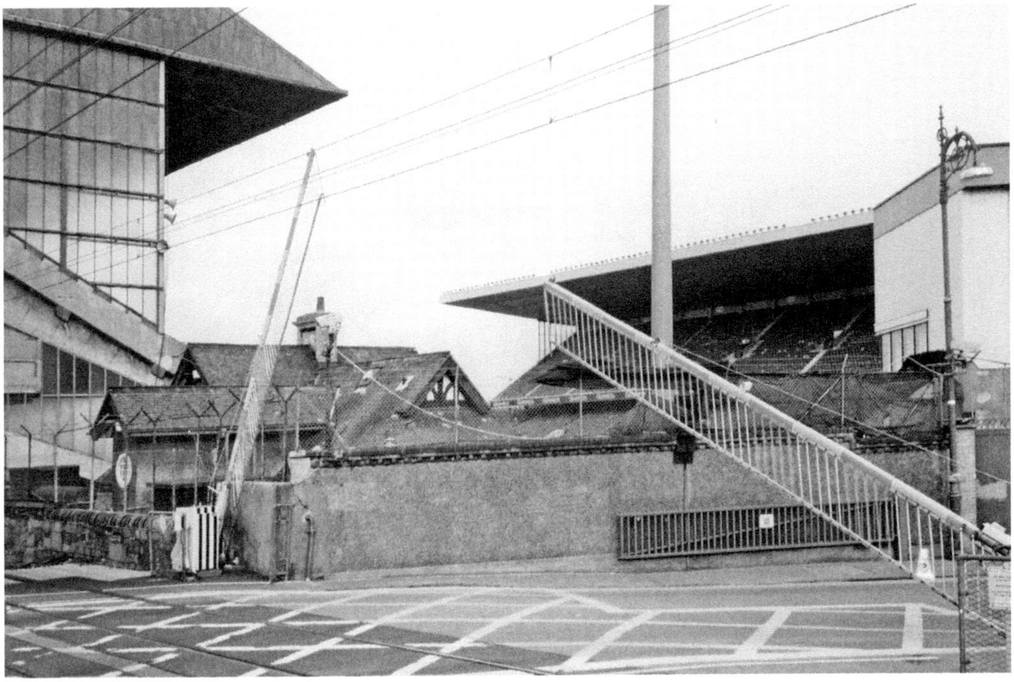

Lansdowne Stadium before the present glass 'space-age' stadium was built in 2010.

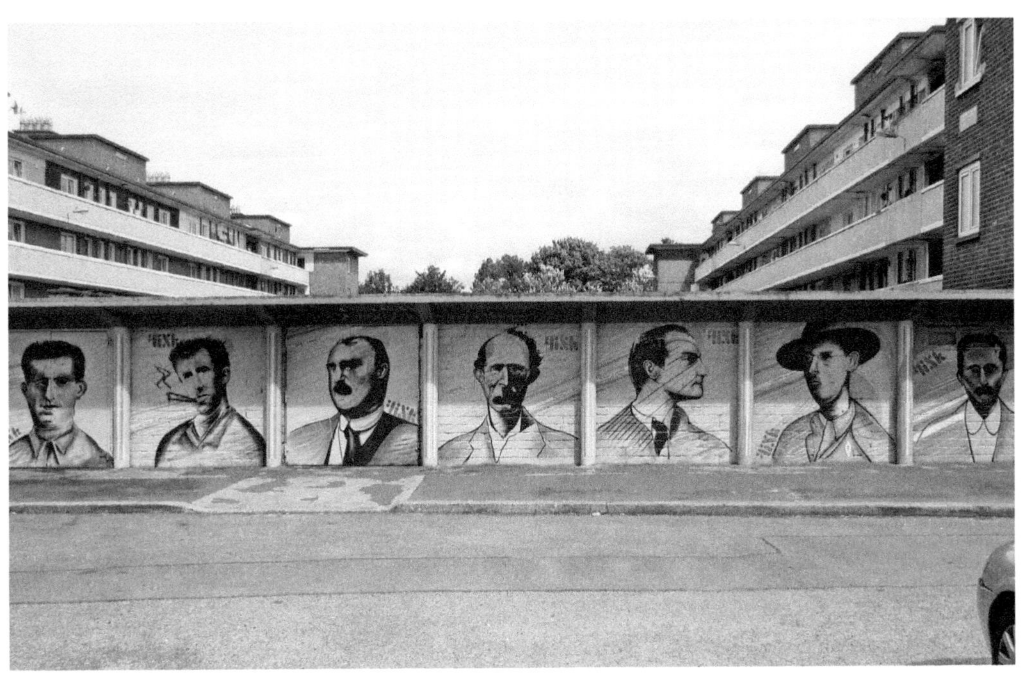

Street art at Canon Mooney Gardens celebrates the centenary of 1916.

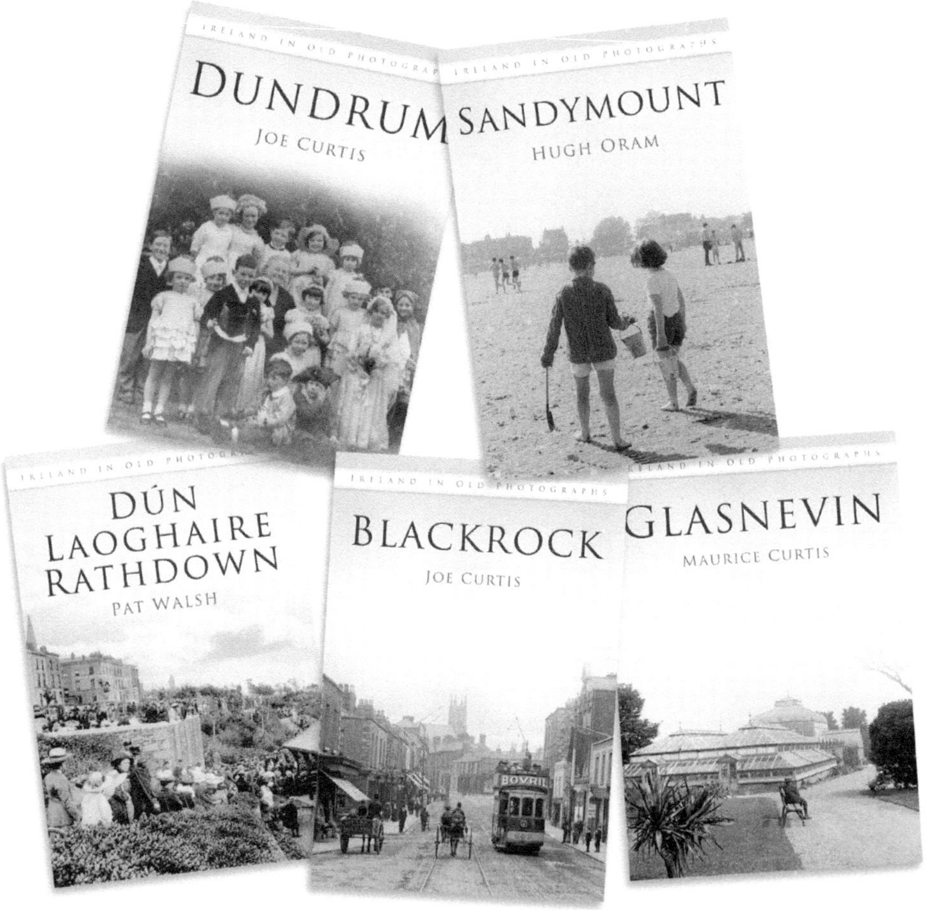